Economics of Monetary Union

Economics of Monetary Union

Fourth Edition

Paul De Grauwe

Professor of Economics, Centre for Economic Studies,
University of Leuven, Belgium

OXFORD
UNIVERSITY PRESS

OXFORD
UNIVERSITY PRESS

Great Clarendon Street, Oxford OX2 6DP
Oxford University Press is a department of the University of Oxford.
It furthers the University's objective of excellence in research, scholarship,
and education by publishing worldwide in
Oxford New York
Athens Auckland Bangkok Bogotá Buenos Aires Calcutta
Cape Town Chennai Dar es Salaam Delhi Florence Hong Kong Istanbul
Karachi Kuala Lumpur Madrid Melbourne Mexico City Mumbai
Nairobi Paris São Paulo Singapore Taipei Tokyo Toronto Warsaw
with associated companies in Berlin Ibadan

Oxford is a registered trade mark of Oxford University Press
in the UK and in certain other countries

Published in the United States
by Oxford University Press Inc., New York

British Library Cataloguing in Publication Data
Data available

Library of Congress Cataloging in Publication Data
Data available
ISBN 0-19-877632-2

3 5 7 9 10 8 6 4

Typeset by RefineCatch Limited, Bungay, Suffolk
Printed in Great Britain
on acid-free paper by
The Bath Press
Bath

Contents

Introduction

DOES a nation increase its welfare when it abolishes its national currency and adopts some currency of a wider area? The eleven EU-countries that joined EMU on 1 January 1999 have given a positive answer. Other EU-countries like the UK, Denmark, and Sweden continue to struggle with this question. Central European countries that are ready to join the European Union will have to analyse that same question.

The issue of whether nations gain by relinquishing their national currencies leads immediately to a new question. Where should the process of monetary integration stop? Should there be one currency for just eleven countries of the present EMU, or for the EU, or for the whole of Europe, or maybe for the whole world? This problem leads us to an analysis of what constitutes an optimal monetary area.

In order to tackle all these problems we have to analyse systematically what the costs and benefits are of having one currency. In the first part of this book we will analyse these issues. We will study the *economic* costs and benefits exclusively. There is also much to be said about the political costs and benefits. These, however, are outside the scope of this book.

The start of EMU on 1 January 1999 was an historic event. Few attempts have been made in history to introduce a monetary union without the force of arms. The new monetary regime in Europe creates new problems that are exciting to analyse. The second part of this book deals with these problems of running a full-fledged monetary union in Europe. We will analyse how the European Central Bank (ECB) was designed to conduct a single monetary policy. We will also discuss some of the shortcomings in this design. The issue of political independence and accountability of the ECB will loom large in this discussion.

Many of the issues with which the ECB is confronted today are practical ones. How does the ECB make a choice between the different targets a central bank should pursue? What are the most appropriate instruments to achieve these targets? Can the ECB deal with financial crises and how? How should the ECB react to different business cycle developments in Euroland? What are the relations between monetary and budgetary policies? These are some of the problems that we will study in the second part of the book.

In the previous editions of this book problems of transition towards EMU received a great deal of attention. They were also the most hotly debated issues in Europe. Since the start of EMU they have become much less important. The focus of the analysis has shifted towards the actual operation of EMU. This is also the reason why the title of the book has been changed to *Economics of Monetary Union*. As a result of these developments much less importance is attached to problems of transition in the current edition. This discussion has not been eliminated altogether, because there are still a lot of outsiders considering joining EMU in the future. Issues of transition remain topical.

The study of the workings of a monetary union is still in its infancy. That is also the reason why it is so fascinating. So many new ideas are still to be discovered. My first hope is that this book can contribute to the discovery of these ideas. My second hope is that I can convey to the reader the same sense of excitement that I have when I study the subject.

This book would not have come about without the intense discussions and debates with colleagues and students over many years. Many of them were kind enough to read parts of the manuscript and to formulate their comments and criticism. In particular, I am grateful to Filip Abraham, Michael Artis, Juan José Calaza, Bernard Delbecque, Harris Dellas, Casper de Vries, Hans Dewachter, Sylvester Eijffinger, Michele Fratianni, Wolfgang Gebauer, Daniel Gros, Henk Jager, Catrinus Jepma, Georgios Karras, Clemens Kool, Ivo Maes, Ugo Marani, Jacques Mélitz, Stefano Micossi, Wim Moesen, Francisco Torres, Alfred Tovias, Niels Thygesen, and Jürgen von Hagen. During the years leading to the fourth edition of this book I have been very much helped by the competent research assistance of Yunus Aksoy, Cláudia Costa, Frauke Skudelny, Magdalena Polan, and Nancy Verret. My gratitute also goes to Gudrun Heyde who patiently checked the manuscript and suggested many improvements. Finally, I am grateful to Francine Duysens for her excellent secretarial assistance.

Costs and Benefits of Monetary Union

Chapter 1
The Costs of a Common Currency

Introduction

THE costs of a monetary union derive from the fact that when a country relinquishes its national currency, it also relinquishes an instrument of economic policy, i.e. it loses the ability to conduct a national monetary policy. In other words, in a full monetary union the national central bank either ceases to exist or will have no real power. This implies that a nation joining a monetary union will not be able any more to change the price of its currency (by devaluations and revaluations), or to determine the quantity of the national money in circulation.

One may raise the issue here of what good it does for a nation to be able to conduct an independent monetary policy (including changing the price of its currency). There are many situations in which these policies can be very useful for an individual nation. The use of the exchange rate as a policy instrument, for example, is useful because nations are different in some important senses, requiring changes in the exchange rate to occur. In the next section we first analyse some of these differences that may require exchange rate adjustments. In later sections we analyse how the loss of monetary independence may be costly in some other ways for an individual nation.

The analysis that follows in this chapter is known as the 'theory of optimum currency areas'. This theory which has been pioneered by Mundell (1961), McKinnon (1963), and Kenen (1969) has concentrated on the cost side of the cost-benefit analysis of a monetary union.[1]

---

[1] For surveys of this literature see Ishiyama (1975) and Tower and Willett (1976).

1 Shifts in demand (Mundell)

CONSIDER the case of a demand shift developed by Mundell in his celebrated article on optimum currency areas.[2] Let us suppose that for some reason EU consumers shift their preferences away from French-made to German-made products. We present the effects of this shift in aggregate demand in Fig. 1.1.

The curves in Fig. 1.1 are the standard aggregate demand and supply curves in an open economy of most macroeconomics textbooks.[3] The demand curve is the negatively sloped line indicating that when the domestic price level increases the demand for the domestic output declines.[4]

The supply curve expresses the idea that when the price of the domestic output increases, domestic firms will increase their supply, to profit from the higher price. These supply curves therefore assume competition in the output markets. In addition, each supply curve is drawn under the assumption that the nominal wage rate and the price of other inputs (e.g. energy, imported inputs) remain constant. Changes in the prices of these inputs will shift these supply curves.

The demand shift is represented by an upward movement of the demand curve in Germany, and a downward movement in France. The result is that output declines in France and that it increases in Germany. This is most likely to lead to additional unemployment in France and a decline of unemployment in Germany.

Figure 1.1 Aggregate demand and supply in France and Germany

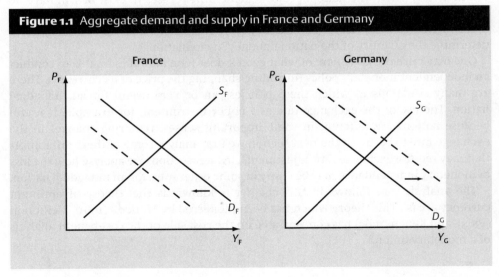

[2] See Mundell (1961).
[3] See Dornbusch and Fischer (1978) or Parkin and Bade (1988).
[4] This is the substitution effect of a price increase. In the standard aggregate demand analysis, there is also a monetary effect: when the domestic price level increases, the stock of real cash balances declines, leading to an upward movement in the domestic real interest rate. This in turn reduces aggregate demand (see P. De Grauwe, 1983). Here we disregard the monetary effect and concentrate on the substitution effect.

The effects on the current accounts of the two countries can also be analysed using Fig. 1.1. We first note that the current account is defined as follows:

current account = domestic output − domestic spending

where these variables are expressed in money terms.

In France the value of domestic output has declined as a result of the shift in aggregate demand. If spending by French residents does not decline by the same amount, France will have a current account deficit. This is the most likely outcome, since the social security system automatically pays unemployment benefits. As a result, the disposable income of French residents does not decline to the same extent as output falls. The counterpart of all this is an increase in the French government budget deficit.

In Germany the situation will be the reverse. The value of output increases. It is most likely that the value of total spending by German residents will not increase to the same extent. Part of the extra disposable income is likely to be saved. As a result, Germany will show a surplus on its current account.

Both countries will have an adjustment problem. France is plagued with unemployment and a current account deficit. Germany experiences a boom which also leads to upward pressures on its price level, and it accumulates current account surpluses. The question that arises is whether there is a mechanism that leads to automatic equilibration, without the countries having to resort to devaluations and revaluations?

The answer is positive. There are two mechanisms that will automatically bring back equilibrium in the two countries. One is based on wage flexibility, the other on the mobility of labour.

1 *Wage flexibility*. If wages in France and Germany are flexible the following will happen. French workers who are unemployed will reduce their wage claims. In Germany the excess demand for labour will push up the wage rate. The effect of this adjustment mechanism is shown in Fig. 1.2. The reduction of the wage rate in France shifts the aggregate supply curve downwards, whereas the wage increases in Germany shift the aggregate supply curve upwards. These shifts tend to bring back equilibrium. In France the price of output declines, making French products more competitive, and stimulating demand. The opposite occurs in Germany. This adjustment at the same time improves the French current account and reduces the German current account surplus.

Note also that the second-order effects on aggregate demand will reinforce the equilibrating mechanism. The wage and price increases in Germany make French products more competitive. This leads to an upward shift in the French aggregate demand curve. Similarly, the decline in French costs and prices makes German products less competitive and shifts the German aggregate demand curve downwards.

2 *Mobility of labour*. A second mechanism that will lead to a new equilibrium involves mobility of labour. The French unemployed workers move to Germany where there is excess demand for labour. This movement of labour eliminates the need to let wages decline in France and increase in Germany. Thus, the French

Figure 1.2 The automatic adjustment process

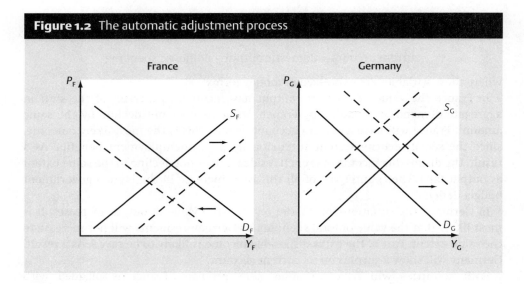

unemployment problem disappears, whereas the inflationary wage pressures in Germany vanish. At the same time the current account disequilibria will also decline. The reason is that the French unemployed were spending on goods and services before without producing anything. This problem tends to disappear with the emigration of the French workers to Germany.

Thus, in principle the adjustment problem for France and Germany will disappear automatically if wages are flexible, and/or if the mobility of labour between the two countries is sufficiently high. If these conditions are not satisfied, however, the adjustment problem will not vanish. Suppose, for example, that wages in France do not decline despite the unemployment situation, and that French workers do not move to Germany. In that case France is stuck in the disequilibrium situation as depicted in Fig. 1.1. In Germany, the excess demand for labour puts upward pressure on the wage rate, producing an upward shift of the supply curve. The adjustment to the disequilibrium must now come exclusively through price increases in Germany. These German price increases make French goods more competitive again, leading to an upward shift in the aggregate demand curve in France. Thus, if wages do not decline in France the adjustment to the disequilibrium will take the form of inflation in Germany.

The German authorities will now face a *dilemma* situation. If they care about inflation, they will want to resist these inflationary pressures (e.g. by restrictive monetary and fiscal policies). However, in that case the current account surplus (which is also the current account deficit of France) will not disappear. If they want to eliminate the current account surplus, the German authorities will have to accept the higher inflation.

This dilemma can only be solved by revaluing the mark against the franc. The effects of this exchange rate adjustment are shown in Fig. 1.3. The revaluation of the mark reduces aggregate demand in Germany, so that the demand curve shifts back to

Figure 1.3 Effects of a revaluation of the DM

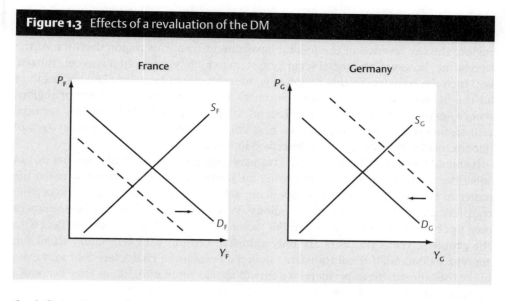

the left. In France the opposite occurs. The devaluation of the franc increases the competitiveness of the French products. This shifts the French aggregate demand curve upwards.

The effects of these demand shifts is that France solves its unemployment problem, and that Germany avoids having to accept inflationary pressures. At the same time, the current account deficit of France and surplus of Germany tend to disappear. This remarkable feat is achieved using just one instrument. (The reader may sense that this is too good to be true. And indeed it is. However, for the moment we just present Mundell's theory. We come back later with criticism.)

If France has relinquished the control over its exchange rate by joining a monetary union with Germany, it will be saddled with a sustained unemployment problem, and a current account deficit that can only disappear by deflation in France. In this sense we can say that a monetary union has a cost for France when it is faced with a negative demand shock. Similarly, Germany will find it costly to be in a monetary union with France, because it will have to accept more inflation than it would like.

Can we solve the dilemma in which the two countries find themselves by using other instruments? The answer, in principle, is yes. The German authorities could increase taxes in Germany so as to reduce aggregate demand. (The aggregate demand curve shifts downwards as it does when the mark is revalued.) These tax revenues are then transferred to France where they are spent. (The aggregate demand curve shifts upwards in France.) France would still have a current account deficit. However, it is financed by the transfer from Germany.

It will be obvious that this solution to the problem is difficult to contemplate between sovereign nations, especially since it would have to be repeated every year if the demand shift that started the problem is a permanent one. This solution, however, is frequently applied between regions of the same nation. Many countries have implicit or explicit regional redistribution schemes through the federal budget.

Implicit regional redistribution within a nation occurs because of the fact that a large part of the government budget is centralized. As a result, when output declines in a region, the tax revenue of the federal government from this region declines. At the same time, however, the social security system (which is quite often also centralized) will increase transfers to this region (e.g. unemployment benefits). The net result of all this is that the central budget automatically redistributes in favour of regions whose income declines. In some federal states there also exist *explicit* regional redistribution schemes. Probably the best known of these is the German system of 'Finanzausgleich'. This system is described in Box 1.

It should be stressed here that fiscal transfers between regions and countries do not solve the adjustment problem following an asymmetric shock. They just make life easier in the country (region) experiencing a negative demand shock and receiving transfers from the other countries (regions). When the demand shock is a permanent one, price and wage adjustments and/or factor mobility will be necessary to deal with the problem. Fiscal transfers are only suited to dealing with temporary shocks in aggregate demand. If fiscal transfers take on a permanent character, they may even make the adjustment to permanent demand shocks more difficult, as they become a substitute for wage and price changes and for mobility of labour.

Let us recapitulate the main points developed in this section. If wages are rigid and if labour mobility is limited, countries that form a monetary union will find it harder to adjust to demand shifts than countries that have maintained their own national moneys and that can devalue (revalue) their currency. In the latter case, the exchange rate adds some flexibility to a system which is overly rigid. Put differently, a monetary union between two or more countries is optimal if one of the following conditions is satisfied: (*a*) there is sufficient wage flexibility, (*b*) there is sufficient mobility of labour. It also helps to form a monetary union if the budgetary process is sufficiently centralized so that transfers can be organized smoothly (and not after a lot of political bickering) between the countries of the union.

From this analysis one might be tempted to conclude that the conditions for forming a monetary union between, say, France and Germany are most probably not satisfied. This would, however, be too rash a conclusion. We have not yet introduced the benefits of a monetary union. After all, one can only draw conclusions after comparing costs with benefits. In addition, there is some criticism to be levied against the preceding analysis. We will come back to this criticism in Chapter 2.

2 Different preferences of countries about inflation and unemployment

COUNTRIES differ also because they have different preferences. Some countries are less allergic to inflation than others. This may make the introduction of a common currency costly. The importance of these differences has been analysed by

Box 1 Fiscal equalization between Länder in Germany

The system came into existence after the Second World War. Its basic philosophy is that Länder (states) whose tax revenues fall below some predetermined range should receive compensation from Länder whose tax revenues exceed that range. The way this range is computed is rather technical (for more detail see Zimmerman (1989)). Simplifying, it consists in first calculating what the normal tax revenue should be for each state. A state whose tax revenues fall below 92% of this norm receives compensation. To cover these transfers the states whose tax revenues exceed the norm by 2% or more contribute to the system. In Table B1.1 we show the amount of redistribution obtained by this system in 1995.

Table B1.1 Amount of redistribution (in millions of DM) through the system of Finanzausgleich in Germany (1995)

Contributing Länder	
North Rhine–Westphalia	3,442
Baden Württemberg	2,804
Bavaria	2,533
Hessen	2,154
Schleswig-Holstein	142
Hamburg	118
Total	11,193

Receiving Länder	
Berlin	4,209
Saxony	1,783
Saxony–Anhalt	1,123
Thüringen	1,017
Brandenburg	865
Mecklenburg–Vorpommern	771
Bremen	562
Rheinland–Palatinate	229
Lower Saxony	451
Saarland	180
Total	11,190

Source: Bundesministerium der Finanzen (1996), 146.

With German unification the system was expanded to incorporate the new Länder. These have all become net receivers of transfers. This system of redistribution (together with the automatic redistribution resulting from the centralization of the Federal budget) has led to a remarkable reduction of regional income inequalities in Germany.

Corden (1972) and Giersch (1973). We present the problem using a simple graphical representation taken from De Grauwe (1975).

Consider two countries. For a change, let us call them Italy and Germany. In Fig. 1.4 we represent the Phillips curves of these two countries, on the right-hand side. The vertical axis shows the rate of change of the wage rate 1,ẇ, the horizontal axis the unemployment rate 1,ů. (We assume for a moment that these Phillips curves are stable, i.e. they do not shift as a result of changes in expectations of inflation. The modern reader will have difficulties swallowing this. Let him/her be patient. We will ask the question of how the analysis is affected once we take into account the fact that these Phillips curves are not stable.)

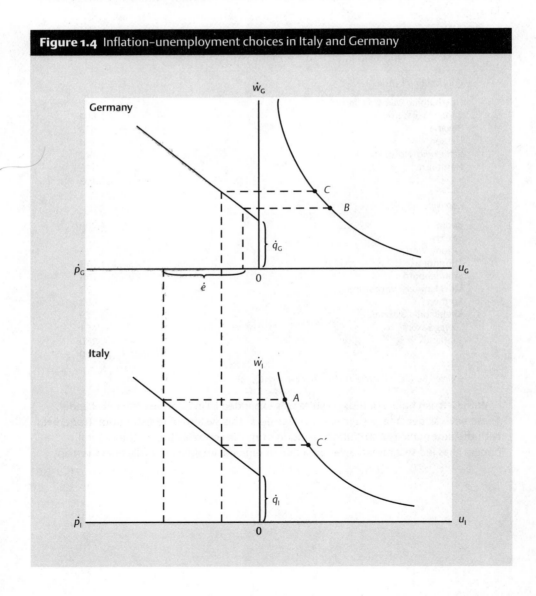

Figure 1.4 Inflation–unemployment choices in Italy and Germany

On the left-hand side we represent the relation between wage changes and price changes. This relationship can be written as follows for Italy and Germany respectively:

$$\dot{p}_I = \dot{w}_I - \dot{q}_I \tag{1.1}$$

$$\dot{p}_G = \dot{w}_G - \dot{q}_G \tag{1.2}$$

where $\dot{p}_I$ and $\dot{p}_G$ are the rates of inflation, $\dot{w}_I$ and $\dot{w}_G$ are the rates of wage increases, and $\dot{q}_I$ and $\dot{q}_G$ are the rates of growth of labour productivity in Italy and Germany. Equations (1.1) and (1.2) can be interpreted by an example. Suppose wages increase by 10% and the productivity of labour increases by 5% in Italy. Then the rate of price increase that maintains the share of profits in total value added unchanged is 5%. Thus equations (1.1) and (1.2) can be considered to define the rate of price changes that keep profits unchanged (as a percentage of value added).[5] These two equations are represented by the straight lines on the left-hand side. Note that the intercept is given by $\dot{q}_I$ and $\dot{q}_G$ respectively. Thus, when the rate of productivity increases in Italy, the line shifts upwards.

The two countries are linked by the purchasing power parity condition, i.e.

$$\dot{e} = \dot{p}_I - \dot{p}_G \tag{1.3}$$

where $\dot{e}$ is the rate of depreciation of the lira relative to the mark. Equation (1.3) should be interpreted as an equilibrium condition. It says that if Italy has a higher rate of inflation than Germany, it will have to depreciate its currency to maintain the competitiveness of its products unchanged. If Italy and Germany decide to form a monetary union, the exchange rate is fixed ($\dot{e} = 0$), so that the rates of inflation must be equal. If this is not the case, e.g. inflation in Italy is higher than in Germany, Italy will increasingly lose competitiveness.

Suppose now that Italy and Germany have different preferences about inflation and unemployment. Italy chooses point A on its Phillips curve, whereas Germany chooses B. It is now immediately obvious that the inflation rates will be different in the two countries, and that a fixed exchange rate will be unsustainable. The cost of a monetary union for the two countries now consists in the fact that if Italy and Germany want to keep the exchange rate fixed they will have to choose another (less preferred) point on their Phillips curves, so that an equal rate of inflation becomes possible. Such an outcome is given by the points C and C' on the respective Phillips curves. (Note that many other points are possible, leading to other joint inflation rates.) Italy now has to accept less inflation and more unemployment than it would do otherwise, Germany has to accept more inflation and less unemployment.

This analysis, which was popular in the 1960s and the early 1970s, has fallen victim to the demise of the Phillips curve. Following the criticisms of Friedman (1968) and Phelps (1968), it is now generally accepted that the Phillips curve is not stable, i.e. that it will shift upwards when expectations of inflation increase. Thus, a country that

---

[5] Suppose a perfect competitive environment. Then profit maximization implies that $w/p = \delta X/\delta L$. If the production function is Cobb–Douglas, $w/p = \alpha X/L$, where α is the labour share in value added. Taking rates of change yields $\dot{w} - \dot{p} = \dot{q}$ (assuming a constant α).

chooses too high an inflation rate will find that its Phillips curve shifts upwards. Under these conditions the authorities have very little free choice between inflation and unemployment. This has also led to the view that the Phillips curve is really a vertical line in the long run, with far-reaching consequences for the costs of a monetary union. We will return to this issue in Chapter 2 when we critically examine the theory of optimum currency areas.

3 Differences in labour market institutions

THERE is no doubt that there are important institutional differences in the labour markets of European countries. Some labour markets are dominated by highly centralized labour unions (e.g. Germany). In other countries labour unions are decentralized (e.g. the UK). These differences may introduce significant costs for a monetary union. The main reason is that these institutional differences can lead to divergent wage and price developments, even if countries face the same disturbances. For example, when two countries are subjected to the same oil price increase the effect this has on the domestic wages and prices very much depends on how labour unions react to these shocks.

Recent macroeconomic theories have been developed that shed some light on the importance of labour market institutions. The most popular one was developed by Bruno and Sachs (1985).[6] The idea can be formulated as follows. Supply shocks, such as the one that occurred during 1979–80, have very different macroeconomic effects depending upon the degree of centralization of wage bargaining. When wage bargaining is centralized (Bruno and Sachs call countries with centralized wage bargaining 'corporatist'), labour unions take into account the inflationary effect of wage increases. In other words they know that excessive wage claims will lead to more inflation, so that real wages will not increase. They will have no incentive to make these excessive wage claims. Thus, when a supply shock occurs, as in 1979–80, they realize that the loss in real wages due to the supply shocks cannot be compensated by nominal wage increases.

Things are quite different in countries with less centralized wage bargaining. In these countries individual unions that bargain for higher nominal wages know that the effect of these nominal wage increases on the aggregate price level is small, because these unions only represent a small fraction of the labour force. There is a free-riding problem. Each union has an interest in increasing the nominal wage of its members. For if it does not do so, the real wage of its members would decline, given that all the other unions are likely to increase the nominal wage for their members. In equilibrium this non-cooperative game will produce a higher nominal wage level

---

[6] It should be stressed that these theories were already available and widely discussed in many European countries before Bruno and Sachs discovered them. Their advantage was that they wrote in English, and thereby succeeded in disseminating the idea internationally.

than the co-operative (centralized) game. In countries with decentralized wage bargaining therefore it is structurally more difficult to arrive at wage moderation after a supply shock. In such a non-cooperative set-up no individual union has an incentive to take the first step in reducing its nominal wage claim. For it risks that the others will not follow, so that the real wage level of its members will decline.

The analogy with the spectators in a football stadium is well known. When they are all seated, the individual spectator has an incentive to stand up so as to have a better view of the game. The dynamics of this game is that they all stand up, see no better, and are more uncomfortable. Once they stand up, it is equally difficult to induce them to sit down. The individual who takes the first step and sits down will see nothing, as long as the others do not follow his example. Since he is sitting, most spectators in the stadium will not even notice this good example.

This co-operation story has been extended by Calmfors and Driffill (1988) who noted that the relationship between centralization of wage bargaining and outcomes is not a linear process. In particular, the more we move towards the decentralized spectrum the more another externality comes to play a role. For in a very decentralized system (e.g. wage bargaining at the firm level), the wage claims will have a direct effect on the competitiveness of the firm, and therefore on the employment prospects of individual union members. Excessive wage claims by an individual union will lead to a strong reduction of employment. Thus, when faced with a supply shock, unions in such a decentralized system may exhibit a considerable degree of wage restraint.

This insight then leads to the conclusion that countries with either strong centralization or strong decentralization of wage bargaining are better equipped to face supply shocks such as the one that occurred during 1979–80 than countries with an intermediate degree of centralization. In these 'extreme' countries there will be a greater wage moderation than in the intermediate countries. As a result, the countries with extreme centralization or decentralization tend to fare better, in terms of inflation and unemployment, following supply shocks, than the others.

Some empirical evidence for this hypothesis is shown in Fig. 1.5. On the horizontal axis we show the degree of centralization of labour markets in a group of industrial countries. (These indices were computed by Calmfors and Driffill (1988).) On the vertical axis the changes in the 'misery' indices of the same countries from the 1970s to the 1980s are represented. These misery indices are the sum of the inflation rate and the unemployment rate.[7] One can see that intermediate countries seem to have experienced a greater worsening of their misery indices than the countries with extreme centralization or decentralization. In other words the labour market institutions of these countries may have made it more difficult to reduce inflation without losses in output following the supply shocks of 1979–80.

It follows that a country might find itself in a situation where wages and prices increase faster than in other countries even when the shock that triggered it all is the same. In terms of the two-country model that we used in Section 1 the supply curve in one country shifts upwards more than in the other country. This will lead to macro-

---

[7] In De Grauwe (1990) econometric evidence is presented giving some support to the non-linear relationship between economic performance and the degree of centralization of labour markets.

Figure 1.5 Change in misery indices (from the 1970s to the 1980s) and labour market centralization

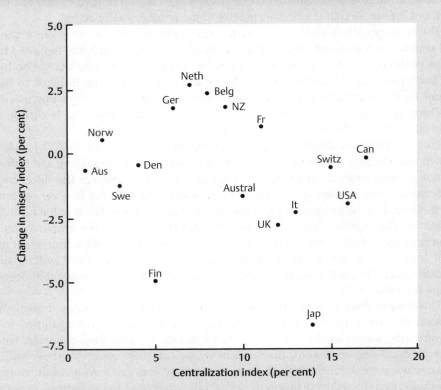

Note: The misery index is the sum of the inflation rate and the unemployment rate. The change in the index is measured from 1973–9 to 1980–8. The centralization index measures the degree of centralization of labour unions. A *low* number implies a *high* degree of centralization.

Sources: Misery index computed from OECD, *Economic Outlook*; index of centralization of wage bargaining from Calmfors and Driffill (1988).

economic adjustment problems that are of the same nature as the ones we analysed in Section 1.

We conclude that countries with very different labour market institutions may find it costly to form a monetary union. With each supply shock, wages and prices in these countries may be affected differently, making it difficult to correct for these differences when the exchange rate is irrevocably fixed.

4 Differences in legal systems

DESPITE decades of integration in the European Union, legal systems continue to be very different in the member states. These differences run deeply and sometimes have profound effects on the way markets function. We concentrate on just a few examples.

The mortgage markets operate very differently in the EU-countries. The main reason is that legal systems differ. In some countries the law protects the banks extending mortgage loans better than in other countries. As a result, mortgages are very different products with different degrees of risk from one country to the other. Because of these differences, banks require mortgages to be backed by 100% collateral in some countries, while in other ones the collateral is substantially below 100% of the value of the loan. Legal differences also lead to differences in the frequency with which interest rates are adjusted. Thus, we find countries where banks offer mortgage loans with a floating/changing interest, while in others mortgage rates are fixed for the whole maturity of the loan. As a result of these differences, the same shocks (e.g. an increase of the interest rate by the European Central Bank) are transmitted very differently across the member states of the monetary union. Recent empirical studies confirm that these differences in the transmission of the same shocks can be substantial (see Dornbusch, Favero, and Giavazzi (1997); Cecchetti (1999); Maclennan, Muellbauer, and Stephens (1999)).

The way companies finance themselves is very different across the European Union. In countries with an Anglo-Saxon legal tradition, firms tend to go directly to the capital market (bond and equity markets) to finance investment projects. As a result, these markets are well developed, sophisticated, and very liquid. In countries with a continental legal tradition firms attract financial resources mainly through the banking system. As a result, capital markets are less developed. Here again these differences lead to the result that the same interest rate disturbances are transmitted very differently. To give an example, take an increase in the interest rate. In the countries with the Anglo-Saxon type of financial system, this is likely to lead to large wealth effects of consumers. The reason is that consumers hold a lot of bonds and stocks. An interest rate increase lowers bond and stock prices, so that the wealth of consumers is likely to decline. Wealth effects will be less pronounced in countries with Continental-type financial markets. In these countries the interest rate increase will affect spending of consumers mainly through the bank-lending channel. A sufficiently high increase in the interest rate will induce banks to start credit rationing.[8] We conclude that the way the same interest rate increase is transmitted into consumption and investment spending will be very different across Union members.

---

[8] For a classic analysis of credit rationing see Stiglitz and Weiss (1981). For an analysis of the implications for monetary union see Cecchetti (1999).

5 Growth rates are different

SOME countries grow faster than others. This is made clear in Table 1.1. We find that during the 1980s some southern European countries (and Ireland) experienced growth rates of their GDP which were higher than in the northern part of Europe. (The same phenomenon is observed during the 1970s.)

Such differences in growth rates could lead to a problem when countries form a monetary union. We illustrate it with the following example. Country A's GDP is growing at 5% per year, country B's GDP at 3% per year. Suppose that the income elasticity of A's imports from B is one, and that similarly B's income elasticity of imports from A is equal to one. Then country A's imports from B will grow at 5% per year, whereas B's imports from A will grow at only 3% per year. This will lead to a trade balance problem of the fast-growing country A, whose imports tend to grow faster than its exports.

In order to avoid chronic deficits of its trade account, country A will have to reduce the price of its exports to country B, so that the latter country increases its purchases of goods from country A. In other words, country A's terms of trade must decline so as to make its products more competitive. Country A can do this in two ways: a depreciation of the currency or a lower rate of domestic price increases than in country B. If it joins a monetary union with country B, however, only the second option will be

Table 1.1 Average yearly growth rates of GDP in the EU, 1981–1998

Country	%
Austria	2.20
Belgium	1.76
Denmark	2.13
Finland	2.34
France	2.00
Germany	2.17
Greece	1.75
Ireland	5.14
Italy	1.81
Netherlands	2.37
Portugal	2.62
Spain	2.55
Sweden	1.56
United Kingdom	2.26

Source: EC Commission, *European Economy*.

available. This will require country A to follow relatively deflationary policies, which in turn will constrain the growth process. Thus, a monetary union has a cost for the fast-growing country. It will find it more advantageous to keep its national currency, so as to have the option of depreciating its currency when it finds itself constrained by unfavourable developments in its trade account.

6 Different fiscal systems and the seigniorage problem

COUNTRIES differ also because they have different fiscal systems. These differences often lead countries to use different combinations of debt and monetary financing of the government budget deficit. When these countries join a monetary union, they will be constrained in the way they finance their budget deficits.

In order to show this, it is useful to start from the government budget constraint:

$$G - T + rB = dB/dt + dM/dt \tag{1.4}$$

where G is the level of government spending (excluding interest payments on the government debt), T is the tax revenue, r is the interest rate on the government debt, B, and M is the level of high-powered money (monetary base).

The left-hand side of equation (1.4) is the government budget deficit. It consists of the primary budget deficit $(G - T)$ and the interest payment on the government debt (rB). The right-hand side is the financing side. The budget deficit can be financed by issuing debt (dB/dt) or by issuing high-powered money dM/dt.

The theory of optimal public finance now tells us that rational governments will use the different sources of revenue so that the marginal cost of raising revenue through these different means is equalized.[9] Thus, if the marginal cost of raising revenue by increasing taxes exceeds the marginal cost of raising revenue by inflation (seigniorage), it will be optimal to reduce taxes and to increase inflation.

The preceding also means that countries will have different optimal inflation rates. In general, countries with an underdeveloped tax system will find it more advantageous to raise revenue by inflation (seigniorage). Put differently, a country with an underdeveloped fiscal system experiences large costs in raising revenue by increasing tax rates. It will be less costly to increase government revenue by inflation.

This reasoning leads to the following implication for the costs of a monetary union. Less developed countries that join a monetary union with more developed countries that have a low rate of inflation will also have to lower inflation. This then means that, for a given level of spending, they will have to increase taxes. There will be a loss of welfare. Some economists (e.g. Dornbusch (1987)) have claimed that this is a par-

---

[9] See Fischer (1982) and Grilli (1989).

ticularly acute problem for the southern EC countries. By joining the low-inflation northern monetary zone they will have to increase taxes, or let the deficit increase further. For these countries the cost of the monetary union is that they will have to rely too much on a costly way of raising revenues.

Table 1.2 gives some empirical evidence on the size of the seigniorage for these southern countries, and compares it with Germany. We observe that up to the middle of the 1980s the southern European countries had high seigniorage revenues. These revenues amounted to 2–3% of GNP in all these countries. This was certainly much more important than in the northern countries. Since the middle of the 1980s, however, seigniorage revenue of these countries has declined significantly, mainly because of the reduction in their inflation rates. This leads to the conclusion that when these countries joined EMU with the low-inflation countries in the 1990s, the additional cost (in terms of public finance) was not very important.

7 Conclusion

IN this chapter we discussed differences between countries. We observed that countries can use exchange rate changes, or other monetary policies, to correct for these differences. We found that in most cases there is an alternative to using the exchange rate as a policy instrument. For example, when confronted with a loss of domestic competitiveness, countries can use contractionary demand policies aiming at regaining competitiveness. However, these alternatives are often more painful, and therefore less desirable. To the extent that these alternative policies are more painful than changing the exchange rate we concluded that the country under consideration does not gain from relinquishing its money and joining a currency union. (Note, however, that we still have not introduced the benefit side of the analysis. It is still

Table 1.2 Seigniorage revenues as per cent of GNP			
	1976–85	1986–90	1993
Germany	0.2	0.6	0.5
Greece	3.4	1.5	0.7
Italy	2.6	0.7	0.5
Portugal	3.4	1.9	0.6
Spain	2.9	0.8	0.6

Sources: Dornbusch (1987); Gros (1990); Gros and Thygesen (1992).

Box 2 Symmetric and asymmetric shocks compared

We have seen that the occurrence of asymmetric shocks creates costs of adjustment in a monetary union if there is a lack of flexibility in the labour markets. Things are very different when symmetric shocks occur. We illustrate this using the same two-country model of aggregate demand and supply as in Fig. 1.1. We now assume that the demand shocks are symmetric. More specifically, we assume that in both France and Germany the demand curve shifts to the left in equal amounts. The result is shown in Fig. B2.1.

Figure B2.1 Symmetric shocks

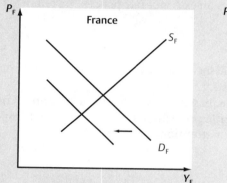
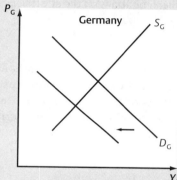

Can France and Germany deal with this negative demand shock when they are in a monetary union? The answer is yes, at least in principle. In a monetary union, monetary policy is centralized in the hands of the union central bank. Call it the European Central Bank (ECB). In addition, in a monetary union there is only one interest rate as the money markets are perfectly integrated. The ECB can now lower the interest rate thereby stimulating aggregate demand in both countries. This contrasts very much with the case of asymmetric shocks. There the ECB will be pretty much paralysed, because it has only one instrument to deal with two problems. If it reduces the interest rate so as to stimulate aggregate demand in France, it increases inflationary pressure in Germany. If on the other hand it increases the interest rate so as to deal with the inflationary pressure in Germany, it reduces aggregate demand in France, and intensifies that country's problem.

It is also interesting to analyse what would happen if the two countries that face a symmetric shock were not in a monetary union. Would a devaluation then be an attractive policy option? The answer is no. Suppose that France would devalue. This would stimulate aggregate demand in France, at the expense of Germany. In France, the aggregate demand curve would shift to the right. The French devaluation would, however, shift the German aggregate demand curve further to the left. The French would essentially solve their problem by exporting it to Germany. It is likely that the latter would react. The danger of a spiral of devaluations and counter-devaluations would be real. In the end the effectiveness of changing the exchange rate would be greatly reduced. In order to avoid such a spiral the two countries would have to coordinate their actions, which is difficult among independent nations. In a monetary union, in contrast, this monetary cooperation is institutionalized. We conclude that a monetary union is a more attractive monetary regime than a regime of independent monetary authorities if shocks that hit the countries are symmetric. When shocks are asymmetric, however, this advantage of a monetary union disappears.

It should be noted that we have assumed that the ECB can manipulate aggregate demand in the union. There are reasons to believe that the effectiveness of monetary policy in raising aggregate demand is limited. The same criticism, however, applies as far as the effectiveness of devaluations is concerned. When countries are independent and when they use the exchange rate as an instrument to deal with asymmetric shocks, they face similar limitations on the effectiveness of exchange rate policies. We return to these issues in Chapter 2.

possible that even if there are costs associated with relinquishing one's national money, the benefits outweigh these costs.)

The analysis of this chapter which is based on the theory of optimum currency areas has been subjected to much criticism. This has led to new and important insights. In the next chapter we turn our attention to this criticism.

Chapter 2
The Theory of Optimum Currency Areas: A Critique

Introduction

IN the previous chapter we analysed the reasons why countries might find it costly to join a monetary union. This analysis, which is known as the theory of optimum currency areas, has come under criticism.[1] This criticism has been formulated at different levels. First one may question the view that the differences between countries are important enough to bother about. Secondly, the exchange rate instrument may not be very effective in correcting for the differences between nations. Thirdly, not only may the exchange rate be ineffective, it may do more harm than good in the hands of politicians.

In this chapter we analyse this criticism in greater detail.

1 How relevant are the differences between countries?

THERE is no doubt that countries *are* different. The question, however, is whether these differences are important enough to represent a stumbling-block for monetary unification.

[1] See EC Commission (1990) and Gros and Thygesen (1991).

1.1 Is a demand shock concentrated in one country a likely event?

The classical analysis of Mundell started from the scenario in which a demand shift occurs away from the products of one country in favour of those of another country. Is such a shock likely to occur frequently between the European countries that form a monetary union? Two views have emerged to answer this question. We will call the first one the European Commission view, which was defended in the report 'One Market, One Money'. The second view is associated with Paul Krugman.

According to the European Commission, differential shocks in demand will occur less frequently in a monetary union. The reason is the following. Trade between the industrial European nations is to a large degree intra-industry trade. The trade is based on the existence of economies of scale and imperfect competition (product differentiation). It leads to a structure of trade in which countries buy and sell to each other the same categories of products. Thus, France sells cars to and buys cars from Germany, and vice versa. This structure of trade leads to a situation where most demand shocks will affect these countries in a similar way. For example, when consumers reduce their demand for cars, they will buy fewer French *and* German cars. Thus, both countries' aggregate demand will be affected in similar ways.

The removal of barriers with the completion of the single market will reinforce these tendencies. As a result, most demand shocks will tend to have similar effects.[2] Instead of being asymmetric, these shocks will tend to be more symmetric.

The second and opposite view has been defended by Paul Krugman. According to Krugman (1991), one cannot discard Mundell's analysis, for there is another feature of the dynamics of trade with economies of scale that may make Mundell's analysis very relevant. Trade integration which occurs as a result of economies of scale also leads to regional concentration of industrial activities.[3] The basic argument here is that when impediments to trade decline this has two opposing effects on the localization of industries. It makes it possible to produce closer to the final markets, but it also makes it possible to concentrate production so as to profit from economies of scale (both static and dynamic). This explains why trade integration in fact may lead to more concentration of regional activities rather than less.

The fact that trade may lead to regional concentration of industrial activities is illustrated rather dramatically by comparing the regional distribution of the automobile production in the USA and in Europe (see Table 2.1). The most striking feature of this table is that the US production of automobiles is much more regionally concentrated than the EU's. (This feature is found in many other industrial sectors; see

---

[2] Peter Kenen (1969) also stressed the importance of the similarity of the trading structure for making a monetary union less costly.

[3] This is an old idea that was developed by Myrdal (1957) and Kaldor (1966). For a survey see Balassa (1961). Krugman (1991) gives a more rigorous underpinning of these ideas.

Table 2.1 Regional distribution of auto production

	USA		EU
Midwest	66.3	Germany	38.5
South	25.4	France	31.1
West	5.1	Italy	17.6
North-east	3.32	UK	12.9

Source: Krugman (1991).

Krugman (1991). There is also no doubt that the US market is more highly integrated than the EU market, i.e. there are fewer impediments to trade in the USA than in the EU. This evidence therefore suggests that when the EU moves forward in the direction of a truly integrated market, it may experience similar kinds of regional concentrations of economic activities to those observed in the USA today. It is therefore possible that the automobile industry, for example, will tend to be more concentrated in, say, Germany (although we are not sure it will be Germany, it could also be another country). Sector-specific shocks may then become country-specific shocks. Countries faced with these shocks may then prefer to use the exchange rate as an instrument of economic policy to correct for these disturbances.

The two views about the relation between economic integration and the occurrence of asymmetric shocks can be analysed more systematically using the graphical device represented in Fig. 2.1. Let us first represent the European Commission view. On the vertical axis we set out the degree of divergent movements of output and employment between groups of countries (regions) which are candidates to form a monetary union.[4] On the horizontal axis we set out a measure of the degree of trade integration between these countries. This measure could be the mutual trade of these countries as a share of their GDP. The European Commission view can then be represented by a downward sloping line. It says that as the degree of economic integration between countries increases, asymmetric shocks will occur less frequently (so that income and employment will tend to diverge less between the countries involved).

We represent the second view, which we label the Krugman view, in Fig. 2.2. Instead of a downward sloping line we have a positively sloped line. Thus, when economic integration increases, the countries involved become more specialized so that they will be subjected to more rather than fewer asymmetric shocks.[5]

What is the right view of the world? A clear-cut answer will be difficult to formulate. Nevertheless it is reasonable to claim that a presumption exists in favour of the

[4] We could take as the measure of divergence one minus the correlation coefficient between the growth rates of output of these countries. Thus when the correlation is one, our measure of divergence is zero. When the correlation is -1 our measure of divergence would be 2, its maximum value.

[5] This view could be associated with Kenen (1969), who stressed that countries with a less diversified output structure are subject to more asymmetric shocks, making them less suitable to form a monetary union. The presumption is that small countries which are highly integrated with the rest of the world are also highly specialized. This leads to the paradox that small and very open countries should keep their own currencies and not join a monetary union (see Frankel and Rose (1996) on this paradox and how it can be resolved).

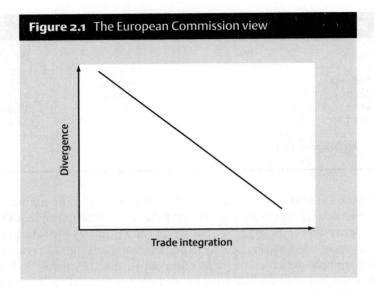

Figure 2.1 The European Commission view

European Commission view. The reason can be formulated as follows. The fact that economic integration can lead to concentration and agglomeration effects cannot be disputed. At the same time, however, it is also true that as market integration between countries proceeds, national borders become less and less important as factors that decide the location of economic activities. As a result, it becomes more and more likely that concentration and agglomeration effects will be blind to the existence of borders. This creates the possibility that the clusters of economic activity will encompass borders. Put differently, it becomes more and more likely that the relevant regions in which some activity is centralized will transgress one or more borders. For example, it could very well be that automobile manufacturing will not be centralized in Germany, but rather in the region encompassing South Germany and Northern Italy. If this is the case, shocks in the automobile industry will affect Germany *and* Italy, so that the DM–lira rate cannot be used to absorb this shock.

Note that the argument we develop here is not that integration does not lead to concentration effects (it probably will), but rather that national borders will increasingly be less relevant in influencing the shape of these concentration effects. As a result, regions may still be very much affected by asymmetric shocks. The probability that these regions overlap existing borders, however, will increase as integration moves on. We conclude that the economic forces of integration are likely to rob the exchange rates between national currencies of their capacity to deal with these shocks.

From the preceding arguments it should not be concluded that economists know for sure what the relationship is between economic integration and the occurrence of asymmetric shocks. All we can say is that there is a theoretical presumption in favour of the hypothesis that economic integration will make asymmetric shocks between nations less likely. The issue remains essentially an empirical one. Frankel and Rose (1996) have undertaken important empirical research relating to this issue. They ana-

Figure 2.2 The Krugman view

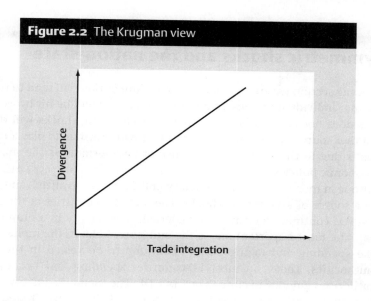

lysed the degree to which economic activity between pairs of countries is correlated as a function of the intensity of their trade links. Their conclusion was that a closer trade linkage between two countries is strongly and consistently associated with more tightly correlated economic activity between the two countries. In terms of Figs. 2.1 and 2.2 this means that the relationship between divergence and trade integration is negatively sloped.

Similar evidence is presented in Artis and Zhang (1995), who find that as the European countries have become more integrated during the 1980s and 1990s, the business cycles of these countries have become more correlated.

There is another piece of empirical evidence that enhances the view that economic integration may not lead to increased asymmetric shocks within a union. This has to do with the rising importance of services. Economies of scale do not seem to matter as much for services as for industrial activities. As a result, economic integration does not lead to regional concentration of services in the way it does with industries. As services become increasingly important (today they account for 70% or more of GDP in many EU-countries) the trend towards regional concentration of economic activities may stop even if economic integration moves forward. There is some evidence that this is already occurring in the USA. In a recent study, the OECD came to the conclusion that the regional concentration of economic activities in the USA started to decline after decades of increasing concentration.[6]

[6] See OECD (1999).

1.2 Asymmetric shocks and the nation-state

In the preceding section we argued that economic integration will tend to reduce the probability that individual nations (in contrast to regions) will be hit by asymmetric shocks. This does not mean, of course, that all asymmetric shocks will disappear. There is another source of asymmetric shocks that will continue to play a role in the future. This is due to the continued existence of nation-states as the main instruments of economic policies.

In the European monetary union, monetary policies are centralized, and therefore cease to be a source of asymmetric shocks. The member countries of the monetary union, however, continue to exercise considerable sovereignty in a number of economic areas. The most important one is the budgetary field. In the monetary union most of the spending and taxing powers continue to be vested in the hands of national authorities. Today, in most EU-countries spending and taxation by the national authorities amount to close to 50% of GDP. The spending and taxing powers of the European authorities represent less than 1.5% of GDP. This situation has not changed since the start of monetary union in 1999. By changing taxes and spending the authorities of an individual country can create large asymmetric shocks. By their very nature these shocks are well contained within national borders. For example, when the authorities of a country increase taxes on wage income, this only affects labour in that country and will influence spending and wage levels in that country. As a result, the aggregate demand and supply curves of the country involved will shift, creating disturbances that will lead to divergent price and wage developments. We are back in the Mundell analysis (of Chapter 1, Section 1) about how to adjust to these asymmetric shocks.

The fact that countries maintain most of their budgetary powers in the monetary union creates the possibility that large asymmetric shocks may occur in the Union. This raises the issue of how budgetary policies should be conducted in a monetary union. We will return to this issue in a separate chapter (see Chapter 9).

There are other aspects of the existence of nation-states that can be a source of asymmetric disturbances. Many economic institutions are national. Wage bargaining systems, for example, differ widely between countries, creating the possibility of asymmetric disturbances. In addition, differences in legal systems and customs generate significant differences in the workings of financial markets. These differences also lead to divergent effects of the same interest rate shocks. We discussed these issues in Sections 3 and 4 of the previous chapter. In the next sections we return to them.

The previous discussion leads to the conclusion that although economic integration is likely to weaken the occurrence of asymmetric shocks, the existence of nation-states with their own peculiarities will be a continued source of asymmetric disturbances in a monetary union, creating the problems of adjustment we discussed in Chapter 1. This had led some economists to argue that a monetary union can only function satisfactorily if further steps towards political unification are taken. In the view of these economists, the absence of a political union will create great risks of difficult adjustments to (political) disturbances in a future monetary union. It is equally possible, however, that the existence of a monetary union will exert sufficient pressure on the member countries to accelerate their efforts towards establishing a political union. In this view, monetary union will work as a device forcing European countries towards political union. Some of the issues relating to the link between monetary union and political union will be taken up again in Chapter 9, where we discuss budgetary policies in a monetary union.

1.3 Institutional differences in labour markets

The differences in the workings of the labour markets in different countries are well documented. These differences, however, have accumulated over the years, partly because European countries have experienced separate policy regimes. The issue is whether monetary integration will not drastically change the behaviour of labour unions, so that the differences we observe today may disappear.[7]

An example may clarify this point. In Fig. 2.3 we present the labour markets of two countries that are candidates for a monetary union. The figure is based on the model of McDonald and Solow (1981).[8] On the vertical axis we have the real wage level, on the horizontal axis the level of employment (N). The convex curves are the indifference curves of the labour union. It is assumed that there is only one labour union in each country. The union maximizes its utility which depends on both the

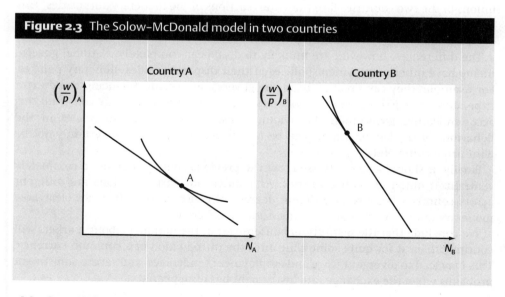

Figure 2.3 The Solow–McDonald model in two countries

[7] See Gros and Thygesen (1991), ch. 9.
[8] For a discussion of this model see Carlin and Soskice (1990).

real wage level and the employment of its members. The negatively sloped line is the economy-wide demand-for-labour curve. For the union, which maximizes its utility, the demand-for-labour curve is a constraint: thus, the union will select a point on it which maximizes its utility. This is represented in Fig. 2.3 by the points A and B.

The interesting feature of this model is that the employment line takes into account the reaction of the authorities to what the labour unions are doing. If we assume that the authorities give a higher weight to employment in their utility function than the labour unions, we may have the following situation. When the labour unions set a wage that reduces the employment level below the level that the authorities find optimal, they will react by changing their policies. For example, they will engage in more expansionary monetary and fiscal policies to absorb the unemployed, they may create public jobs, etc. To the extent that labour unions take this reaction of the authorities into account, the constraint the unions face will change. More specifically, the employment line becomes steeper because an increase in the real wage level reduces private employment and, thus, induces the authorities to intensify their job-creating policies. As a result, an increase in the real wage level has a less pronounced effect on the total level of employment.[9] Thus, the steepness of this employment line also reflects the willingness of the authorities to engage in expansionary employment policies when the wage rate increases.

In Fig. 2.3 we have drawn the employment line of country B steeper than that of country A, assuming that the authorities of country B are more willing to accommodate the unions' wage-setting behaviour by expansionary employment policies. Monetary union now changes the possibility for the national governments to follow such accommodating policies. Monetary policies are now centralized, so that the unions of the two countries face the same reactions of the monetary authorities. This makes the employment lines similar, so that the two unions tend to select a similar combination of wage rates and employment levels.

The differences, however, are unlikely to disappear completely. National governments have other employment policies at their disposal besides monetary policies. For example, they can create jobs in the government sector, financing these extra expenditures by issuing debt. A monetary union does not necessarily constrain this accommodating government behaviour. Thus, although the differences in the behaviour of the labour unions will be less pronounced, they will certainly not be eliminated completely.

Finally, it should also be stressed that the previous analysis assumes a completely centralized union in both countries. As pointed out earlier, unions are different across countries because of different degrees of centralization. It is not clear how monetary union will change these institutional differences.

We conclude that the institutional differences in the national labour markets will continue to exist for quite some time after the introduction of a common currency. This may lead to divergent wage and employment tendencies, and severe adjustment problems when the exchange rate instrument has disappeared.

---

[9] This employment line must in fact be interpreted as the reaction curve of the government. The union operates as a 'Stackelberg' leader and selects the optimal point on this reaction line.

1.4 Different legal systems and financial markets

Financial markets continue to work differently across the EU, creating the risk that the same monetary shocks are transmitted very differently. This is mainly due to different legal systems in the member-states. Not all the differences in the workings of financial markets, however, are due to different legal systems. Some of them have arisen over time because of the fact that countries followed different monetary policies. An example will clarify this point. Some countries have managed to keep inflation low (e.g. Germany). Other countries have experienced relatively large inflation (e.g. Italy). These systematic differences in inflation have affected the workings of financial markets in these countries. In an environment of high inflation investors are typically very reluctant to buy long-term bonds. The reason is very simple. The price of long-term bonds is very sensitive to unexpected inflation. Small increases in the latter can lead to large declines in the price of long-term bonds. This is much less the case for short-term bonds. As a result, in high-inflation countries, the long-term bond market barely exists. Instead, most issues of bonds are made in the short-term market. Thus in Italy, a large part of the government debt is short term. This is not the case in low-inflation countries, like Germany. Because the inflation risk is low, investors are willing to invest in long-term bonds, and governments will tend to supply these long-term bonds. We show some evidence in Table 2.2.

All this caused asymmetries in the way EU-governments reacted to the same interest rate changes in the past. When the interest rate increased, the Italian government budget was immediately affected. Because of the short maturity of the Italian debt, an increase in the interest rate forced the Italian government quickly to spend more on interest payments, so that the budget deficit increased significantly. In low-inflation countries like Germany, the budgetary effects of an interest rate increase were much slower to materialize.

These differences which were due to differences in inflation will disappear in the monetary union. Over time, the maturity structure of the bonds issued by the Italian and German governments will converge, and so will the budgetary implications of the same interest rate shock.[10] Thus, monetary union by itself will eliminate some of

Table 2.2 Maturity distribution of government bonds (% of total)

	Short-term (<1 year)	Medium and long term (>1 year)	Of which long term (>5 years)
Italy	49.4	50.6	24.8
Germany	18.5	81.5	–
Netherlands	6.7	93.3	63.0

Source: OECD, Economic Surveys, Italy, no. 1, 1999.

[10] For a recent analysis of these issues, see Arnold and de Vries (1999).

the institutional differences that exist between national financial systems. However, 'deeper' differences, i.e. those that are the result of different legal systems, will only disappear by a convergence of national legal systems. This can only be brought about by further political integration.

1.5 Do differences in growth rates matter?

Fast-growing countries experience fast-growing imports. In order to allow exports to increase at the same rate, these countries will have to make their exports more competitive by real depreciations of their currencies. If they join a monetary union, this will be made more difficult. As a result, these countries will be constrained in their growth. This popular view of the constraint imposed on fast-growing countries that decide to join a monetary union has very little empirical support.

In Fig. 2.4. we present data on the growth rates of EC countries during 1981–98 and real depreciations (or appreciations) of their currencies. The fast-growers are above the horizontal line, the slow-growers below. We observe that among the low-growers there are countries that saw their currency appreciate and others depreciate. The fast-growers experienced real appreciations (and not depreciations).[11]

This lack of relation between economic growth and real depreciations has been given an elegant interpretation by Paul Krugman (1989). Economic growth has relatively little to do with the static view implicit in the story told in the earlier sections. Economic growth implies mostly the development of new products. Fast-growing countries are those that are able to develop new products, or old products with new qualitative features. The result of this growth process is that the income elasticities of the exports of fast-growing countries are typically higher than those of slow-growers. More importantly, these income elasticities of the export goods of the fast-growers will also typically be higher than the income elasticities of their imports. (See Krugman (1989) for empirical evidence.) As a result, these countries can grow faster without incurring trade balance problems. This also implies that the fast-growers can increase their exports at a fast pace without having to resort to real depreciations.

There is a second reason why the fast-growing countries should not worry too much that joining a monetary union will constrain their potential for growth. This has to do with the existence of capital flows. A fast-growing country is usually also a country where the productivity of capital is higher than in slow-growing countries. This difference in the productivity of capital will induce investment flows from the slow-growing countries to the fast-growing countries. These capital flows then make it possible for the fast-growing country to finance current account deficits without any need to devalue the currency.

[11] This visual evidence is confirmed by the regression equation

$$GDP = 0,0 + 0,2 \; REER;$$
$$\quad\quad (0,0) \;\; (0,4)$$

Corrected $R^2 = 0,02$;

where GDP = growth rate of GDP minus EC growth, and REER = the average growth rate of unit labour costs relative to Community partners. Standard errors are in brackets. It can be seen that the coefficient of REER is not statistically different from zero.

Figure 2.4 Real depreciation and growth, 1981–1998

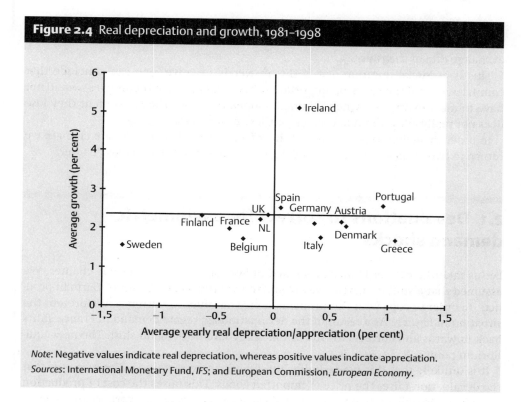

Note: Negative values indicate real depreciation, whereas positive values indicate appreciation.
Sources: International Monetary Fund, *IFS*; and European Commission, *European Economy*.

There is even an argument to be made here that fast-growing countries that join a monetary union with slow-growing countries will find it easier to attract foreign capital. With no exchange rate uncertainty, investors from the slow-growing area may be more forthcoming in moving their capital to the fast-growing country in order to profit from the larger returns.

One can conclude that differences in the growth rates of countries cannot really be considered as an obstacle to monetary integration. In other words, fast-growing countries will, in general, not have to reduce their growth rates by joining a monetary union.

2 Nominal and real depreciations of the currency

THE cost of relinquishing one's national currency lies in the fact that a country cannot change its exchange rate any more to correct for differential developments in demand, or in costs and prices. The question, however, is whether these exchange rate changes are effective in making such corrections. Put differently, the question that arises is whether *nominal* exchange rate changes can permanently alter the *real* exchange rate of the country.

This is a crucial question. For if the answer is negative, one can conclude that countries, even if they develop important differences between themselves, would not have to meet extra costs when joining a monetary union. The instrument they lose does not really allow them to correct for these differences.

In order to analyse this question of the effectiveness of exchange rate changes we return to two of the asymmetric disturbances analysed in the previous chapter.

2.1 Devaluations to correct for asymmetric demand shocks

Let us take the case of France developed in Section 1.1 of the previous chapter. We assumed that a shift occurred away from French products in favour of German products. In order to cope with this problem France devalues its currency. We present the situation in Fig. 2.5. As a result of the devaluation aggregate demand in France shifts back upwards and corrects for the initial unfavourable demand shift. The new equilibrium point is *F*.

It is unlikely that this new equilibrium point can be sustained. The reason is that the devaluation raises the price of imported goods. This raises the cost of production directly. It also will increase the nominal wage level in France as workers are likely to be compensated for the loss of purchasing power. All this means that the aggregate supply curve will shift upwards. Thus, prices increase and output declines. These price increases feed back again into the wage-formation process and lead to further

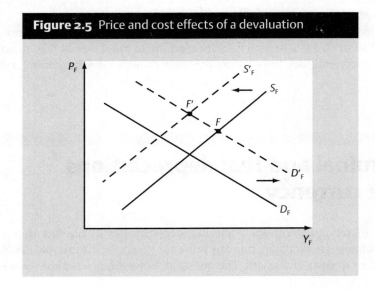

Figure 2.5 Price and cost effects of a devaluation

upward movements of the aggregate supply curve. The final equilibrium will be located at a point like F'. The initial favourable effects of the devaluation tend to disappear over time. It is not possible to say here whether these favourable effects will disappear completely. This depends on the openness of the economy, on the degree to which wage-earners will adjust their wage claims to correct for the loss of purchasing power. There is a lot of empirical evidence, however, that for most of the European countries this withering away of the initially favourable effects of a devaluation will be strong.[12]

The previous conclusion can also be phrased as follows. Nominal exchange rate changes have only temporary effects on the competitiveness of countries. Over time the nominal devaluation leads to domestic cost and price increases which tend to restore the initial competitiveness. In other words, nominal devaluations only lead to temporary *real* devaluations. In the long run nominal exchange rate changes do not affect the real exchange rate of a country.

Does this conclusion about the long-run ineffectiveness of exchange rate changes imply that countries do not lose anything by relinquishing this instrument? The answer is negative. We also have to analyse the short-term effects of an exchange rate policy aiming at correcting the initial disturbance, and we have to compare these to alternative policies that will have to be followed in the absence of a devaluation. This is done in Fig. 2.6. We have added here a line (TT) which expresses the trade account equilibrium condition. It is derived as follows. Trade account equilibrium is defined as equality between the value of domestic output and the value of spending by residents (sometimes also called absorption). Thus we have equilibrium in the trade account if and only if:

$$P_d Y = P_a A \tag{2.1}$$

where P_d is the price of the domestic good, Y the domestic output level, P_a is the average price index of the domestic and the imported good, A is absorption (in real terms). The level of real absorption depends on many factors (e.g. government spending, the real interest rate). If these are fixed, we can derive a negative relation between P_d and Y which maintains the equality (2.1), in other words which maintains trade account equilibrium. The negative relationship follows from the fact that as P_d increases, P_a (which contains the import price) increases less than proportionately, so that the left-hand side increases relative to the right-hand side of (2.1). Thus, when P_d increases, the value of output increases relative to the value of absorption, tending to produce a trade account surplus. It follows that domestic output should decline to maintain trade account equilibrium. Put differently an increase in P_d (for a given import price) is equivalent to an improvement in the terms of trade. This allows the country to reduce domestic output and still maintain equilibrium in the trade account.

Points to the left of this TT-line are ones where the country has a trade deficit, i.e. the level of domestic output is too low compared to the level of absorption. Points to the right of the TT-line are those where the country produces more than it spends.

---

[12] See EC Commission (1990), ch. 6.

Figure 2.6 Devaluation and deflationary policies compared

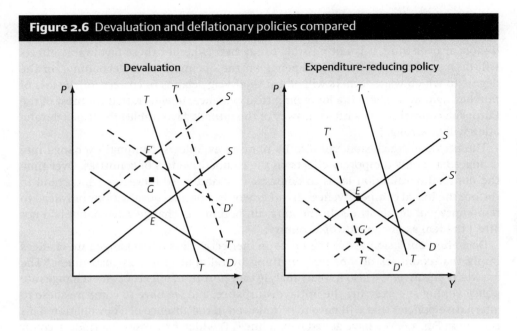

In Fig. 2.6, we assume that the country has been hit by a negative demand shock which has brought the output point to *E*. As a result, the country has a trade account deficit which will have to be corrected. One way to correct the disequilibrium is to devalue the currency. The dynamics of the adjustment after the devaluation are shown in the left-hand panel of Fig. 2.6. The devaluation shifts the demand and the supply curves upwards, as explained earlier. However, it also shifts the *TT*-curve to the right (to *T'T'*). This follows from the fact that the devaluation increases the price of imports. Thus, in equation (2.1), P_a increases. It follows that P_d and/or *Y* must increase to maintain trade account equilibrium (at least if the real level of absorption *A* remains unchanged).

The new equilibrium in the goods market is now located at point *F'*. It can be seen that there is still a trade account deficit because the new output point is located to the left of the *T'T'* line. In order to restore trade account equilibrium the government will have to follow policies reducing real absorption. These policies have the effect of shifting the *T'T'* line to the left. The reason is that with a lower level of absorption (due to say lower government spending) the level of output that maintains trade account equilibrium is also reduced. These expenditure-reducing policies also affect the demand curve, however. In general expenditure-reducing policies reduce domestic demand for the domestic good. It can be shown that there exists a combination of devaluation and expenditure-reducing policy that will bring the economy to a point like *G*, located vertically above the initial output point.[13] In the end the devaluation is neutral in that it does not affect output permanently.

In the right-hand panel of Fig. 2.6 we present the case where the country chooses

[13] See De Grauwe (1983), ch. 9.

not to devalue. Since in the initial situation (point *E*) there is a trade account deficit, the authorities will have to do something to correct this. This will necessarily have to be a policy which reduces absorption. Thus, deflationary monetary and/or fiscal policies will have to be instituted. These shift the trade account equilibrium line *TT* to the left.

These expenditure-reducing policies, however, also reduce aggregate demand for the domestic goods. Thus, the aggregate demand line also shifts to the left. The economy will go through a deflationary process, which reduces output. With sufficient wage and price flexibility, this will also tend to shift the supply line downwards, because the decline in prices leads to lower nominal wages. If wages and prices are not very flexible, this may require a considerable time. In the long run, the economy will settle at a point like *G'*. The output level is equal to its initial level, and the trade account is in equilibrium.

We conclude that in *the long run* the two policies (devaluation and expenditure-reducing) lead to the same effect on output and the trade account. Put differently, in the long run the exchange rate will not solve problems that arise from differences between countries that originate in the goods markets. This result is also in the tradition of the classical economists. These stressed that money is a veil. Structural differences should be tackled with structural policies. Manipulating money (its quantity or its price) cannot change these real differences.

The difference between the two policies, a devaluation or an expenditure-reducing policy, is to be found in their *short-term dynamics*. When the country devalues, it avoids the severe deflationary effects on domestic output during the transition. The cost of this policy is that there will be inflation. With the second policy, inflation is avoided. The cost, however, is that output declines during the transition period. In addition, as we have seen, this second policy may take a long time to be successful if the degree of wage and price flexibility is limited.

One can conclude that although a devaluation does not have a permanent effect on competitiveness and output, its dynamics will be quite different from the dynamics engendered by the alternative policy which will necessarily have to be followed if the country has relinquished control over its national money. This loss of a policy instrument will be a cost of the monetary union.

In Box 3 we present a case-study of a devaluation (Belgium in 1982) that helped this country to restore domestic and trade account equilibrium at a cost that was most probably lower than if it had not used the exchange rate instrument. There were other noteworthy and successful devaluations during the 1980s. The French devaluations of 1982–3 (coming after a period of major policy errors) stand out as success stories (see Sachs and Wyplosz (1986)). Similarly, the Danish devaluation of 1982 was quite successful in re-establishing external equilibrium without significant costs in terms of unemployment (see De Grauwe and Vanhaverbeke (1990)).

Box 3 The devaluation of the Belgian franc of 1982

In 1982 Belgium devalued its currency by 8.5%. In addition, fiscal and monetary policies were tightened, and an incomes policy, including temporary abolition of the wage-indexing mechanism, was instituted. This decision came after a period of several speculative crises during which the BF was put under severe pressures. These crises were themselves triggered by the increasing loss of competitiveness (in turn due to excessive wage increases) which the Belgian economy experienced during the 1970s. This led to unsustainable current account deficits.

It can now be said that the devaluation (together with the other policy measures) was a great success. Not only did it lead to a rapid turnaround in the current account of the balance of payments (see Table B3.1). It managed to do so without imposing great deflationary pressures on the Belgian economy. As Table B3.2 shows, there was a pronounced recovery in employment after 1983. This recovery in employment proceeded at a pace that was not significantly different from the rest of the Community after that date.

Table B3.1 Current account of Belgium (as a per cent of GDP)

1981	−3.8
1982	−3.6
1983	−0.6
1984	−0.4
1985	0.5
1986	2.0

Source: EC Commission (1990).

Table B3.2 Growth rate of employment

	Belgium	EC
1981	−2.0	−1.2
1982	−1.3	−0.9
1983	−1.1	−0.7
1984	0.0	0.1
1985	0.8	0.6
1986	1.0	0.8

Source: EC Commission (1990).

2.2 Devaluations to correct for different policy preferences

In the previous chapter we presented a model of two countries in which the authorities have different preferences concerning the choice between inflation and unemployment. It was argued that by making suitable exchange rate adjustments countries could choose a preferred point on their Phillips curve. Italy, for example, could by a policy of continuous depreciations of the lira ensure that it could 'buy' a low unemployment rate by accepting more inflation. The cost for Italy of joining the monetary union is that it would have to accept more unemployment than it desired in exchange for less inflation.

We have already mentioned that this analysis depends on the assumption that the Phillips curve is a stable one, and does not move with changes in expected inflation. The monetarist critique of the Phillips curve has changed all this, and therefore also the analysis of the costs of a monetary union.

The core of the monetarist critique is that a country which chooses too high an inflation rate (and in the process is forced to let its currency depreciate) will find that its Phillips curve shifts upwards. In this monetarist view of the world, the Phillips curve is really a vertical line in the long run. The implications for the costs of a monetary union are analysed in Fig. 2.7, where we represent both the short-term and the long-term (vertical) Phillips curves. The intercept of the long-run vertical Phillips curve with the x axis represents the 'natural' rate of unemployment. We now observe that, in the long run, the authorities cannot choose an optimal combination of inflation and unemployment. The latter is determined by the natural rate of unemployment and is independent of inflation.

There is therefore also nothing to be gained by Italy and Germany from having two different inflation rates. They can set their inflation rates equal to each other by fixing their exchange rates, without any cost in terms of unemployment. Italy and Germany can form a monetary union without costs. Put differently, the fact that Italy and Germany cannot follow independent monetary policies in a monetary union is no loss at all, since an independent monetary policy (and therefore inflation rate) does not bring about lower unemployment.

This analysis is now generally accepted. There remains the problem, however, of the short-term costs of joining a monetary union. Although in the long run, countries cannot really choose between inflation and unemployment, the short-run Phillips curve is still alive. That is, countries that want to reduce inflation will most probably be faced with a temporary increase in the unemployment rate. The experiences of the 1980s make this clear. In Box 4 we present a few case-studies that illustrate how policies of disinflation during the early 1980s led to significant increases in unemployment in major industrial countries.

The problem that arises then is whether the decision to join a monetary union by a country with a high rate of inflation (Italy in our example of Fig. 1.4) may not lead to a temporary but significant unemployment cost. In Fig. 1.4, the decision by Italy to

Figure 2.7 Monetary union in a world of vertical Phillips curves

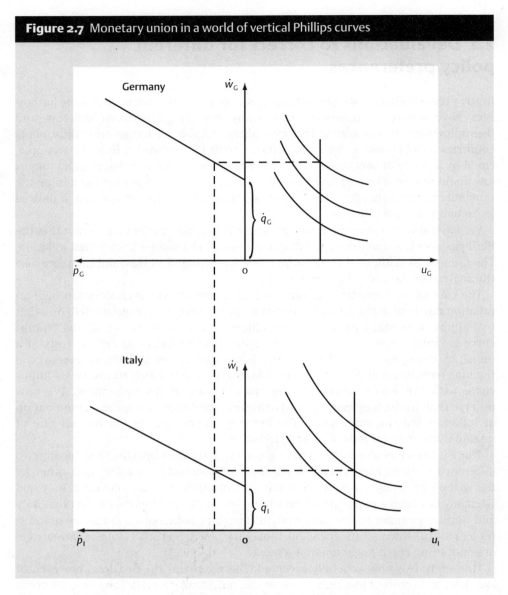

form a monetary union with Germany raises unemployment in Italy from *A* to *C'*. Over time the Italian Phillips curve will shift downwards because of lower expectations of inflation. However, during the transition, Italy is faced with high unemployment.

It should be stressed that this cost of disinflating the economy should not necessarily be called a cost of monetary union. If Italy has too high an inflation, it will have to take action to reduce it. It will then face the short-term unemployment cost whether it is part of a monetary union or not. The issue then really boils down to the question of whether it will be less costly for Italy to reduce the rate of inflation when it forms a monetary union with Germany than when it does it alone. This question has been discussed in great detail recently. We shall return to it in Section 3, where we discuss issues of the credibility of monetary policies.

The model of Fig. 2.7 allows us to highlight another important source of possible differences between countries. Suppose the growth rate of productivity $\dot{q}$ is higher in Germany than in Italy. If both countries decide to form a monetary union this implies that the nominal wage increases in Italy must be lower than in Germany. This can be seen by setting $\dot{e} = 0$ in equation (1.3), so that $\dot{p}_G = \dot{p}_I$. From equations (1.1) and (1.2) it then follows that

$$\dot{w}_G - \dot{q}_G = \dot{w}_I - \dot{q}_I \tag{2.2}$$

or

$$\dot{w}_G - \dot{w}_I = \dot{q}_G - \dot{q}_I. \tag{2.3}$$

If, following monetary unification, the German and the Italian labour unions should centralize their wage bargaining and aim for equal nominal wage increases despite the differences in productivity growth, this would spell trouble. Italian industry would become increasingly less competitive. Therefore, a condition for a successful monetary union is that labour unions should *not* centralize their wage bargaining when productivity growth rates differ.

We can summarize the main points of this section as follows. Countries differ in terms of their preferences towards inflation and unemployment. These differences, however, cannot be a serious obstacle to forming a monetary union, if one accepts that countries cannot really choose an optimal point on their Phillips curves. The only serious issue that arises in this connection is that (high-inflation) countries that join in a union may face a transitory cost in terms of unemployment.

To conclude, it should be stressed that the analysis of the Phillips-curve model in this section and the analysis of the aggregate demand and supply model in the previous section are very similar. In both sections we have stressed that policies of inflation and devaluations of the currency have only temporary effects on output and employment. In the long run, inflation and depreciations of the currency have no or only limited effects on these variables. In the monetarist models of the world (e.g. a vertical long-run Phillips curve, or a vertical long-run aggregate supply curve) inflation and depreciations of the currency have no effects on output and employment. As a result, in this monetarist world the cost of a monetary union is really zero.

2.3 Productivity and inflation in a monetary union

Up to now we have assumed that national inflation rates will be equalized in a monetary union. This is not necessarily true. We often observe that in existing monetary unions there are regional differences in inflation rates. Although these differences are relatively small, they can be significant.

The model underlying equation (2.3) allows us to understand this phenomenon. We

Fig. B4.1*a–f* presents data on inflation and unemployment in the major industrialized countries during the 1980s. We observe that in all countries the supply shocks of the 1979–80 period led to an increase in the inflation rate. Most countries then started a process of disinflation, which contributed to an increase in the unemployment rate. Some countries (France, Germany, and Italy) experienced significantly more difficulties in reducing their inflation rates, that is, the cost in terms of unemployment seems to have been considerable. In other words it took many years for the respective Phillips curves to move inwards. For France and Italy the inward movements of the Phillips curves at the end of the 1980s were very small. This suggests two possible interpretations. One is that inflationary expectations were very slow to come down; the other is that the natural rate of unemployment may have increased in these countries.

Countries like the USA and the UK experienced less difficulty in shifting their Phillips curves downward. In De Grauwe (1990) an interpretation is given of this phenomenon. We return to this issue when we discuss the functioning of the European Monetary System in Chapter 5.

Finally, note the special position of Japan, which seems to have been able to reduce inflation without any apparent cost in terms of unemployment.

Figure B4.1 Inflation and unemployment in major industrial countries 1970–1993

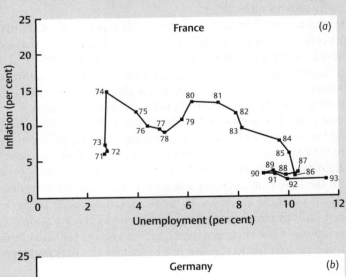

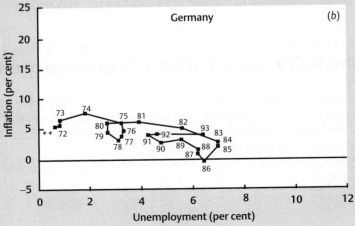

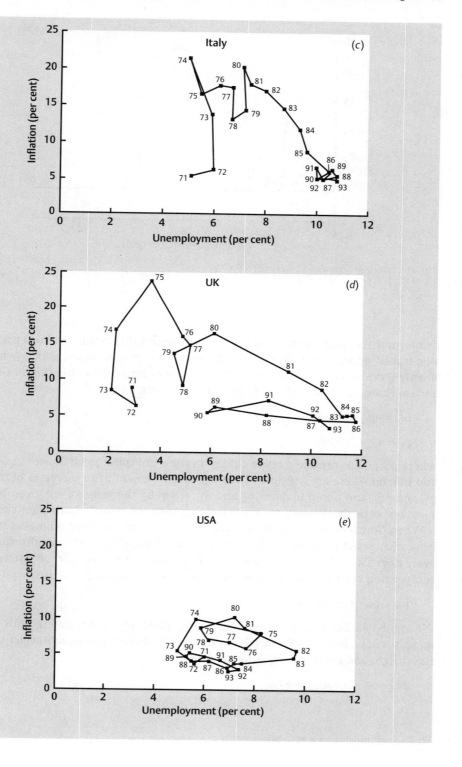

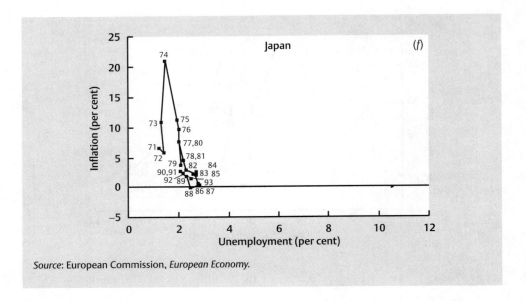

Source: European Commission, *European Economy*.

reinterpret the model as follows.[14] Let us introduce a distinction between traded and non-traded goods. We will assume that the price of non-traded goods (which are mostly services) consists of wage costs only. Let us now define inflation in Germany and (to change our example) Ireland in the following way:

$$\dot{p}c_G = \alpha \dot{p}_G + (1 - \alpha)\dot{w}_G \tag{2.4}$$

$$\dot{p}c_I = \alpha \dot{p}_I + (1 - \alpha)\dot{w}_I \tag{2.5}$$

where $\dot{p}c_G$ and $\dot{p}c_I$ are the rates of change in the *consumption* price indices in Germany and Ireland. These are a weighted average of the rates of price increases of tradables ($\dot{p}_G$ and $\dot{p}c_I$), and non-tradables ($\dot{w}_G$ and $\dot{w}_I$), whereby the weights are given by α and $1 - \alpha$, respectively. (We assume these weights to be the same in both countries.)

When Germany and Ireland are in a monetary union, competition makes sure that price changes of tradable goods are equalized. Thus $\dot{p}_G = \dot{p}_I$. Such equalization, however, does not occur in the non-tradable goods sector, because no international competition occurs there. We can now subtract (2.5) from (2.4) and use $\dot{p}_G = \dot{p}_I$:

$$\dot{p}c_G - \dot{p}c_I = (1 - \alpha)(\dot{w}_G - \dot{w}_I) \tag{2.6}$$

We argued earlier that in a well-functioning monetary union, differentials in wage increases must reflect differentials in productivity growth (see equation (2.3)). We use this insight and substitute equation (2.3) into (2.6).

$$\dot{p}c_G - \dot{p}c_I = (1 - \alpha)(\dot{q}_G - \dot{q}_I) \tag{2.7}$$

---

[14] The basic insights come from Balassa (1964).

From equation (2.7) we conclude the following. If there are differentials in productivity growth between countries in a monetary union then the inflation rates (measured by the consumption price index) must also differ. For example, if productivity grows faster in Ireland than in Germany, then Irish inflation will have to exceed German inflation in a monetary union.

It is important to understand that these inflation differentials should not be a source of worry. On the contrary, they are the result of an equilibrating mechanism. It is because (in our example) productivity grows faster in Ireland than in Germany that wages (and thus prices of non-tradables) must increase faster in Ireland than in Germany so as to keep the competitive position of both countries' tradable goods sectors unchanged.[15]

The previous analysis should not be interpreted to mean that all observed differences in inflation rates in a monetary union are the result of this equilibrating mechanism. Sometimes regional inflation differentials are the result of the asymmetric developments in aggregate demand. As we have argued earlier, these are a source of concern, because they can change the competitive position of countries (regions) leading to difficult adjustment problems.

3 Devaluation, time consistency, and credibility

THE idea that when the government follows particular policies it plays a game with the private sector has conquered macroeconomic theory since the publication of the path-breaking articles of Kydland and Prescott (1977) and Barro and Gordon (1983).[16] This literature stresses that economic agents follow optimal strategies in response to the strategies of the authorities, and that these private sector responses have profound influences on the effectiveness of government policies. In particular, the reputation governments acquire in pursuing announced policies has a great impact on how these policies are going to affect the economy.

This literature also has important implications for our discussion of the costs of a monetary union. It leads to a fundamental criticism of the view that the exchange rate is a policy tool that governments have at their disposal to be used in a discretionary way. In order to understand this criticism it will be useful to present first the Barro–Gordon model for a closed economy, and then to apply it to an open economy, and to the choice of countries whether or not to join a monetary union.

---

[15] Canzoneri *et al.* (1996) provide an interesting empirical analysis of these productivity-induced inflation differentials in Europe.

[16] The Barro–Gordon model has been applied to open economies by Mélitz (1988) and Cohen and Wyplosz (1989) among others.

3.1 The Barro–Gordon model: a geometric interpretation

Let us start from the standard Phillips curve which takes into account the role of inflationary expectations. We specify this Phillips curve as follows:

$$U = U_N + a(\dot{p}^e - \dot{p}) \tag{2.8}$$

where U is the unemployment rate, U_N is the natural unemployment rate, $\dot{p}$ is the observed rate of inflation, and $\dot{p}^e$ is the expected rate of inflation.

Equation (2.8) expresses the idea that only unexpected inflation affects the unemployment rate. Thus, when the inflation rate $\dot{p}$ is higher than the expected rate of inflation, the unemployment rate declines below its natural level.

We will also use the rational expectations assumption. This implies that economic agents use all relevant information to forecast the rate of inflation, and that they cannot be systematically wrong in making these forecasts. Thus, *on average* $\dot{p} = \dot{p}^e$, so that *on average* $U = U_N$.

We represent the Phillips curve in Fig. 2.8.[17] The vertical line represents the 'long-term' vertical Phillips curve. It is the collection of all points for which $\dot{p} = \dot{p}^e$. This vertical line defines the natural rate of unemployment U_N which is also called the NAIRU (the non-accelerating-inflation rate of unemployment).

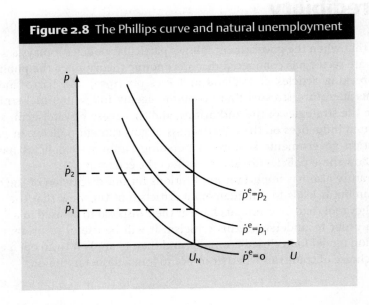

Figure 2.8 The Phillips curve and natural unemployment

---

[17] Note that we set the inflation rate on the vertical axis. This contrasts with the representation used in Sect. 2 of Ch. 1, where we had the rate of wage inflation on the vertical axis. We can, however, easily go from one representation to the other, considering that $\dot{w} = \dot{p} + \dot{q}$, where we assume that the rate of productivity growth, $\dot{q}$ is a constant.

Figure 2.9 The preferences of the authorities

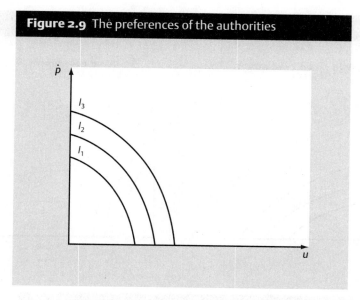

The second step in the analysis consists in introducing the preferences of the monetary authorities. The latter are assumed to care about both inflation and unemployment.

We represent these preferences in Fig. 2.9 in the form of a map of indifference curves of the authorities. We have drawn the indifference curves concave, expressing the idea that as the inflation rate declines, the authorities become less willing to let unemployment increase in order to reduce the inflation rate. Put differently, as the inflation rate declines the authorities tend to attach more weight to unemployment. Note also that the indifference curves closer to the origin represent a lower loss of welfare, and are thus preferred to those farther away from the origin.

The slope of these indifference curves expresses the relative importance the authorities attach to combating inflation or unemployment. In general, authorities who care much about unemployment ('wet' governments) have steep indifference curves, i.e. in order to reduce the rate of unemployment by one percentage point, they are willing to accept a lot of additional inflation.

On the other hand, 'hard-nosed' monetary authorities are willing to let the unemployment rate increase a lot in order to reduce the inflation rate by one percentage point. They have flat indifference curves. At the extreme, authorities who care only about inflation have horizontal indifference curves. We represent a few of these cases in Fig. 2.10.

We can now bring together the preferences of the authorities and the Phillips curves to determine the equilibrium of the model. We do this in Fig. 2.11.

In order to find out where the equilibrium will be located, assume for a moment that the government announces that it will follow a monetary policy rule of keeping the inflation rate equal to zero. Suppose also that the economic agents believe this announcement. They therefore set their expectations for inflation equal to zero. If the government implements this rule we move to point A.

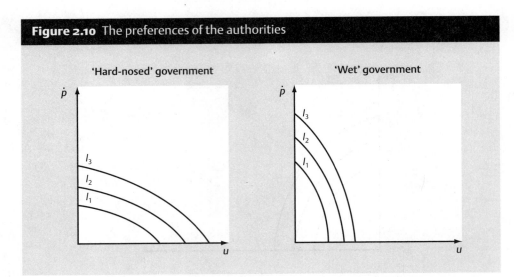

Figure 2.10 The preferences of the authorities

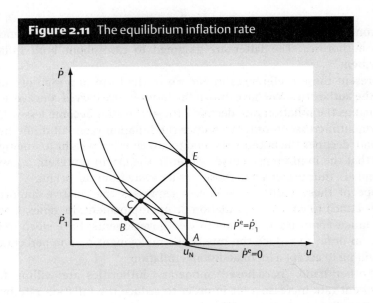

Figure 2.11 The equilibrium inflation rate

It is now clear that the government can do better than point *A*. It could cheat and increase the rate of inflation unexpectedly. Thus, suppose that after having announced a zero inflation, the authorities increase the inflation rate unexpectedly. This would bring the economy to point *B*, which is located on a lower indifference curve. One can say that the government has an incentive to renege on its promise to maintain a zero inflation rate.

Will the government succumb to this temptation to engineer a surprise inflation? Not necessarily. The government also knows that economic agents are likely to react by increasing their expectations of inflation. Thus during the next period, the Phillips curve is likely to shift upwards if the government decides to increase the rate of inflation unexpectedly. The government should therefore evaluate the short-term gain from cheating against the future losses that result from the fact that the Phillips curve shifts upwards.

But suppose now that the government consists of short-sighted politicians who give a low weight to future losses, and that it decides to cheat. We then move to point B. This, however, will trigger a shift of the Phillips curve upwards. Given these new expectations, it will be optimal for the authorities to move to point C. This will go on until we reach point E. This point has the following characteristics. First, it is on the vertical Phillips curve, so that agents' expectations are realized. They have therefore no incentives any more to change their expectations further. Secondly, at E the authorities have no incentive any more to surprise economic agents with more inflation. A movement upwards along the Phillips curve going through E would lead to an indifference curve located higher and therefore to a loss of welfare.

Point E can also be interpreted as the equilibrium that will be achieved in a rational expectations world when the authorities follow a *discretionary* policy, i.e. when they set the rate of inflation optimally each period given the prevailing expectations.

It is clear that this equilibrium is not very attractive. It is however the only equilibrium that can be sustained, given that the authorities are sufficiently short-sighted, and that the private sector knows this. The zero inflation rule (or any other constant inflation rule below the level achieved at E) has no credibility in a world of rational economic agents. The reason is that these economic agents realize that the authorities have an incentive to cheat. They will therefore adjust their expectations up to the point where the authorities have no incentive to cheat any more. This is achieved at point E. A zero inflation rule, although desirable, will not come about automatically.[18]

It should be stressed that this model is a static one. If the policy game is repeated many times, the government will have an incentive to acquire a reputation of low inflation. Such a reputation will make it possible to reach a lower inflation equilibrium. One way the static assumption can be rationalized is by considering that in many countries political institutions favour short-term objectives for politicians. For example, the next election is never far away, leading to uncertainty whether the present rulers will still be in place next period. Thus, what is implicitly assumed in this model is that the political decision process is inefficient, leading politicians to give a strong weight to the short-term gains of inflationary policies. The politicians as individuals are certainly as rational as private agents; the political decision process, however, may force them to give undue weight to the very short-term results of their policies.

Before analysing the question of how a monetary union might help the authorities to move to a more attractive equilibrium, it is helpful to study what factors determine the exact location of the 'discretionary' equilibrium (point E).

We distinguish two factors that affect the location of the discretionary equilibrium, and therefore also the equilibrium level of inflation.

---

[18] In the jargon of the economic literature it is said that the policy rule of zero inflation is 'time-inconsistent', i.e. the authorities face the problem each period that a better short-term outcome is possible. The zero inflation rule is incentive-incompatible.

(a) The preferences of the authorities. In Fig. 2.12 we present the cases of the 'wet' (steep indifference curves) and the 'hard-nosed' (flat indifference curves) governments. Assuming that the Phillips curves have the same slopes, Fig. 2.12 shows that in a country with a 'wet' government, the equilibrium inflation will be higher than in the country with a 'hard-nosed' government.

Note also that the only way a zero rate of inflation rule can be credible is when the authorities show no concern whatsoever for unemployment. In that case the indifference curves are horizontal. The authorities will choose the lowest possible horizontal indifference curve in each period. The inflation equilibrium will then be achieved at point A.[19]

(b) The level of the natural rate of unemployment. Suppose the level of the natural unemployment rate increases. It can then easily be shown that if the preferences of the authorities remain unchanged, the new equilibrium inflation rate increases. This is made clear in Fig. 2.13 which shows the case of an increase of the NAIRU. Its effect is to shift the equilibrium point from E to E′.

Figure 2.12 Equilibrium with 'hard-nosed' and 'wet' governments

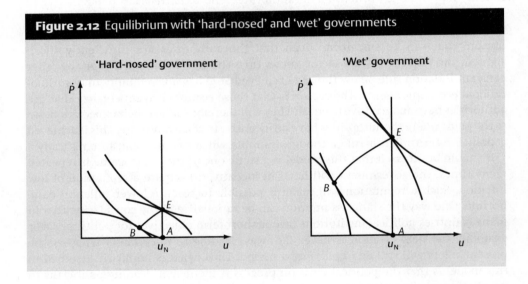

3.2 The Barro–Gordon model in open economies

In the previous sections we showed how a government, which is known to care about inflation and unemployment, will not credibly be able to announce a zero inflation rate. It is therefore stuck in a suboptimal equilibrium with an inflation rate that is too high.

This analysis can be extended to open economies. Let us now assume that there are

---

[19] Rogoff (1985b) has suggested that the best thing that could happen to a country is that its monetary policy be run by an orthodox central banker.

two countries. We call the first country Germany, and assume its government is 'hard-nosed'. The second country is called Italy, where the government is 'wet'. As in the model presented in Section 2 of Chaper 1, we use the purchasing-power parity condition, i.e.

$$\dot{e} = \dot{p}_I - \dot{p}_G \qquad\qquad (2.9)$$

We show the inflation outcome in Fig. 2.14. Italy has a higher equilibrium rate of inflation than Germany. Its currency will therefore have to depreciate continuously. The problem of Italy is that it could achieve a much lower inflation equilibrium than

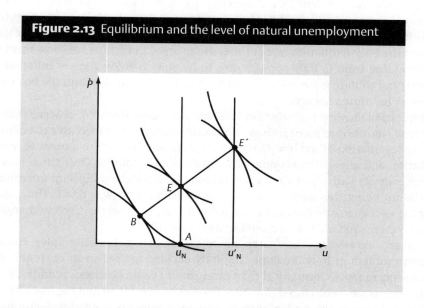

Figure 2.13 Equilibrium and the level of natural unemployment

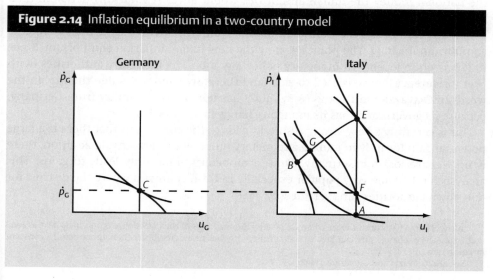

Figure 2.14 Inflation equilibrium in a two-country model

point E if its government were able to convince its citizens that, once at point A, it would not try to reach point B.

This Barro–Gordon model for open economies allows us to add important insights into the discussion of the costs of a monetary union.

3.3 Credibility and the cost of a monetary union

Can Italy solve its problem by announcing that it will join a monetary union with Germany? In order to answer this question, suppose, first, that Italy announces that it will fix its exchange rate with the German mark. Given the purchasing-power parity, this fixes the Italian inflation rate at the German level. In Fig. 2.14 we show this by the horizontal line from C. Italy appears now to be able to enjoy a lower inflation rate. The potential welfare gains are large, because in the new equilibrium the economy is on a lower indifference curve.

The question, however, is whether this rule can be credible. We observe that once at the new equilibrium point F, the Italian authorities have an incentive to engineer a surprise devaluation of the lira. This surprise devaluation leads to a surprise increase in inflation and allows the economy to move towards point G. Over time, however, economic agents will adjust their expectations, so that the equilibrium inflation rate will end up being the same as before the exchange rate was fixed. Thus, merely fixing the exchange rate does not solve the problem, because the fixed exchange rate rule is no more credible than a fixed inflation rate rule.[20]

There are, however, other arrangements that can potentially solve the high-inflation problem in Italy. Imagine that Italy decided to abolish its currency and to adopt the currency of Germany. If that arrangement could be made credible, i.e. if the Italian citizens were convinced that once this decision is taken and the mark becomes the national money the Italian authorities would never rescind this decision, then Italy could achieve the same inflation equilibrium as Germany. In Fig. 2.14 the horizontal line connecting the German inflation equilibrium with Italy defines a credible equilibrium for Italy. The point F is now the new Italian inflation equilibrium. Since Italy has no independent monetary policy any more, its monetary authorities (with 'wet' preferences) have ceased to exist and therefore cannot devalue the lira. In the words of Giavazzi and Pagano (1987), Italy has borrowed credibility from Germany, because its government has its monetary hands firmly tied.[21]

This is certainly a very strong result. It leads to the conclusion that there is a large potential gain for Italy in joining a monetary union with Germany. In addition, there is no welfare loss for Germany. Thus, a monetary union only leads to gains. This analysis has become very popular especially in Latin countries where the distrust for one's own authorities runs very deeply.

[20] We will come back to this issue when we discuss the workings of the EMS. Some economists have argued that fixing the exchange rate can be a rule that inherently has more credibility than announcing a constant inflation rate rule.

[21] See also Giavazzi and Giovannini (1989).

There are two considerations, however, that tend to soften this conclusion. First, it should be clear from the previous analysis that only a full monetary union establishes the required credibility for Italy. That is, Italy must be willing to eliminate its national currency, very much like East Germany did on 1 July 1990 when it adopted the West German mark. Anything less than full monetary union will face a credibility problem.[22] As was pointed out, when Italy fixes its exchange rate relative to the mark and keeps its own currency, the credibility of this fixed exchange rate arrangement will be in doubt.

Secondly, and more importantly for our present purpose, we have assumed that the central bank of the monetary union is the German central bank. In this arrangement, Italy profits from the reputation of the German central bank to achieve lower inflation. Suppose, however, that the new central bank is a new institution, where both the German and the Italian authorities are represented equally. Would that new central bank have the same reputation as the old German central bank? This is far from clear. If the union central bank is perceived to be less 'hard-nosed' than the German central bank prior to setting up the union, the new inflation equilibrium of the union will be higher than the one which prevailed in Germany before the union. Italy may still gain from such an arrangement. Germany, however, would lose, and would not be very enthusiastic to form such a union. We return to these issues in Chapter 8 where we discuss problems of devising institutions that enhance the low-inflation reputation of the European central bank.

We conclude from the preceding analysis that problems of credibility are important in evaluating the costs of a monetary union. First, the option to devalue the currency is a two-edged sword for the national authorities. The knowledge that it may be used in the future greatly complicates macroeconomic policies. Secondly, the time-consistency literature also teaches us some important lessons concerning the costs of a monetary union: a devaluation cannot be used to correct every disturbance that occurs in an economy. A devaluation is not, as it is in the analysis of Mundell, a flexible instrument that can be used frequently. When used once, it affects its use in the future, because it engenders strong expectational effects. It is a dangerous instrument that can hurt those who use it. Each time the policy-makers use this instrument, they will have to evaluate the advantages obtained today against the cost, i.e. that it will be more difficult to use this instrument effectively in the future.

This has led some economists to conclude that the exchange rate instrument should not be used at all, and that countries would even gain from irrevocably relinquishing its use. This conclusion goes too far. There were many cases, observed in Europe during the 1980s, in which devaluations were used very successfully (see the previous section). The ingredients of this success have typically been that the devaluation was coupled with other drastic policy changes (sometimes with a change of government, e.g. Belgium in 1982 and Denmark in the same year). As a result, the devaluation was perceived as a unique and an extraordinary change in policies that

---

[22] Some countries (e.g. Argentina, Hong Kong) have experimented with currency boards. These are more constraining monetary regimes than fixed exchange rates, but fall short of a full monetary union. As a result, these countries have occasionally been subjected to intensive speculative attacks.

could not easily be repeated in the future. Under those conditions the negative repu-tation effects could be kept under control. Some countries, in particular Denmark in 1982, even seem to have improved their reputation quickly after the devaluation. Relinquishing the possibility of using this instrument for the indefinite future does imply a cost for a nation.

4 The cost of monetary union and the openness of countries

IN this chapter we have developed several ideas that bear on the question of how the openness of a country affects the cost of the monetary union. Here we concentrate on two of these which, as will be seen, have opposite effects. First, there is the rela-tion between the degree of openness (the degree to which a country is integrated with the rest of the world) and the occurrence of asymmetric shocks. We have presented two views: the European Commission view, which sees this as a negative relation-ship, and the Krugman view, which sees this as a positive one. According to the first view, we can conclude that more openness reduces the cost of a monetary union, as it reduces the probability that asymmetric shocks occur. On the second view, however, this conclusion is reversed: the costs of a monetary union increase with the degree of openness of countries.

The second idea which matters in our analysis of how openness affects the cost of monetary union has to do with the effectiveness of the exchange rate in dealing with asymmetric shocks. Let us return to Fig. 2.5, where we analysed the effects of a devaluation. We now consider two countries, one relatively open, the other relatively closed. We represent these two countries in Fig. 2.15. Both the demand and the supply effects of a devaluation differ between the two countries. As far as the demand-side effects are concerned, the same devaluation has a stronger effect in the relatively open economy than in the relatively closed one. To understand this, consider two extreme cases. Suppose the relatively open economy exports 99% of its GDP, whereas the relatively closed one only exports 1% of its GDP. The same devaluation, say 10%, is bound to raise aggregate demand more in the former country than in the latter. In Fig. 2.15 we show this difference by the fact that the demand curve in the relatively open country shifts further outward than in the relatively closed country.

The two countries also differ with respect to the supply-side effects of the devalu-ation. One can expect that in the relatively open economy, the upward shift of the supply curve following the devaluation is more pronounced than in the relatively closed economy. This has to do with the fact that the more open economy imports more (as a per cent of total consumption) so that the CPI increases more, leading to a stronger wage–price spiral than in the relatively closed economy.

We now arrive at the following conclusion. The combined demand and supply effects of a devaluation in the two countries are such that we cannot say a priori in

Figure 2.15 Effectiveness of devaluation as a function of openness

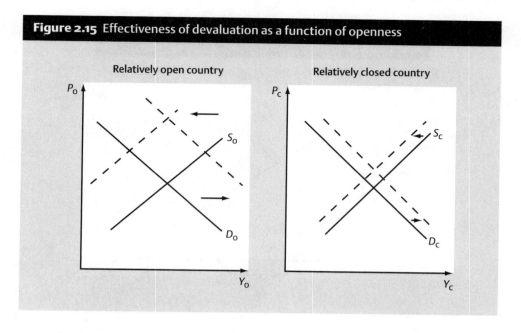

which country the devaluation is most effective in stimulating output. What we can conclude, however, is that the devaluation will be felt more strongly on the aggregate price level in the more open economy than in the relatively closed economy. This means that the systematic use of the exchange rate instrument will lead to more price variability in the more open economy than in the relatively closed one. To the extent that price variability involves costs, the systematic use of the exchange rate instrument in the more open economy will be more costly. This point was first recognized by McKinnon (1963) in his important contribution to the theory of optimum currency areas.

From this discussion of the effectiveness of a devaluation in open and (relatively) closed economies one can conclude that for the same effect on output, the devaluation is likely to be more costly in the open economy because of the higher price variability involved. Thus the loss of the exchange rate instrument is likely to be less costly for the relatively open economy than for the relatively closed one.

Combining the analysis of the effectiveness of a devaluation with the analysis of the relationship between openness and asymmetric shocks, one can derive the conclusion that the cost of monetary union most likely declines with the degree of openness of a country. We show this in Fig. 2.16, which is borrowed from Krugman (1990). On the vertical axis the cost of a monetary union is set out (i.e. the cost of relinquishing the exchange rate instrument). This cost is expressed as a per cent of GDP. On the horizontal axis the openness of the country relative to the countries with whom it wants to form a monetary union is set out. This openness is represented by the trade share in the GDP of the country considered here. We see that as the openness increases the cost of joining a monetary union declines.

This conclusion, however, does not hold in general. We cannot exclude the possi-

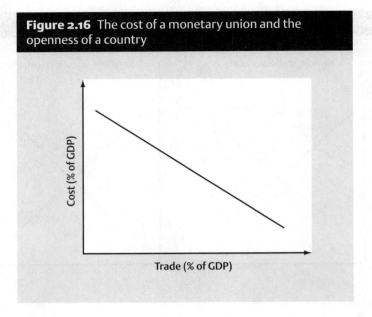

Figure 2.16 The cost of a monetary union and the openness of a country

bility that the relationship is positively sloped. This situation may occur when the probability of asymmetric shocks increases significantly with the degree of openness of a country (the Krugman scenario). The presumption, however, is that this case is unlikely to happen. First, it is more likely that with trade integration, asymmetric shocks become less likely (see our analysis of the European Commission view). Second, even if trade integration leads to more asymmetric shocks, the cost of using the exchange rate instrument is likely to offset the former effect in more highly integrated economies. We will therefore maintain our presumption that the cost of the monetary union declines with openness.

5 Conclusion

T**HE** criticism against the traditional theory of optimal currency areas, as developed by Mundell and McKinnon, has enabled us to add important nuances to this theory. In particular, it has changed our view about the costs of a monetary union. The traditional theory of optimal currency areas tends to be rather pessimistic about the possibility for countries to join a monetary union at low cost. The criticism we have discussed in this chapter is much less pessimistic about this, i.e. the costs of forming a monetary union appear to be less forbidding.[23] The main reasons why we came to this conclusion are twofold.

---

[23] See Tavlas (1993) for some further thoughts.

First, the ability of exchange rate changes to absorb asymmetric shocks is weaker than the traditional (Keynesian-inspired) OCA-theory has led us to believe. Exchange rate changes usually have no permanent effects on output and employment.

Second, countries that maintain independent monetary and exchange rate policies often find out that the movements of exchange rates become a source of macroeconomic disturbances, instead of being instruments of macroeconomic stabilization. Contrary to the old view, exchange rate changes are not instruments that policy-makers can use flexibly and costlessly.

Does this mean that the insights of the traditional OCA-theory have become irrelevant? The answer is no. Despite our criticism the hard core of the OCA-analysis still stands. This can be put as follows.

There are important differences between countries that are not going to disappear in a monetary union. Many, if not most, of these differences have a political and institutional origin. The nation-states, which are now making up the monetary union in Europe, have maintained many of their national peculiarities. Labour markets continue to have special national institutional features. Legal systems are not identical, creating differences in the functioning of financial markets, of the housing markets, and possibly of other markets. The governments of the member-states of the monetary union use different tax systems and follow different spending policies. EMU will by itself erase some of these differences, but certainly not all. The remaining ones some day will lead to divergent movements in national output and prices, creating the need for difficult national adjustments. The absence of national exchange rate policies to assist in this adjustment process will then be felt as a cost of the monetary union. In this sense one can say that the EU-countries that joined EMU on 1 January 1999 took a calculated risk. It also follows that the theory of optimal currency areas remains relevant for those countries that contemplate joining EMU, or for countries in the rest of the world moving into monetary unions of their own.

The risk of high adjustment costs in the face of asymmetric disturbances can be reduced by implementing two strategies. One consists in making markets more flexible, so that asymmetric shocks can be adjusted better. The other consists in speeding up the process of political unification. This will reduce national idiosyncrasies and thus the occurrence of asymmetric disturbances that have a political or institutional origin.

Chapter 3
The Benefits of a Common Currency

Introduction

WHEREAS the costs of a common currency have much to do with the *macroeconomic* management of the economy, the benefits are mostly situated at the *microeconomic* level. Eliminating national currencies and moving to a common currency can be expected to lead to gains in economic efficiency. These gains in efficiency have two different origins. One is the elimination of transaction costs associated with the exchanging of national moneys. The other is the elimination of risk coming from the uncertain future movements of the exchange rates. In this chapter we analyse these two sources of benefits of a monetary union.

1 Direct gains from the elimination of transaction costs

ELIMINATING the costs of exchanging one currency into another is certainly the most visible (and most easily quantifiable) gain from a monetary union. We all experience these costs whenever we exchange currency. These costs disappear when countries move to a common European currency.

How large are the gains from the elimination of transaction costs? The EC Commission has estimated these gains, and arrives at a number between 13 and 20 billion ECUs per year.[1] This represents one-quarter to one-half of one per cent of the

---

[1] See EC Commission (1990).

Community GDP. This may seem peanuts. It is, however, a gain that has to be added to the other gains from a single market.

It should be noted here that these gains that accrue to the general public have a counterpart somewhere. They are mostly to be found in the banking sector. Surveys in different countries indicate that about 5% of the banks' revenues are the commissions paid to the banks in exchange of national currencies. This source of revenue for the banks will disappear with a monetary union.

The preceding should not give the impression that the gain for the public is offset by the loss of the banks. The transaction costs involved in exchanging money are a *deadweight* loss. They are like a tax paid by the consumer in exchange for which he gets nothing. Banks, however, will have a problem of transition: they will have to look for other profitable activities. When this has been done, society will have gained. The banks' employees, previously engaged in exchanging money, will now be free to perform more useful tasks for society.

Two other points should be mentioned here. First, the full gains from the elimination of transaction costs can only be reaped when national currencies are replaced by a common currency. As long as national currencies remain in existence, even if the exchange rates are irrevocably fixed, residents of each country will continue to use their home currency (banknotes, coins) in preference to foreign ones. This is the present situation in Euroland until the year 2002, when the single currency will replace the national currencies. Until that date, there will continue to be a need to convert one currency into another. Those that provide this service will charge a price. Transactions costs will not be eliminated.

Second, as long as payments systems are not fully integrated, bank transfers between member countries of EMU will remain more expensive than bank transfers within the same country. This is the case today (2000) in Euroland. The reason is that although the national payments systems are now linked up by the so-called TARGET system, these national systems are still very much in place. As a result, cross-border bank transfers follow a different, and more expensive, route than bank transfers within the same country.

2 Indirect gains from the elimination of transaction costs

THE elimination of transaction costs will also have an indirect (albeit less easily quantifiable) gain. It will reduce the scope for price discrimination between national markets.

There is a lot of evidence that price discrimination is still practised widely in Europe. In Table 3.1 we illustrate this phenomenon in the automobile market. It can be seen that the same automobiles are priced very differently (net of taxes) in the European Union.

Table 3.1 Average price differentials (net of taxes) for the same automobile in Europe, 1993, 1995, and 1997 (cheapest country = 100)

	1993	1995	1997
Belgium	116	122	106
France	121	121	106
Germany	124	128	112
Ireland	115	112	112
Italy	100	100	109
Netherlands	115	121	100
Portugal	108	108	—
Spain	108	105	104
United Kingdom	120	120	140

Source: European Commission (various years).

Such price discrimination is only possible because national markets are still segmented. That is, there are relatively large transaction costs for the consumer who would buy a car in another country. If these transaction costs did not exist, consumers would not hesitate to purchase these goods in the countries where they are cheap. Of course, there are many sources of transaction costs (e.g. administrative regulations, differences in taxation), and eliminating the cost of buying and selling foreign currencies may not even be the most important one. However, together with the other measures to create a single market, they would make price discrimination much more difficult. This would be a benefit for the European consumer.

The importance of the existence of national currencies in segmenting markets should not be underestimated. In a recent study Charles Engel and Richard Rogers[2] analysed the factors that influence the price differentials of the same goods in different locations. They did this by studying the price differentials of the same pairs of goods in different North American cities (in the USA and Canada). What they found is quite revealing. First, distance matters. Price differentials between Los Angeles and New York are larger than between Los Angeles and San Francisco (this is not really surprising). Second, and more importantly, crossing a border (in this case the US–Canadian border) is equivalent to travelling 2,500 miles within the same country. In other words, price differentials between Detroit and Windsor (which is just across the border) are of the same order of magnitude as the price differentials between New York and Los Angeles. Thus, borders are quite powerful in segmenting markets and in introducing large variations in the movements of prices. Of course, crossing borders not only involves exchanging moneys. As mentioned earlier, borders create other impediments to trade. Nevertheless, the fact that at borders moneys have to be exchanged is a significant factor in explaining why markets remain segmented.

The previous discussion also makes clear that a monetary union will have a great potential further to integrate markets in the European Union, in the same way as

---

[2] See Engel and Rogers (1995).

having the same currency, the dollar, has been of great significance for the United States in creating a truly single market in that country.

3 Welfare gains from less uncertainty

THE uncertainty about future exchange rate changes introduces uncertainty about future revenues of firms. It is generally accepted that this leads to a loss of welfare in a world populated by risk-averse individuals. These will, generally speaking, prefer a future return that is more certain than one that is less so, at least if the expected value of these returns is the same. Put differently, they will only want to take the more risky return if they are promised that it will be higher than the less risky. Eliminating the exchange risk reduces a source of uncertainty and should therefore increase welfare.

There is one important feature of the theory of the firm that may invalidate that conclusion. Take a profit-maximizing firm which is a price-taker in the output market. We represent its marginal cost curve and the price of its output in Fig. 3.1. Suppose there are two regimes. In the first regime (presented in the upper panel) the price is constant and perfectly predictable by the firm. In the second regime (lower panel) the price fluctuates randomly. We assume here that the price fluctuates symmetrically between p_2 and p_3.

In the first regime of certainty the profit of the firm in each period is given by the shaded area minus the area FGp_1. In the second uncertain regime the profit will fluctuate depending on whether the price p_2 or p_3 prevails. We can now see that the profit will be larger on average in the uncertain regime than in the certain regime. When the price is low the profit is lower than in the certainty case by the area p_1BCp_2. When the price is high, the profit is higher than in the certainty case by the area p_3EBp_1. It can now easily be seen that P_3EBp_1 is larger than p_1BCp_2. The difference is given by two darkened triangles.

This result has the following interpretation. When the price is high the firm increases output so as to profit from the higher revenue per unit of output. Thus, it gains a higher profit for each unit of output it would have produced anyway, and *in addition* it expands its output. The latter effect is measured by the upper darkened triangle. When the price is low, however, the firm will do the opposite, it will reduce output. In so doing it limits the reduction in its total profit. This effect is represented by the lower darkened triangle.

There are many complications that can be added to this theory. One can introduce the assumption of imperfect competition, or the assumption that firms face adjustment costs when they vary output. Also, when downward price changes are large enough, some firms will make losses, and may have to close down. The cost of reallocating the factors of production employed by these firms may be substantial. All these complications provide important insights into the effect of price uncertainty on

Figure 3.1 Profits of the firm under price certainty and uncertainty

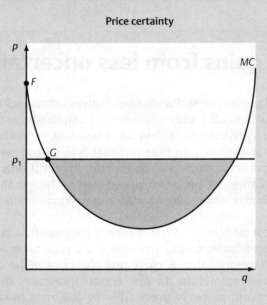

Price certainty

Price uncertainty

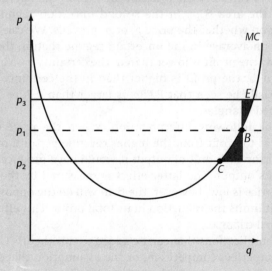

average profits. In more complicated models, however, it is generally the case that price uncertainty *may* increase average profits of the firm.

If one wants to make welfare comparisons between a regime of price certainty and one of price uncertainty, the positive effect of price uncertainty on the average profits should be compared to the greater uncertainty about these profits. The higher average profit increases the utility of the firm, whereas the greater uncertainty about these profits reduces the utility of the (risk-averse) firm. It is, therefore, unclear whether welfare will decline when exchange rate uncertainty increases, or, conversely that we can say with great confidence that the welfare of firms will increase when national currencies are eliminated and a common currency is introduced.

Another way to put the preceding analysis is to recognize that changes in the exchange rate do not only represent a risk, they also create opportunities to make profits. When the exchange rate becomes more variable the probability of making very large profits increases. In a certain sense, exporting can be seen as an *option*. When the exchange rate becomes very favourable the firm exercises its option to export. With an unfavourable exchange rate the firm does not exercise this option. It is well known from option theory that the value of the option increases when the variability of the underlying asset increases. Thus, the firm that has the option to export is better off when the exchange rate becomes more variable.

The same argument can be developed for the *consumer*. In Fig. 3.2 we present the demand function of a representative consumer. Suppose again that there are two regimes of price volatility. In the first regime the price is constant and perfectly predictable. In the second regime the price fluctuates randomly between p_2 and p_3. We find that in the second regime of price uncertainty the consumer surplus is higher on average than in the first regime of price certainty. The reason is the same as in the case of the firm. When the price is low, the consumer increases his demand to profit from the low price. When the price is high he does the opposite, and thereby

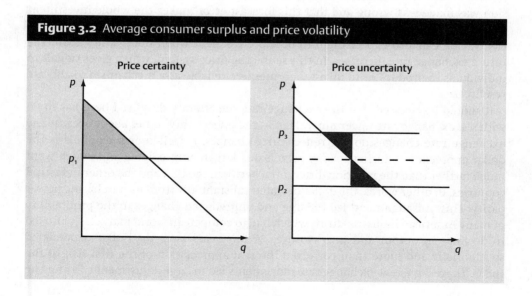

Figure 3.2 Average consumer surplus and price volatility

limits the negative effect the price increase has on his welfare. Thus, on average, the consumer gains when prices fluctuate.

This positive effect of price uncertainty on the average consumer surplus has to be compared to the increased risk. To the extent that consumers are risk-averse they will give a lower utility value to the higher (but uncertain) consumer surplus than to the lower consumer surplus obtained in a regime of certainty. Our conclusion from the static theory of the consumer is that we do not know whether consumers gain from lower price variability. We also conclude that if gains from a common currency and the ensuing reduction in risk are to be expected, they should probably be found elsewhere than in the static welfare gains that we have analysed in this section.

4 Exchange rate uncertainty and the price mechanism

THERE is another area where more substantial gains from a reduction of the exchange rate risk can be expected. Exchange rate uncertainty introduces uncertainty about the future prices of goods and services. Economic agents base their decisions concerning production, investment, and consumption on the information that the price system provides for them. If these prices become more uncertain the quality of these decisions will decline.

We can make these general statements more concrete by considering an example. Suppose a firm decides to invest in a foreign country. It bases this decision on many variables. One of these is the expected future exchange rate. Suppose then that after having made the investment, it turns out that the exchange rate on which the decision was made was wrong and that this forecast error makes the whole investment unprofitable so that the firm decides to close its foreign operation. Such errors will be costly. One can also expect them to be more frequent when uncertainty about the future exchange rate increases. In this sense, the price system, which gives signals to individuals to produce or to invest, becomes less reliable as a mechanism to allocate resources.

It should be stressed that the exchange rate uncertainty discussed here has to do with *real* exchange rate uncertainty. That is, the uncertainty comes about because the exchange rate changes do not reflect price changes. A well-known example is the dollar appreciation during 1980–5, which was largely unpredicted and which went much farther than the inflation differential between the USA and the other industrial countries. In other words, the dollar deviated substantially from its purchasing power parity. This 'misalignment' led to large and unpredicted changes in the profitability of many American industrial firms which had to compete in world markets. It also led to declines in output and firm closures. A few years later the dollar depreciated substantially and more than corrected the real appreciation of the first half of the 1980s. These large real exchange rate movements led to large adjustment costs for the

American economy. (For a well-known analysis of the effects of misalignment see Williamson (1983).)

A decline in real exchange rate uncertainty, due for example to the introduction of a common currency, can reduce these adjustment costs. As a result, the price system becomes a better guide to make the right economic decisions. These efficiency gains are difficult to quantify. They are no less important for this. Their importance becomes all the more visible when we look at what happens in countries that experience hyperinflation. We observe in these countries that the wrong production and investment decisions are made on a massive scale. Quite often we observe that output and investment booms in countries with hyperinflation. However, these increases in output and investment frequently occur in the wrong sectors or product lines. After a while these productions and investments have to be abandoned. Massive amounts of resources are wasted in the process.

There is a second reason why greater price and exchange rate uncertainty may reduce the quality of the information provided by the price mechanism. An increase in risk, due to price uncertainty, will in general increase the real interest rate. This follows from the fact that when the expected return on investment projects becomes more uncertain, risk-averse investors will require a higher risk premium to compensate them for the increased riskiness of the projects. In addition, in a riskier economic environment, economic agents will increase the discount rate at which they discount future returns. Thus, exchange rate uncertainty which leads to this kind of increased systemic risk also increases the real interest rate. Higher interest rates, however, lead to increased problems in selecting investment projects in an efficient way. These problems have to do with *moral hazard* and *adverse selection*.

The *moral hazard problem* arises because an increase in the interest rate changes the incentives of the borrower. The latter will find it more advantageous to increase the riskiness of his investment projects. This follows from an asymmetry of expected profits and losses. If the investment project is successful the extra profits go to the borrower. If the investment project turns out badly and if the borrower goes bankrupt, his loss is limited to his equity share in the project. With a higher interest rate this moral hazard problem becomes more intense. This asymmetry gives the borrower the incentive to select more risky projects. Thus, on average, investment projects will become riskier when the real interest rate increases. Lenders, however, will try to defend themselves by asking for an additional risk premium, which in turn intensifies the problem. In general, the moral hazard problem may lead the lender to apply credit ceilings as a way to reduce his risk.[3]

The *adverse selection problem* leads to a similar result. When the interest rate increases, the suppliers of low-risk investment projects will tend to drop out of the credit market. They will find it less attractive to borrow at the higher interest rate for projects that do not represent a high risk. Thus, on average, the riskiness of investment projects will increase when the interest rate increases.

Both phenomena, moral hazard and adverse selection, lead to the selection of more risky investment projects. Thus, the systemic risk increases. Eliminating that risk by

---

[3] See the classic article of Stiglitz and Weiss (1981).

moving towards a common currency reduces the amount of risky projects that are selected by the market.

We can conclude this section by noting that the movement towards a common currency will eliminate the exchange risk, and thereby will lead to a more efficient working of the price mechanism. Although this effect cannot easily be measured, it is likely to be an important benefit of the introduction of one currency in Europe.

It should be noted here that not all economists will share this conclusion. Some have argued that the elimination of the exchange risk can only be obtained by introducing more risk elsewhere in the economic system. As a result, we are not sure whether the systemic risk is reduced by eliminating just one source of risk. We return to this issue in Box 5 where we evaluate this argument.

5 Exchange rate uncertainty and economic growth

THE argument that the elimination of the exchange risk will lead to an increase in economic growth can be made using the neoclassical growth model, and its extension to situations of dynamic economies of scale. This analysis features prominently in the EC report 'One Market, One Money' (1990) which in turn was very much influenced by Baldwin (1989).

The neoclassical growth model is represented in Fig. 3.3. The horizontal axis shows the capital stock per worker, the vertical axis the output per worker. The line $f(k)$ is the production function which has the usual convex shape, implying diminishing marginal productivities. The equilibrium in this model is obtained where the marginal productivity of capital is equal to the interest rate consumers use to discount future consumption. This is represented in Fig. 3.3 by the point A, where the line rr (whose slope is equal to the discount rate) is tangent to the production function $f(k)$. In this model, growth can only occur if the population grows or if there is an exogenous rate of technological change. (Note also that in this neoclassical model the savings ratio does not influence the equilibrium growth rate.)

We can now use this model as a starting-point to evaluate the growth effects of a monetary union. Assume that the elimination of the exchange risk reduces the systemic risk so that the real interest rate declines. We represent this effect in Fig. 3.4. The reduction of the risk-adjusted rate of discount makes the rr-line flatter. As a result, the equilibrium moves from A to B. There will be an accumulation of capital and an increase in the growth rate while the economy moves from A to B. In the new equilibrium, output per worker and the capital stock he has at his disposal will have increased. Note, however, that the growth rate of output then returns to its initial level, which is determined by the exogenous rate of technological change and the rate of growth of the population. Thus, in this neoclassical growth model the reduction of the interest rate due to the monetary union *temporarily* increases the rate of

Figure 3.3 The neoclassical growth model

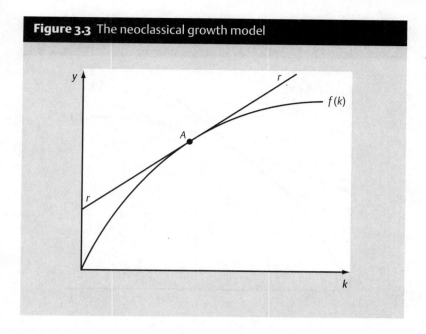

growth of output. In the new equilibrium the output *level* per worker will have increased. (Note also that the productivity of capital has declined.)

This model has been extended by introducing dynamic economies of scale.[4] Suppose the productivity of capital increases when the capital stock increases. This may arise because with a higher capital stock and output per worker there are learning effects and additional knowledge is accumulated. This additional knowledge then increases the labour productivity in the next period. There may also be a public goods aspect to knowledge. Thus, once a new machine is in place the knowledge it embodies is freely available to the worker who uses it. All these effects produce increases in the productivity of labour over time when capital accumulates.

One of the interesting characteristics of these new growth models is that the growth path becomes endogenous, and is sensitive to the initial conditions. Thus, an economy that starts with a higher capital stock per worker can move on a permanently higher growth path.

A lowering of the interest rate can likewise put the economy on a permanently higher growth path. We represent this case in Fig. 3.5. As a result of the lower interest rate the economy accumulates more capital. Contrary to the static case of Fig. 3.4, however, this raises the productivity of the capital stock per worker. This is shown by the upward movement of the $f(k)$ line. The economy will be on a higher growth path.

The previous analysis sounds very promising for the growth effects of a monetary union.[5] It is, however, most probably a little too optimistic, for it ignores the point

---

[4] See Romer (1986). What is new here is the formalization of old ideas. Many economists in the past have stressed that the growth phenomenon is based on dynamic economies of scale and learning effects.

[5] This analysis was also implicit in the hope of the founding fathers of the EMS that the greater exchange rate stability provided by the system would stimulate the growth of investment, output, and trade in Europe.

Figure 3.4 The effect of lower risk in the neoclassical growth model

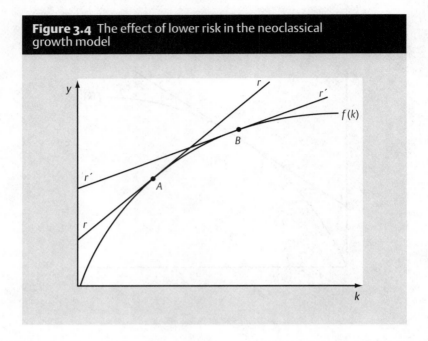

that was made in Section 3 above, that is, a reduction of exchange rate variability also reduces the expected value of future profits of firms. Thus, a lower risk due to less exchange rate variability has a double effect. It reduces the real interest rate (which in the previous analysis generated the growth effect) *and* it reduces the expected return of investment. As a result, this reduction in risk has an ambiguous effect on investment activity, and thus also on the growth of output.

This point is not generally recognized by the public. Quite often it is stated that a reduction of the risk will boost investment activity. Economic theory does not allow us to draw this conclusion. The question whether a reduction of the exchange risk increases investment, therefore, is an empirical one. What does the empirical evidence tell us?

There has been a large amount of empirical analysis of the relation between exchange rate uncertainty and international trade and investment. (For a survey, see IMF (1984).) On the whole it is fair to say that very little relation has been found. In other words, the increased variability of the exchange rates, and in particular the large and unpredictable variability of the real exchange rates, does not seem to have had very significant effects on international trade and investment. This implies that the link between exchange rate uncertainty and economic growth is empirically also a very weak one.

We illustrate this lack of empirical relationship between exchange rate variability and the growth of output and investment in Table 3.2. We show the growth rates of GDP and of investment in industrial countries during the period when the EMS (with narrow bands) existed. We classify these countries into two groups, those that have experienced relatively stable (nominal and real) exchange rates (mainly the EMS

Figure 3.5 Endogenous growth in the 'new' growth model

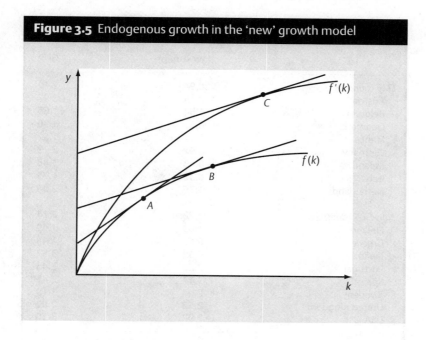

countries) and those that have seen their (nominal and real) exchange rates fluctuate a lot. In general, the latter countries have experienced exchange variability (both nominal and real) that is three to five times as large as the former.

The figures of Table 3.2 are striking. The greater exchange rate stability that the EMS countries have experienced during the 1980s does not seem to have provided a great boost to the growth rates of output and investment.[6] As a matter of fact, the growth rates of output and investment have on average been somewhat lower in the EMS countries than in the non-EMS countries that experienced relatively large movements in their exchange rates.

Another way to illustrate this lack of a robust relationship between economic growth and exchange rate risk is to look at the growth rate of countries as a function of their size. Large countries have a large monetary zone within which there is no exchange rate uncertainty. Firms in small countries typically face much more exchange rate uncertainty because they sell a larger proportion of their final output to countries in different monetary areas. Thus, a large part of these sales face exchange rate uncertainty. Therefore one would expect that if a reduction of exchange rate uncertainty stimulates economic growth, larger countries will on average experience a higher growth rate of output than small countries. We show some evidence in Fig. 3.6. On the vertical axis we present the growth rates during 1981–98, on the horizontal axis the size of these countries as measured by their GDP

---

[6] For more evidence on the growth effects of the EMS see De Grauwe (1987). Note that it is not implied here that the greater exchange rate stability observed in the EMS has not been beneficial for the EMS countries. What is implied is that this greater exchange rate stability does not seem to have had much beneficial effect on the growth rates of output and investment.

Table 3.2 Growth of GDP and investment, 1981–1993

	Investment	GDP
EMS countries	*0.94*	*2.10*
Austria	2.15	2.07
Belgium	1.54	1.65
Denmark	0.52	1.80
France	1.11	1.87
Germany	0.92	2.12
Ireland	−0.43	3.48
Italy	0.32	1.75
Netherlands	1.36	2.04
Non-EMS countries	*1.72*	*2.14*
Finland	−1.63	1.49
Greece	−0.07	1.44
Japan	4.35	3.57
Portugal	2.52	2.45
Spain	3.17	2.45
Sweden	−0.04	1.19
United Kingdom	2.52	2.02
USA	2.92	2.50

Source: EC Commission, *European Economy*.
Note: Spain, Portugal, and the UK belonged to the EMS during a short period from 1990 on.

(in 1998). It is immediately clear that there is no relationship between the size of countries and their growth rates.

The previous evidence is of course only meant to be suggestive. Most of the many econometric studies that have been performed recently tend to confirm that the degree of exchange rate variability has a very weak impact on the growth rates of investment, trade, and output. Thus, the weakness of the theoretical argument for such a relationship is confirmed by a weakness of the empirical relationship.

There are, however, two other possible explanations for our failure to find a significant empirical relationship between exchange rate uncertainty and economic growth.

A first alternative explanation is that when we compare the experience of the EMS countries with the other countries, we fail to take into account the fact that the exchange rate uncertainty within the EMS, although reduced, had not been eliminated. It may be that the movement to full monetary union with a common currency is the step we need to eliminate the exchange rate uncertainty, and to stimulate economic growth. (Note, however, that this interpretation of the empirical results is less convincing when we look at the evidence concerning the size of countries.)

A second more promising explanation is that the reduction in exchange rate uncertainty may not necessarily reduce the systemic risk. Less exchange rate uncertainty may be compensated by greater uncertainty elsewhere, e.g. output and

Figure 3.6 GDP level (1998) and its average growth rate (1981–1998)

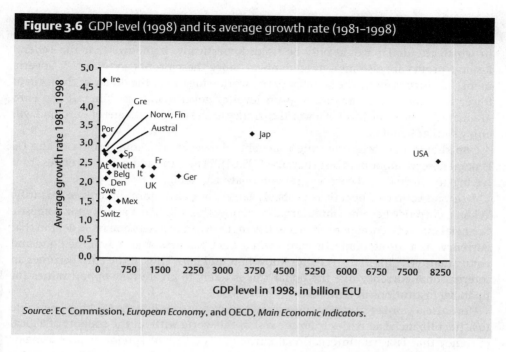

Source: EC Commission, *European Economy*, and OECD, *Main Economic Indicators*.

employment uncertainty. As a result, firms that operate in a greater monetary zone may not on average operate in a less risky environment. There is a whole theoretical literature, starting with William Poole (1970), that has analysed this problem. We have presented the main results in Box 5.

6 Benefits of an international currency

WHEN countries form a monetary union the new currency that comes out of this union is likely to weigh more in international monetary relations than the sum of the individual currencies prior to the union. As a result, the new common currency is likely to find increasing use outside the union. This creates additional benefits of the monetary union. In this section we analyse the nature of these benefits. In a later chapter we turn to the issue of whether and how quickly the euro can become an international currency like the dollar, and thereby reap the benefits that will be described here.

The advantages of having a currency, which is used as a unit of account and a medium of exchange in the rest of the world, are significant. We distinguish two sources of benefits.

First, when a currency is used internationally, the issuer of that currency obtains additional revenues. For example, in 1999 more than half of the dollars issued by the

Federal Reserve were used outside the USA. This situation has the effect of more than doubling the size of the balance sheet of the Federal Reserve compared to a situation in which the dollar would only be used domestically. It follows that the Federal Reserve profits are also more than doubled. Since these profits go to the US Government, US citizens enjoy the benefits of the worldwide use of the dollar in the form of lower taxes needed to finance a given level of government spending. If the euro graduates to the same level of a world currency as the dollar, citizens of Euroland will enjoy similar benefits.

One should not exaggerate these benefits, however. The total profits of the US Federal Reserve amount to less than 1% of US GDP. Thus, the additional revenues from having an international currency remain relatively small.

A second source of benefit is probably larger, but also more difficult to quantify. When a currency becomes an international one, this will boost activity for domestic financial markets. Foreign residents will want to invest in assets and issue debt in that currency. As a result, domestic banks will attract business, and so will the bond and equity markets. This in turn creates know-how and jobs. Thus, if the euro becomes an international currency like the dollar this is likely to create new opportunities for financial institutions in Euroland.

Here also a word of caution is necessary. Some countries like the UK have been able to attract financial activities from the rest of the world without the support of a local currency that is a true international currency. The City of London is now a major centre of international finance, despite the fact that the pound sterling does not play a major role in the world any more. Thus, having an international currency is not a necessary condition for generating financial services that the rest of the world is willing to pay for. Nor is it a sufficient condition for that matter. We come back to this issue in Chapter 10 when we discuss the conditions under which the euro will become a world currency.

7 Benefits of a monetary union and the openness of countries

As in the chapter on the costs of a monetary union, we can also derive a relationship between the *benefits* of a monetary union and the openness of a country. The welfare gains of a monetary union that we have identified in this chapter are likely to increase with the degree of openness of an economy. For example, the elimination of transaction costs will weigh more heavily in countries where firms and consumers buy and sell a large fraction of goods and services in foreign countries. Similarly, the consumers and the firms in these countries are more subject to decision errors because they face large foreign markets with different currencies. Eliminating these risks will lead to a larger welfare gain (per capita) in small and open economies than in large and relatively closed countries.

We can represent this relationship between the benefits of a monetary union and the openness of the countries that are candidates for a union graphically. This is done in Fig. 3.7. On the horizontal axis we show the openness of the country relative to its potential partners of the monetary union (measured by the share of their bilateral trade in the GDP of the country considered). On the vertical axis we represent the benefits (as a percentage of GDP). With an increasing openness towards the other partners in the union, the gains from a monetary union (per unit of output) increase.

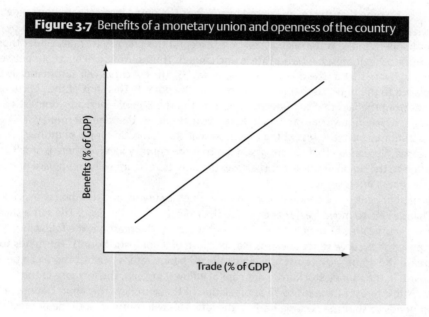

Figure 3.7 Benefits of a monetary union and openness of the country

Box 5 Fixing exchange rates and systemic risk

In a path-breaking article William Poole (1970) showed that fixing interest rates does not necessarily reduce the volatility of output compared to fixing the money stock. The argument Poole developed can easily be extended to the choice between joining a monetary union (irrevocably fixing the exchange rate) and staying outside the union (allowing for a flexible exchange rate).

We consider first *random shocks occurring in the domestic goods market* (business cycle shocks for example). We present this by shifts in the *IS* curve. The latter now moves unpredictably between IS_U and IS_L.

Assume first that the country is a part of a monetary union. Thus, there is no exchange rate any more to worry about. This implies that the domestic interest rate is equal to the union interest rate set by the union central bank. We represent the model graphically in Fig. B5.1.

Let us assume that the union central bank keeps the union interest rate unchanged. This is a rather strong assumption since the central bank is likely to be influenced by what happens in the country analysed here, except if this country is small. Under those conditions the domestic interest rate is unchanged. Thus, output will fluctuate between y_L and y_U. Note that as the *IS* curve moves to, say, IS_U the *LM* curve will automatically be displaced to the right, so that it intersects IS_U at the point *F*. This shift of the *LM* curve comes from the fact that the upward movement of the *IS* curve increases domestic income, which in turn leads to an increase of the domestic demand for money. This will attract money from the rest of the union, so that the domestic supply of money increases. Note again that we are assuming that the country involved here is small in relation to the union. If this is not the case, the domestic boom will put upward pressure on the union interest rate.

What happens if the country is not in the monetary union, and if it then allows its exchange rate to move freely? In this case the *LM* curve remains fixed. The same shocks in the *IS* curve now have no effect on the output level. The reason is the following. Suppose the *IS* curve shifts upwards (say because of a domestic boom). This tends to increase the domestic interest rate. Since the exchange rate is flexible, there can be no increase in the money stock from net capital inflows. Instead, the increase in the domestic interest rate leads to an appreciation of the currency. This appreciation, in turn, tends to shift the *IS* curve back to the left. This will continue until the domestic interest rate returns to its initial level, which is only possible when the *IS* curve returns to its initial position.

We conclude from this case that being a member of the monetary union has led to more variability in the output market (and therefore also in the labour market) compared to being outside the union and letting the exchange rate vary. Joining the monetary union and thereby irrevocably fixing the exchange rate does not necessarily reduce systemic risk, because it leads to more uncertainty elsewhere in the system. Note that this is in essence the same conclusion as in the traditional theory of optimum currency areas in the presence of asymmetric shocks in the output market.[7]

[7] In a recent study, the OECD provides some interesting evidence relating to this issue. It finds that output variability tends to be higher in member-states of monetary unions. See OECD (1999).

Figure B5.1 Shocks in the *IS* curve

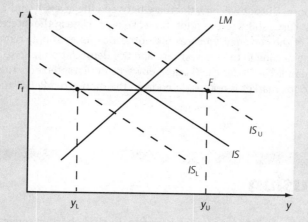

Figure B5.2 Shocks in the *LM* curve

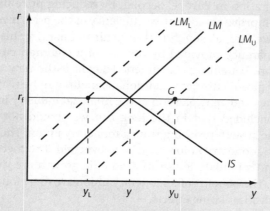

This result, however, very much depends on the nature of the random shocks, that were assumed to come from the goods markets. Things are quite different if the random shocks originate from the money market.

Suppose that we have *random disturbances in the demand for money* (disturbances in velocity). We represent these by movements in the *LM* curve between the limits LM_L and LM_U in Fig. B5.2. Let us again consider the case where the country is in the monetary union. As before, this means that the domestic interest rate is fixed (assuming no shocks in the *union* interest rate). It can now immediately be established that there will be no change in output. The reason is the following. Suppose that the domestic demand for money has declined leading to a rightward shift of the *LM* curve. This tends to reduce the interest rate. Such a reduction, however, is prevented by an immediate outflow of liquidity. The *LM* curve must return to its initial level. Thus, the domestic goods market is completely insulated from domestic money market disturbances when the country is in the union.

If the country is outside the union and allows the exchange rate to float, this will not be the case any more. Output will now fluctuate between the levels Y_L and Y_U. The intuition is that if the *LM* curve shifts to the right, the ensuing decline in the interest rate leads to a depreciation of the currency, whereas the domestic money supply remains unchanged. The decline in the interest rate and the depreciation tend to stimulate aggregate demand. This shifts the *IS* curve upwards until it intersects the LM_U line at point *G*. The goods market is not insulated from the money market disturbances.

8 Conclusion

A COMMON currency has important benefits. In this chapter several of these benefits were identified. First, a common currency in Europe decreases transaction costs. This will not only produce direct, but also indirect benefits in that it will stimulate economic integration in Europe. Second, by reducing price uncertainty, a common currency will improve the allocative efficiency of the price mechanism. This will certainly improve welfare, although it is difficult to quantify this effect. Third, the greater price transparency provided by the use of a common currency is likely to increase competition, benefiting consumers. Fourth, if the new common currency graduates to a truly global currency, additional benefits can be reaped in the form of government revenues and an expansion of the financial industry in the union.

We have also concluded that in the long run we should not expect too much additional economic growth resulting from a monetary union. The potential growth-boosting effects of a monetary union have been oversold. The theoretical reasons for a monetary union to stimulate long run economic growth are weak, and so is the empirical evidence. The benefits of a monetary union are to be found elsewhere than in its alleged growth-stimulating effects.

Chapter 4
Costs and Benefits Compared

Introduction

IN the previous chapters the costs and benefits of a monetary union were identified. In this chapter we conclude this discussion by comparing the benefits with the costs in a synthetic way. This will allow us to evaluate the wisdom of the EU-countries when they decided to launch EMU, and the risks they took. In addition this will make it possible to draw some conclusions about the economic desirability of joining EMU by those countries which today still hesitate to do so.

1 Costs and benefits compared

IT is useful to combine the figures (derived in the previous chapters) relating benefits and costs to the openness of a country. This is done in Fig. 4.1. The intersection point of the benefit and the cost lines determines the critical level of openness that makes it worthwhile for a country to join a monetary union with its trading partners. To the left of that point, the country is better off keeping its national currency. To the right it is better off when it relinquishes its national money and replaces it with the money of its trading partners.

Fig. 4.1 allows us to draw some qualitative conclusions concerning the importance of costs and benefits. The shape and the position of the cost schedule depend to a large extent on one's view about the effectiveness of the exchange rate instrument in correcting for the effects of different demand and cost developments between the countries involved.

Figure 4.1 Costs and benefits of a monetary union

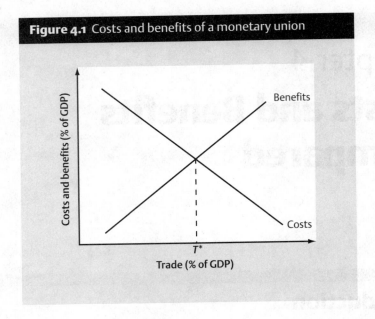

At one extreme, there is a view, which will be called '*monetarist*', claiming that exchange rate changes are ineffective as instruments to correct for these different developments between countries. And even if they are effective, the use of exchange rate policies typically make countries worse off. In this 'monetarist' view[1] the cost curve is very close to the origin. We represent this case in Fig. 4.2a. The critical point that makes it worth while to form a union is close to the origin. Thus, in this view, many countries in the world would gain by relinquishing their national currencies, and by joining a monetary union.

At the other extreme, there is the 'Keynesian' view that the world is full of rigidities (wages and prices are rigid, labour is immobile), so that the exchange rate is a powerful instrument in eliminating disequilibria. This view is well represented by the original Mundell model discussed in Chapter 1. In this view, the cost curve is far away from the origin, so that relatively few countries should find it in their interest to join a monetary union. It also follows from this view that many large countries that now have one currency would be better off (economically) splitting the country into different monetary zones.

It is unmistakable that since the early 1980s the 'monetarist' view has gained adherents, and has changed the view many economists have about the desirability of a monetary union. The popularity of monetarism helps to explain why EMU became a reality in the 1990s.

What does this analysis teach us about the issue of whether EMU is an optimal currency area? In order to answer this question we first present some data on the importance of intra-EU trade for each EU country. The data are in Table 4.1, whose

---

[1] This is the view taken by the drafters of the influential EC Commission report (1990).

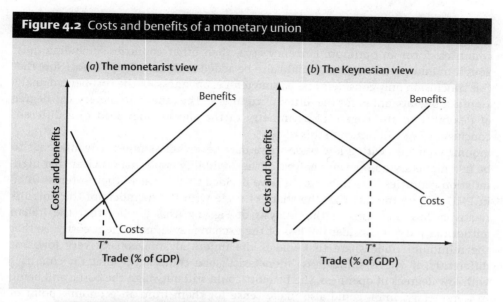

Figure 4.2 Costs and benefits of a monetary union

Table 4.1 Intra-Union exports and imports of EU countries (as per cent of GDP) in 1996

	Exports	Imports
Ireland	45.7	27.8
Belgium and Lux.	41.9	40.8
The Netherlands	32.1	24.9
Portugal	19.4	25.5
Sweden	18.4	17.0
Finland	16.9	14.3
Denmark	16.3	16.6
EU-15	14.7	14.0
Austria	14.3	21.6
United Kingdom	12.8	13.3
Germany	12.7	10.9
Spain	12.2	13.7
France	11.7	11.1
Italy	11.0	10.0
Greece	5.7	16.1

Note: as a percentage of GDP at market prices.
Source: EC Commission, *European Economy*, 61 (1996).

most striking feature is the large difference in openness of EU countries with the rest of the Union. This leads immediately to the conclusion that the cost-benefit calculus is likely to produce very different results for the different EU-countries. For some countries with a large degree of openness relative to the other EU partners, the cost-benefit calculus is likely to show net benefits of being in EMU. This is most likely to be the case in the Benelux countries and Ireland.

Note that Germany and France have low degrees of openness towards the rest of the EU. Thus, if as is often said, France and Germany, together with the Benelux countries, form an optimum currency area, then other countries, including most Southern European countries, should also be added to this monetary area. (Note that this conclusion only considers one parameter, i.e. openness, in the cost-benefit analysis of a monetary union for the different countries. The other parameters, e.g. degree of flexibility or the degree of asymmetry in the shocks, may lead to a different conclusion. We will return to this issue.)

Some countries with a low trade share may nevertheless find it advantageous to be in a monetary union. Our analysis of the credibility issues makes clear that high-inflation countries, like Italy, might have decided that it was in their interest to be in EMU despite the fact that the share of trade with the members of the union is relatively low. In terms of the analysis of Fig. 4.2, this implies that the Italian authorities did not consider the loss of the exchange rate instrument costly, so that the minimum trade share that makes the union advantageous is very low. Put differently, if one is sufficiently 'monetarist', one could argue that for countries with low degrees of openness, the benefits could still outweigh the costs, and being in a monetary union could also make sense for them from an economic point of view.

2 Monetary union, price and wage rigidities, and labour mobility

THE cost-benefit calculus of a monetary union is also very much influenced by the degree of wage and price rigidities. As stressed in Chapter 1, countries in which the degree of wage and price rigidities is low experience lower costs when they move towards a monetary union. We show this in Fig. 4.3.

A decline in wage and price rigidities has the effect of shifting the cost-line in Fig. 4.3 downwards. As a result, the critical point at which it becomes advantageous for a country to relinquish its national currency is lowered. More countries become candidates for a monetary union.

In a similar way, an increase in the degree of mobility of labour shifts the cost curve to the left and makes a monetary union more attractive. In this sense it can be said that, if it increases labour mobility, the single market will make EMU more attractive for EU-countries. It should be noted, however, that not all forms of integration have these effects. As stressed in Chapter 2, economic integration can also lead to more regional concentration of industrial activities. This feature of the integration process changes the cost-benefit calculus, in that it shifts the cost curve to the right and makes a monetary union less attractive.

Figure 4.3 Costs and benefits with decreasing rigidities

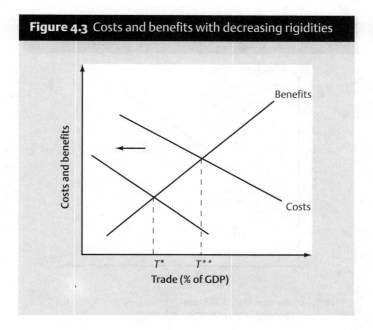

3 **Asymmetric shocks and labour market flexibility**

NOT only the degree of labour market flexibility (wage flexibility and labour mobility) matters for determining whether a monetary union will be attractive to countries. Also the size and the frequency of asymmetric shocks to which they are subjected matters. This means that countries that experience very different demand and supply shocks (because their industrial structures differ very much) will find it more costly to form a monetary union. In the framework of Fig. 4.3 this means that the cost-line shifts to the right.

We are now in a position to analyse the relation between labour market flexibility and asymmetric shocks in a monetary union. This is done graphically in the following way (see Fig. 4.4). On the vertical axis we set out the degree of 'real' divergence between regions (countries) which are candidates to form a monetary union. With real divergence is meant here the degree to which growth rates of output and employment tend to diverge as a result of asymmetric shocks.[2] On the horizontal axis we have the degree of flexibility of the labour markets in these regions (countries).

[2] The latter are those that occur independently from the monetary regime, and were described in Ch. 1. Asymmetric shocks that are the result of divergent national monetary policies are not included here. In a monetary union these would disappear.

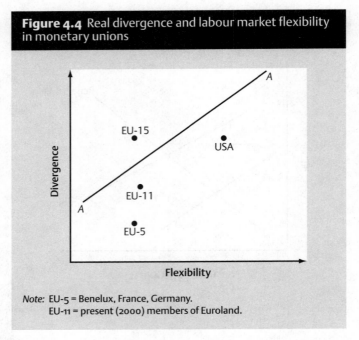

Figure 4.4 Real divergence and labour market flexibility in monetary unions

Note: EU-5 = Benelux, France, Germany.
EU-11 = present (2000) members of Euroland.

The flexibility here relates to wage flexibility and interregional (international) mobility of labour.

The central insight of the theory of optimum currency areas is that countries or regions that experience a high divergence in output and employment growth need a lot of flexibility in their labour markets if they want to benefit from monetary union, and if they wish to avoid major adjustment problems. The larger the degree of 'real divergence', the greater is the need for flexibility in the labour markets to make a smoothly functioning monetary union possible. This relationship between real divergence and flexibility is represented by the upward sloping line *AA*. Countries or regions located below the *AA* line can form a monetary union without 'excessive' adjustment costs. By excessive is meant here that the adjustment costs exceed the benefits of a monetary union. Countries above the *AA* line will experience a lot of adjustment costs in a monetary union. In other words, these countries have too low a degree of flexibility in their labour markets (given the level of real divergence). They do not form an optimum currency area. They are, therefore, well advised to maintain some degree of exchange rate flexibility. Of course, these countries are still free to form a monetary union. The theory, however, predicts that they will suffer economically from this decision.

Where should the European Union be located in Fig. 4.4? There is now a broad consensus among economists, who have tried to implement the theory empirically, that the *EU-15 is not an optimum currency area.* (See Eichengreen (1990); Neumann and von Hagen (1991); Bayoumi and Eichengreen (1993)(1997); De Grauwe and Heens (1993); De Grauwe and Vanhaverbeke (1993).)[3] Thus, according to these empirical

---

[3] A dissenting view is presented in EC Commission (1990). See also Gros and Thygesen (1992).

studies, the EU as a whole (EU-15) is located above the *AA* line. As a result, from an economic point of view, a monetary union involving all EU member countries is a bad idea. The economic costs of a monetary union are likely to be larger than the benefits for a significant number of countries.

Whereas there is a strong consensus among economists that the EU-15 should not form a monetary union, there is an equally strong conviction that *there is a subset of EU countries which form an optimum currency area*. The minimum set of countries that could form a monetary union is generally believed to include Germany, the Benelux countries, and France (EU-5). This conclusion is buttressed by the same empirical studies as those quoted earlier.

Recent empirical analysis, however, has tended to enlarge the group of EU-countries that would benefit from monetary union. The study of Artis and Zhang (1995) shows that the business cycles of EU-countries (including Southern European countries) have become more correlated since the early 1980s. Thus, there are now fewer asymmetric shocks among a relatively large group of EU-countries than 15 years ago.[4] This seems to confirm what we said earlier, i.e. that with economic integration the occurrence of asymmetric shocks tends to diminish.

Other recent studies have cast further doubts on the core–periphery view of monetary integration in the EU. Erkel-Rousse and Mélitz (1995) and Canzoneri *et al.* (1996) find that in most EU-countries monetary policies are powerless to affect real variables like output and employment. Thus, even if EU-countries are confronted with asymmetric shocks, their national monetary policy instruments cannot be used to deal with them effectively. As a result, the loss of these instruments for most of the EU-countries is not very costly.[5]

Finally, another series of empirical studies has found that a large part of the asymmetric shocks in the EU-countries occur at the sectoral level and not so much at the national level. Put differently, a large part of the changes in output and employment in a country are the result of different developments as between sectors (e.g. due to demand shifts or to differential technological changes). These shocks cannot be dealt with by exchange rate changes. (See Bini-Smaghi and Vori (1993); Bayoumi and Prassad (1995); and Gros (1996).)

Thus, the most recent empirical studies lead to more optimism concerning the question of how many EU-countries will profit from EMU. This number could be significantly larger than the five or six core countries usually mentioned in this context. These recent empirical studies, however, do not seem to undermine our conclusion that the EU-15 as a whole does not constitute an optimum currency area. There is no consensus, however, about the size of the subset of countries that will profit from monetary union. In Fig. 4.4 we have placed the core group of countries (EU-5), about which there is a relatively wide consensus, below the *AA* line. (Note that within these countries the degree of labour market flexibility is not higher than among the member countries of the EU-15. The empirical evidence seems to indicate that the degree

[4] The authors credit the European Monetary System (EMS) for this. The EMS has forced countries to follow similar monetary policies. In so doing it has reduced the possibility of following independent monetary policies. The latter are a major source of asymmetric shocks.

[5] For a recent study of Portugal confirming this, see Costa (1996).

of real divergence is lower.) There are other subsets of countries, however (e.g. EU-10 = EU-5 + Austria, Ireland, Portugal, Spain, Italy), that according to the more recent studies could also form an optimum currency area. Because of the many difficulties in quantifying the costs of a monetary union, it will remain difficult, however, to obtain clear-cut results in this area.

In Fig. 4.4 we have also located the USA below the *AA* line. We are, of course, not really sure that the USA forms an optimum currency area. We are, however, much less uncertain about the relative position of the EU and the USA. Note that we have placed the USA at about the same vertical level as the EU-15, expressing the fact that the degree of real divergence between regions in the USA is not much different from the real divergence observed between countries in the EU (see Krugman (1993) on this). The major difference between the USA and the EU seems to be the degree of flexibility of labour markets. Many empirical studies have recently been done documenting this difference in the degree of flexibility of the labour markets in the USA and in Europe. For example, there is ample evidence that real wages in Europe respond less to unemployment than in the USA.[6] Similarly, there is ample evidence that labour mobility is much higher within the USA than it is between member countries of the EU.

It should be stressed here that the analysis underlying Fig. 4.4 is based on the traditional theory of optimum currency areas. It does not deal with some of the problems we have discussed in Chapter 2. For example, countries may experience asymmetric shocks because their monetary policies are independent. Some of them may find it difficult, for reasons of credibility, to follow low-inflation policies. The formation of a monetary union may reduce these problems. In addition, part of the asymmetric shocks one observes today in Europe may be the result of the absence of a monetary union. For example, the unsynchronized nature of the business cycle between Euroland and the UK may be due to the fact that the UK follows a monetary policy independent of the monetary policies on the continent. If the UK joins EMU these divergences are likely to become less important. As a result, one cannot really be sure that the EU-15 would not gain from a monetary union. Nevertheless, with the present state of our knowledge, it is not unreasonable to maintain our conclusion that the EU-15 is not an optimum currency area.

The challenge for the EU-15 is to move to the other side of the *AA* curve, i.e. to make a monetary union less costly. How can this be achieved? There are essentially two strategies. One is to reduce the degree of real divergence, the other is to increase the degree of flexibility.

The difficulty of the first strategy is that the degree of real divergence is to a large extent dependent on factors over which policy-makers have little influence. For example, the degree of industrial specialization matters in determining how important asymmetric shocks are. There is very little policy-makers can do, however, to change regional specialization patterns.

There is one area, however, where policy-makers can do something to reduce the degree of real divergence. This is in the field of political unification. We argued earlier that an important source of asymmetric shocks is the continued existence of nation-

---

[6] See Grubb *et al.* (1983) and Bruno and Sachs (1985).

states with their independent spending and taxing policies, and with their own pecu-liarities as far as economic institutions are concerned. In order to reduce asymmetric shocks, more economic policy co-ordination and institutional streamlining will be necessary. (A special problem arises here: How should labour unions be organized in a monetary union? We take up this issue in Box 6.)

The other strategy for moving the whole of the EU to the other side of the *AA* curve consists in increasing the degree of flexibility of labour markets (real wages and/or labour mobility). This strategy implies a reform of labour market institutions. Although such reforms are difficult to implement, they are necessary if one wants to have a monetary union involving the whole of the European Union.

4 A case-study

IN this section we present a case-study that vividly demonstrates the difference in the adjustment process following shocks that affect regions (or countries) differently.

During the early 1980s the industrial world was hit by a severe recession. This worldwide downturn of economic activity hit regions of the world very differently. In general, regions with an older industrial structure suffered more severely. We take two examples, Michigan in the USA, and Belgium in Europe. Both regions are of a comparable size. In Figs 4.5 and 4.6 we present the evolution of the unemployment rate in these two regions and compare them with the total US and European unemployment.

We observe from these figures that unemployment increased significantly more in Michigan and Belgium than in the USA and in Europe, respectively. It should also be noted that the fact that the USA is much more integrated economically than Europe did not prevent large differentials in unemployment from emerging. In fact the dif-ferential development in unemployment rates appears to be even more pronounced in the USA than in Europe. We discussed this phenomenon in Chapter 2, where we argued that integration also leads to regional concentration. In the case of the USA, integration has also led to a large regional concentration of the automobile sector in Michigan. This sector was severely hit by the recession of the early 1980s. This also explains the intensity of the unemployment problem in Michigan during that period.

How did these two regions adjust? The nature of the adjustment was very dif-ferent in the two cases. In the case of Michigan a significant part of the adjustment was taken care of by outward migration. This is shown in Fig. 4.7, borrowed from Eichengreen (1990), which compares the differential of the Michigan–US unemploy-ment rate with the rate of emigration from Michigan (as a percentage of the Michigan population). Note that the percentages are not fully comparable because the denominators are different. In the case of the emigration figures, the denominator is total population, whereas in the case of the unemployment figures the denominator

Box 6 Labour unions and monetary union

During our discussion of the costs and benefits of a monetary union we have stressed, on several occasions, the role of labour unions in determining the costs of a monetary union. Let us bring these insights together.

We established two rather opposite requirements for the optimal organization of labour unions in a monetary union.

First, we stressed that in the presence of *asymmetric* shocks, wages should be flexible, i.e. they should have different rates of change as between countries (and regions). An example we gave is a differential in productivity growth between countries. In that case nominal wage growth should be different and should reflect the differences in productivity growth between these countries (see Chapter 2). This implies that centralized wage bargaining would be harmful. By imposing the same nominal growth rates of wages it would lead to great losses of competitiveness of the country (region) with a low growth of labour productivity. This problem exists today within individual countries. A recent example is Germany where labour unions imposed centralized wage bargaining on the former East Germany. As a result, many East German firms failed to survive the shock of unification and employment was negatively affected. A similar problem exists in Italy where centralized wage bargaining has hurt the south of the country, where productivity is growing slower than in the north. The effect of this is that unemployment in the south of Italy is four to five times higher than in the north.

A second insight we obtained is that in the presence of the same, *symmetric* shock different wage bargaining systems may lead to a different wage–price spiral and therefore to divergent developments in competitiveness between countries (see Chapter 2). This seems to suggest that when symmetric shocks prevail the wage bargaining systems should be made more uniform across countries. Does this mean that a centralized wage bargaining system at the level of the union becomes desirable? Most probably not. The reasons are the following. First, we have noted that although in a unified Europe asymmetric shocks *between countries* may become less prevalent, specialization would still lead to large regional divergences. These regional asymmetries may even increase in a more unified Europe. The characteristic feature of this specialization is that it would likely cross borders. In such an environment, a centralized wage bargaining system would be harmful for many of the European regions. Second, we have also stressed that technological changes tend to lead to uneven changes in output and employment between sectors. There is even a lot of empirical evidence indicating that many of the asymmetric shocks occur within the same sectors (see Davis *et al.* (1996)). Again, a centralized wage bargaining system would be very detrimental to output and employment in sectors that experience less favourable developments and for firms that lag behind other ones in the same sectors.

To conclude, the future organization of labour unions in a monetary union will have to respect the inevitable requirements of flexibility in a world where shocks occur mostly at the sectoral and micro-economic level.

Figure 4.5 Unemployment rate, Michigan and USA

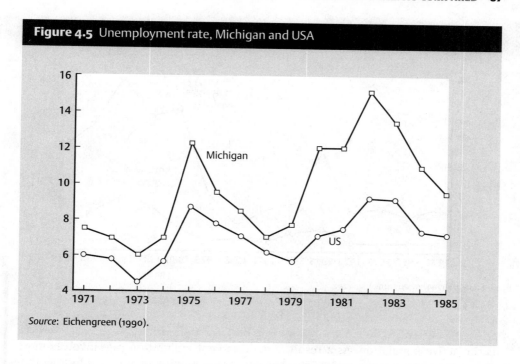

Source: Eichengreen (1990).

Figure 4.6 Unemployment rate, Belgium and EC-9

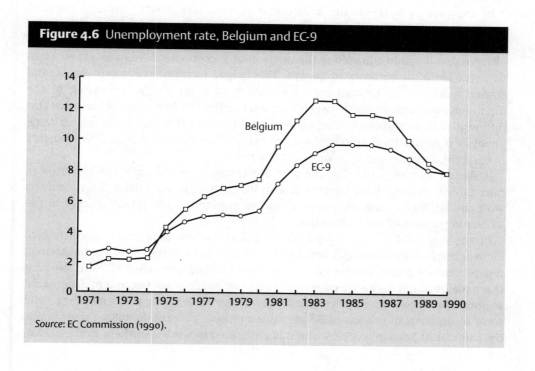

Source: EC Commission (1990).

Figure 4.7 Michigan unemployment differential and emigration

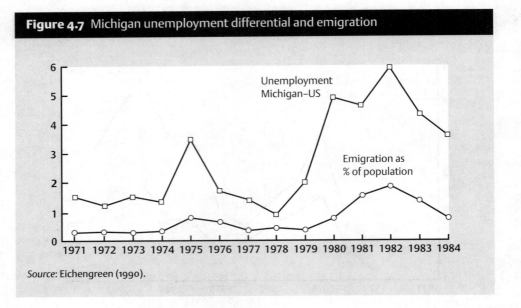

Source: Eichengreen (1990).

is the active population. As a result, a one per cent emigration rate involves more than twice the numbers implicit in a one per cent unemployment rate. It follows that emigration from Michigan was a sizeable fraction of the unemployed, and helped to reduce the unemployment rate of that state.

In the case of Belgium the adjustment process was mainly through the real exchange rate changes. In Fig. 4.8, we show the differential of the Belgian-EC unemployment rate together with the real exchange rate of the Belgian franc. We observe that Belgium adjusted to the unfavourable economic developments by a real depreciation of its currency of 20–25%. This helped to restore competitiveness, and started a process of gradual recovery leading to a significant narrowing of the unemployment differential between Belgium and the EC. At the end of the 1980s this differential had completely disappeared. About half of this real depreciation came about by nominal devaluations, the other half by lower cost and price developments in Belgium, compared to its main trading partners.

It should also be noted that the real depreciations of the early 1980s started to have effects on the unemployment rate in Belgium with some delay. This contrasts with the Michigan experience where the emigration reacted rather quickly to the worsening unemployment situation.

In the case of Michigan very little real depreciation took place. According to Eichengreen, regional changes in the real exchange rates in the USA were limited to a few percentage points during that period. (See Eichengreen (1990: 7). Note also that these real regional exchange rates in the USA can only change because of differential regional developments in prices.) In Belgium very little of the adjustment took the form of outward migration of Belgian unemployed workers. In 1984, for example, the number of Belgian workers who had emigrated to work elsewhere in the EC (i.e.

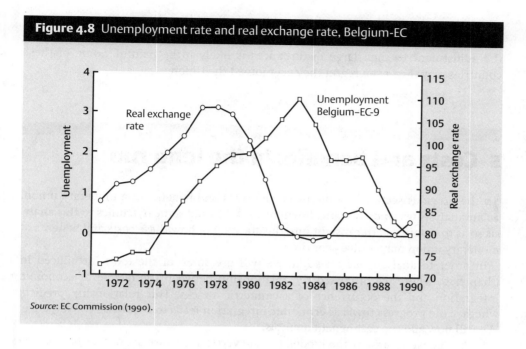

Figure 4.8 Unemployment rate and real exchange rate, Belgium-EC

Source: EC Commission (1990).

the sum of the emigrations from all previous years) amounted to barely 40,000. This is 0.4% of the Belgian population.[7]

There is another important difference in the adjustment mechanism in these two regions. This has to do with fiscal policies. A separate chapter will be devoted to the role of fiscal policies in monetary unions. It is important to note here how differently fiscal policies work within and outside monetary unions.

In the case of Michigan the Federal budget tended to transfer purchasing power automatically to Michigan. This result came about mainly through the Federal transfers for the unemployed, and through the reduction in Federal tax revenues from Michigan. It has been estimated by Sachs and Sala-i-Martin (1989) that for every decline in state income of $1 the Federal budget transfers back 40 cents to the state.[8]

Belgium could not profit from such an intra-European redistribution. Instead, Belgium let its government budget deficit increase spectacularly and borrowed heavily in the foreign capital markets. This allowed it to soften the blow of the recession. It also implied that the *interregional* solidarity which was present in the USA was substituted for by an *intergenerational* solidarity within Belgium, where future generations of Belgians will have to service the government debt.

This case-study suggests that even small countries like Belgium, for which the benefits of being in EMU probably outweigh the costs, have taken some risk. When in the future they will be subject to large shocks (and surely this will happen in some

[7] See Straubhaar (1988).
[8] Von Hagen (1991) has argued that this number overestimates the automatic fiscal transfers in the USA.

countries at some time) they will not have a national monetary and exchange rate instrument to soften the blow. As a result, given the rigidity of their labour markets, the adjustment to such large disturbances is likely to be painful. Some of these countries may then even regret they ever joined the Union.

5 Costs and benefits in the long run

IN the previous sections we discussed the costs and benefits of a monetary union. Our analysis was mostly static. It will be useful to add some dynamics to this analysis so as to obtain a better insight into the question of how these costs and benefits of monetary union may evolve over time.

In order to analyse this question, we will use some of the tools introduced in Chapter 2, where we discussed the relationship between the degree of economic integration and the occurrence of asymmetric shocks. This relationship predicts whether the progress towards economic integration leads to economic convergence. We will now add the cost-benefit analysis.

In Fig. 4.9 we represent the model. On the vertical axis, we set out, as before, the degree of economic divergence between groups of countries. On the horizontal axis we have the degree of trade integration between the same groups of countries. The downward sloping line (TT) says that as trade integration increases the degree of economic divergence between the countries involved declines, i.e. countries become more alike and face fewer asymmetric shocks. (We called this the European

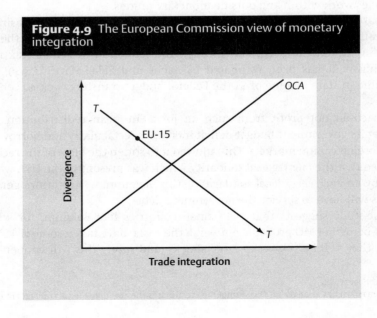

Figure 4.9 The European Commission view of monetary integration

Commission view in Chapter 2. We will return to the Krugman view later.) The upward sloping line (called *OCA*) represents the combinations of divergence and trade integration that make monetary union a break-even operation (costs = benefits). It is derived as follows. As trade integration increases, the net gains of a monetary union increase (see the previous sections). At the same time, when economic divergence increases, the costs of a monetary union increase. The two phenomena together allow us to derive the *OCA* schedule: when trade integration increases the net gains of the monetary union rise. These gains will be compensated by an increase in economic divergence. All points on the *OCA* line are then combinations of divergence and integration for which the monetary union has a zero net gain. Note that all the points to the right of the *OCA* line are points for which the benefits of monetary union exceed the costs. We call it the *OCA* zone.

In Fig. 4.9 we have put the EU-15 on the downward sloping *TT* line to the left of the *OCA* line, reflecting the conclusion that we arrived at in Section 3, i.e. that today (in 2000) the EU-15 is probably not an optimum currency area. As trade integration within the EU proceeds, however, this point will move downwards along the *TT* line. This will inevitably bring us into the *OCA* zone, at least if we can assume that the dynamics of integration will continue to work within the EU. Thus, in this view, monetary unification will over time be perceived to be beneficial for all countries in the European Union. In this sense monetary union among all EU-countries is inevitable.

This is the optimistic view about the long-term prospects for monetary integration in Europe. There is, however, also a pessimistic view which one can derive from the Krugman analysis. It will be remembered that in the Krugman analysis, economic integration leads to more economic divergence between countries. This is represented in Fig. 4.10 by the upward sloping *TT* and *T'T'* lines.

We now have to consider two possibilities for the long-term prospects of monetary union. One is represented by the *TT* line, the slope of which is flatter than the slope of the *OCA* line. In this case, although today the EU-15 may not be an optimum currency area, it will move into the *OCA* zone over time. In this case more integration leads to more specialization and thus more asymmetric shocks. However, the benefits of a monetary union also increase steeply with the degree of integration. As a result, despite the increase in asymmetric shocks, more integration will lead us into the *OCA* zone.

The second case is represented by the steep *T'T'* line. Here integration brings us increasingly farther away from the *OCA* zone. This is so because the net gains of a monetary union do not increase fast enough with the degree of integration. As a result, the costs of divergence overwhelm all the other benefits a monetary union may have. In the long run the prospects for a monetary union of the EU-15 are poor. It should be noted that this case leads to an anomaly. It implies that a lowering of trade integration can bring us into the *OCA* zone. Thus if the EU-countires would go back and disintegrate, monetary union would become attractive. An odd result.

From the discussion of the Krugman model we conclude that even if integration leads to more asymmetric shocks, this may still lead to increasing net gains of a monetary union for the EU-15. We cannot exclude, however, the possibility that the process of integration will make monetary union for the EU-15 more and more unattractive.

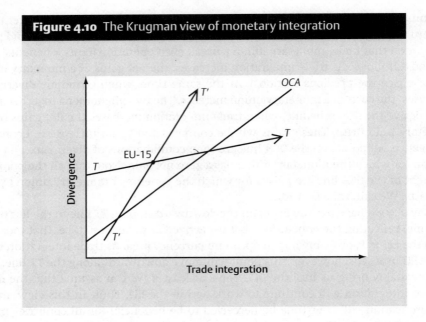

Figure 4.10 The Krugman view of monetary integration

The reader should keep in mind what we said earlier about the relevance of the Krugman scenario. First, the theoretical presumption is not in favour of this scenario. Second, recent empirical evidence seems to sustain this theoretical presumption.

A last point about the long-run dynamics of monetary integration is the following. The decision by an individual country to join the monetary union is likely to speed up the integration process. In Chapter 2 we documented this by referring to empirical studies indicating how the existence of different national currencies helps to segment national markets. A decision by an individual country to join EMU, even if it does not satisfy the *OCA* criteria, would have a self-fulfilling character, at least if Fig. 4.9 is the right view of the world. In this case the process of integration would be sped up by the very decision to join the monetary union, so that this new country grouping moves faster into the *OCA* zone.

6 Conclusion

THE arguments developed in this chapter have led to the following conclusions. First, it is unlikely that the EU as a whole constitutes an optimal monetary union. Put differently, not all EU-countries have the same interest in relinquishing their national currencies and in adhering to a European monetary union. The cost-benefit analysis of this chapter therefore also implies that a monetary unification in Europe better suits the economic interests of the different individual countries if it can proceed at different speeds, i.e. if some countries who today feel that it is not in their national interest to do so, have the option to wait before joining the union.

Second, the number of countries that benefit from monetary union is probably larger than most economists thought just a few years ago. In addition, as the process of integration moves on, the number of countries that are likely to benefit from monetary union will increase. Thus, in the long run monetary union will be an attractive proposition for most, if not all, EU-countries.

Third, even the countries that are net gainers from a monetary union take a risk by joining the union. The risk is that when large shocks occur (like the one that occurred in some countries in the early 1980s), they will find it more difficult to adjust, having relinquished their national currencies.

The discussion of this and the previous chapters has been based on an *economic* cost-benefit analysis. Countries may also decide to adopt a common currency for *political* reasons. A common currency may be the first step towards a political union that they wish to achieve. The economic cost-benefit analysis remains useful, however, because it gives an idea of the price some countries will have to pay to achieve these political objectives.

Part II

Monetary Union

Chapter 5

Incomplete Monetary Unions: The European Monetary System

Introduction

IN the previous chapters we discussed the costs and benefits of full monetary union. In the real world, there exist many monetary arrangements between nations that are far removed from full monetary union, and yet also follow rules, and constrain the national monetary policies of the participants. These are arrangements whereby the monetary authorities peg their exchange rates. The best-known examples of such 'incomplete' monetary unions in the post-war period are the Bretton Woods system and the European Monetary System.

In this chapter we will focus on the European Monetary System, which started in 1979 and ceased to exist on 31 December 1998 when EMU came into existence. The system went through several crises, the most important one occurring in 1992-3, when several major countries left it, and when the system was transformed fundamentally. In the second half of the 1990s, however, as the start of EMU approached, the system found a new and surprising stability. In this chapter, we will analyse two questions. First, why is it that in general, pegged exchange rate regimes, like the EMS, turn out to be so fragile? Second, what factors led to the surprising stability of the fixed exchange rate commitment while countries approached the entry into EMU?

The fragility of a fixed exchange rate system has everything to do with credibility. When the authorities of a country announce that they will fix the exchange rate they are making a promise: they pledge to keep the exchange rate fixed today and in the future. The problem with any promise, however, is that doubts may arise as to whether it will be kept. In other words, all promises lead to problems of credibility. This is, in a nutshell, the essential problem of fixed exchange rates.

Box 7 The European Monetary System: some institutional features

The European Monetary System was instituted in 1979. It came as a reaction to the large exchange rate variability of Community currencies during the 1970s, which was seen as endangering the integration process in Europe.[1]

The EMS consisted of two features. The 'Exchange Rate Mechanism' (ERM) and the ECU.

Like the Bretton Woods system, the ERM was an 'adjustable peg' system. That is, countries participating in the ERM determined an official exchange rate (central rate) for all their currencies, and a band around these central rates within which the exchange rates could fluctuate freely. This band was set at +2.25% and −2.25% around the central rate for most member countries (Belgium, Denmark, France, Germany, Ireland, and the Netherlands). Italy was allowed to use a larger band of fluctuation (+6% and −6%) until 1990 when it decided to use the narrower band. The three newcomers to the system, Spain (1989), the UK (1990), and Portugal (1992), used the wider band of fluctuation. The UK dropped out of the system in September 1992. In August 1993 the band of fluctuation was raised to +15% and −15%. On 1 January 1999 the EMS ceased to exist.

When the limits of the band (the margins) were reached, the central banks of the currencies involved were committed to intervene so as to maintain the exchange rate within the band. (This intervention was called 'marginal' intervention, i.e. intervention at the margins of the band.) The commitment to intervene at the margins, however, was not absolute. Countries could (after consultation with the other members of the system) decide to change the parity rates of their currency (a realignment).

These realignments were very frequent during the first half of the 1980s, when more than ten took place. They became much less frequent after the middle of the 1980s. During 1987–92 no realignment took place. In 1992–3 several realignments occurred. (In Section 7 we discuss post-1993 developments in the EMS.)

The second feature of the EMS was the existence of the ECU. The ECU was defined as a basket of currencies of the countries that are members of the EMS. (This was a larger group of countries than the ERM members. It included all the EU-countries except Austria, Finland, and Sweden.)

The value of the ECU in terms of currency i (the ECU rate of currency i) was defined as follows:

$$ECU_i = \Sigma_j \, a_j \, S_{ji} \qquad\qquad (B7.1)$$

where a_j is the amount of currency j in the basket; S_{ji} is the price of currency j in units of currency i (the bilateral exchange rate).

On 1 January 1999 the ECU was transformed into the euro at the rate of 1 ECU = 1 euro. Since the euro became a currency on its own, the basket definition ceased to exist.

---

[1] For a fascinating account of the discussions that led to the establishment of the EMS, see Ludlow (1982). For a more detailed description of some institutional features of the system see van Ypersele (1985).

The next question then is why countries would want to go back on a promise they made in the past. (Presumably, when they pledged to fix the exchange rate they must have considered that it was in their national interest to do so.) The answer is that there may arise circumstances in which the fixed exchange rate arrangement ceases to be seen as serving the national interest of the country. In that case the country will have an incentive to renege on its promise. Economic agents will suspect this and will attack the currency. We have a speculative crisis.

We will analyse several problems that bring countries into situations in which they want to re-evaluate their commitment. One we will call the reputation problem, the second the adjustment problem, and third the $n-1$ problem.

1 Differences in reputation lead to low credibility of a fixed exchange rate

THE Barro–Gordon model, which we discussed in Chapter 2, allows us to analyse problems of reputation. This analysis led to the conclusion that the high-inflation country (Italy) has a lot to gain from pegging its currency to the currency of the low-inflation country. However, Italy will find it difficult to fix its exchange rate credibly. We repeat the analysis here but refine it in one crucial manner. We assume that there is some cost, C_D, to devalue the currency. This cost could be interpreted to include the political cost of a devaluation, i.e. the politicians who decide to devalue have to face the prospect that their promises have become less credible. Many politicians are therefore reluctant to devalue. We show the case of Italy in Fig. 5.1. We assume that it has pegged to the German mark. As a result, the announcement of a fixed exchange rate amounts to an announcement that the Italian inflation rate will be equal to the German one. In order to facilitate the graphical analysis we set the German inflation rate equal to zero. This means that Italy must keep its inflation equal to zero. In order to keep the exchange rate fixed, the economy must be in point B. Once the exchange rate is fixed, the Italian authorities have an incentive to follow inflationary policies and to devalue by surprise, so as to obtain a more favourable inflation-unemployment outcome. One can measure the welfare gain for the authorities of such a surprise inflation (devaluation) by the distance AB (this is the welfare gain expressed in units of unemployment). If AB is larger than the fixed cost of the devaluation, C_D (measured in units of unemployment), economic agents will attack the currency. As a result, the economy will move to F and ultimately to E, when all adjustments in expectations will have occurred.

The only way the fixed exchange rate can be made credible is when the cost of the devaluation exceeds the distance AB. In that case speculators know that despite the temptation, the authorities will not devalue. The fixed exchange rate is then credible and can be sustained.

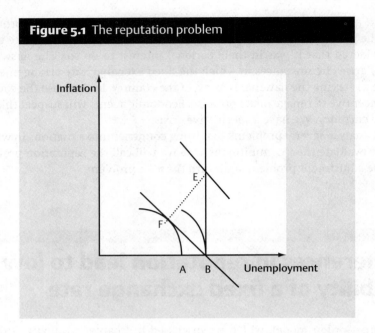

Figure 5.1 The reputation problem

We will return to this model later in this chapter when we first analyse the crisis of the EMS during 1992–3, and the subsequent stabilization in the progress towards EMU.

2 The adjustment problem

COUNTRIES are often subjected to shocks that may lead them to re-evaluate their commitment to a fixed exchange rate. We show such a shock in the context of the Barro–Gordon model (see Fig. 5.2). We assume that the short-term Phillips curve shifts to the right (from point B to point D). We will also assume that the cost of devaluing C_D is larger than AB so that prior to the shock, the fixed exchange rate commitment was credible. What happens after the shock? The authorities now have an incentive to go to point G, i.e. they would like to accommodate the negative shock by stimulating the economy. The fixed exchange rate, however, constrains them to stay in point D. This is certainly worse than point G, given the preferences of the authorities as represented by the indifference curves. The distance ED measures the welfare cost for the authorities (expressed in units of unemployment) of maintaining the exchange rate fixed.

We can now come to the following conclusion. If the cost of a devaluation, C_D, is smaller than ED, then a devaluation will be inevitable. The authorities will have an incentive to devalue. Speculators realize this, and will therefore attack the currency.

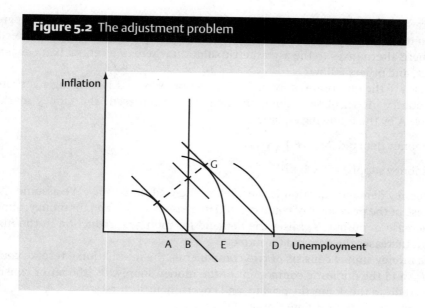

Figure 5.2 The adjustment problem

Note that the fact that prior to the shock the cost of a devaluation exceeds AB, does not guarantee that after the shock, C_D will also exceed ED. The reason is that with a large enough shock, as shown in Fig. 5.2, the cost of maintaining the fixed exchange rate can become very large. The shock then changes the calculus of the authorities and undermines the credibility of the fixed exchange rate.

We have called this the adjustment problem of a fixed exchange rate because the authorities feel that they can reduce the adjustment costs after the shock by some expansionary monetary policies. In a fixed exchange rate regime, the adjustment costs are perceived to be larger.

3 The $n - 1$ problem in pegged exchange rate systems

EVERY system of fixed exchange rates faces the problem of how to set the system-wide level of the money stock and interest rate. This issue essentially arises from the so-called $n - 1$ problem. In a system of n countries, there are only $n - 1$ independent exchange rates.[2] Therefore $n - 1$ monetary authorities will be forced to adjust their monetary policy instrument so as to maintain a fixed exchange rate. There will be one monetary authority which is free to set its monetary policy independently. Thus, the

---

[2] There are more exchange rates (actually the number is $n(n - 1)/2$. Arbitrage, however, ensures that only $n - 1$ are independent.

system has one degree of freedom. This leads to the problem of how this degree of freedom will be used. Who will be the central bank that uses this degree of freedom? Are there alternatives to the asymmetric solution where one central bank does what it likes, and others follow?

These are the questions analysed in this section. We do this by using a very simple two-country model of the money markets. Let us represent the money market of country A by the following equations:

money demand: $M_A^D = P_A L_A(Y_A, r_A)$ (5.1)

money supply: $M_A^S = R_A + D_A$ (5.2)

The money demand equation is specified in the traditional way. We assume that an increase in the price level of country A (P_A) increases the demand for money. Similarly an increase in output, Y_A raises the demand for money. A reduction in the interest rate r_A, increases the demand for money.

The money supply consists of two components, the international reserve component, R_A, and the domestic component of the money supply, D_A (the latter consists of bank credit to the domestic, private, and government sectors).

For country B we postulate similar equations, i.e.

money demand: $M_B^D = P_B L_B(Y_B, r_B)$ (5.3)

money supply: $M_B^S = R_B + D_B$ (5.4)

We will assume that there is perfect mobility of capital between these two countries. This allows us to use the interest parity condition, which we specify as follows:

$r_A = r_B + \mu$ (5.5)

where μ is the expected rate of depreciation of the currency of country A.[3]

This relationship is also called the 'open interest parity'. It says that if economic agents expect a depreciation of currency A, the interest rate of country A will have to exceed the interest rate of country B in order to compensate holders of assets of country A for the expected loss.

Now suppose countries A and B decide to fix their exchange rate. Let us also assume that economic agents do not expect that the exchange rate will be adjusted in the future. This means that μ = zero. The interest rates in the two countries will be identical.

We can now represent the equilibrium of this system graphically as follows (Fig. 5.3). The downward-sloping curve is the money demand curve. The money supply is represented by the vertical lines M_A^1 and M_B^1. Money market equilibrium in both countries is obtained where demand and supply intersect (points E and F). In addition, given the interest parity condition, the interest rates must be equal.

It is clear from Fig. 5.3 that there are many combinations of such points that bring about equilibrium in this system. Consider, for example, the points G and H. At these two points demand and supply of money in the two countries are equal, and the

---

[3] In Box 8 more explanation is given about how this expression is derived.

Figure 5.3 The $n-1$ problem in a two-country monetary model

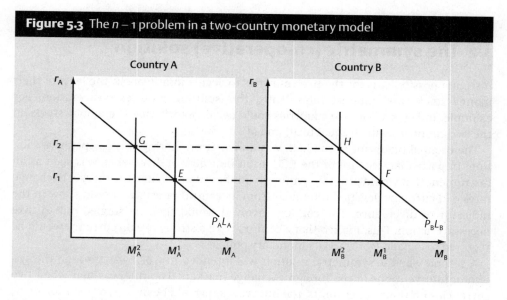

interest rates are also equalized. It is easy to see that there are infinitely many combinations that will satisfy these equilibrium conditions. Each of these combinations will produce one level of the interest rate and one of the money stock. One can say that the fixed exchange rate arrangement is compatible with any possible *level* of the interest rates and of the money stocks. There is a fundamental indeterminacy in this system. This follows from the $n-1$ problem, which, as we have seen, produces one degree of freedom in the system.

How can this indeterminacy be solved? We discuss two possible solutions: one is asymmetric (hegemonic), the other is symmetric (co-operative).

3.1 The asymmetric (hegemonic) solution

The first solution to the problem consists in allowing one country to take a leadership role. Suppose, for example, that country A is the leader and that it fixes its money stock independently, say at the level M_A^1 (see Fig. 5.3). This then fixes the interest rate in country A at the level r_1. Country B now has no choice any more. Its interest rate will have to be the same as in country A. Given the money demand in country B, this then uniquely determines the money supply in country B (M_B^1) that will be needed to have equilibrium. Country B has to accept this money supply. It cannot follow an independent monetary policy.

In this asymmetric arrangement, country A takes on the role of anchoring the money stock in the system. The degree of freedom in the system is used by country A to set its monetary policy independently.

3.2 The symmetric (co-operative) solution

A second possibility is for the two countries to decide jointly about the level of their money stocks and interest rates. Thus, this solution requires co-operation. For example, in Fig. 5.3, the two countries could decide jointly that the money stocks in the two countries will be equal to M_A^1 and M_B^1.

The original blueprint of the EMS was aimed at promoting this co-operative solution. In particular, the use of the ECU as an indicator of divergence was seen as an instrument that would promote symmetry in the system. When the market exchange rates of a currency deviated too much from its central rates, this would show in the indicator of divergence. The country involved would then be singled out to take necessary action. This implied that a country with a strong (weak) currency would be required to expand (contract) its monetary policies.

A second way the symmetric solution was intended to work was through the system of interventions in the foreign exchange markets. The rule was that when two currencies hit their upper limits, the intervention would be in each other's currency, so that the monetary effect in the two countries would be symmetrical.

We illustrate this symmetric intervention system in Fig. 5.4. We assume that doubts have arisen about the fixity of the exchange rate of currency A against currency B, and that economic agents expect a *future* devaluation of currency B. According to the interest-parity condition, this requires an increase in the interest rate of country B relative to the interest rate of country A. In the foreign exchange market the following will happen. The expectation of a future devaluation of currency B leads speculators to sell currency B against currency A. In order to prevent the market rate of currency B from dropping below its limit against A, the central bank of country B

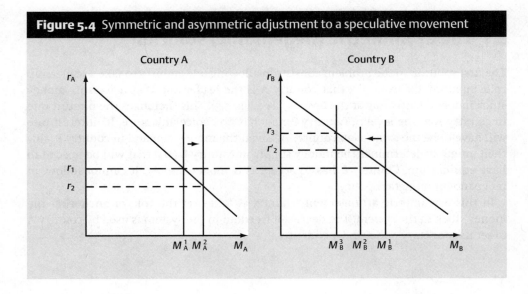

Figure 5.4 Symmetric and asymmetric adjustment to a speculative movement

must buy its own currency and sell currency A. (The latter it will typically obtain through the system of short-term financing, which forces country A to provide the necessary amounts of its currency to country B.) The result of this intervention on the money stocks is symmetric: country B's money stock declines, and country A's money stock increases. The latter arises from the fact that the sale of currency A by country B increases the amount of currency A in circulation. We represent this symmetric effect in Fig. 5.4 by a leftward shift of the money stock line in country B (from M_B^1 to M_B^2) and a rightward shift of the money stock line in country A (from M_A^1 to M_A^2). As a result, the interest rate in country B increases to r'_2, whereas it declines in country A to r_2. Thus, the speculative disturbance is taken care of by a symmetric adjustment, in which country A allows its money stock to increase and its interest rate to decline, and country B allows the opposite to occur.

As a matter of fact, the symmetric solution, as we just described it, has generally not worked well. In particular, when a speculative crisis arose, requiring intervention in the foreign exchange market, the strong-currency country (Germany) has generally been unwilling to allow its money stock to increase and its interest rate to decline. This Germany has achieved by using *sterilization policies*, i.e. by offsetting the expansionary effects of the interventions in the foreign exchange market by reverse operations of the Bundesbank. Thus, when the central bank of the weak-currency country sold marks (against its own currency), the Bundesbank has usually bought these marks back through open market operations. The effect of these sterilization policies then typically was that the German money stock was not (or only slightly) affected by the foreign exchange market operations of the weak-currency countries.

The implication of this asymmetry is that the weak currency is forced to do all the monetary adjustment. In Fig. 5.4 we see that country B is now forced to reduce its money stock to the level given by M_B^3, and to allow the interest rate to increase to r_3. The money stock of country A remains unchanged at M_A^1 in this asymmetric adjustment system.

Despite the original intentions of the founding fathers of the EMS, the system has evolved into an asymmetric one.[4] Such asymmetric arrangements are very common in fixed exchange rate systems. In the Bretton Woods system, the USA took on this role. In the EMS, Germany has taken the anchoring role.

Several issues arise here. First, the question is why a particular country is selected as a leader, and not another one. Why did Germany become the leader in the EMS? This question will be analysed in Section 3. 4 below. Secondly, what are the characteristics of these asymmetric (sometimes also called hegemonic) arrangements as compared to symmetric systems, where countries decide jointly about the system-wide money stock and interest rate, or where they allow rules to lead to symmetric adjustments?

---

[4] There has been a lively academic discussion on the question of how important the dominant position of Germany has been during the EMS period. Econometric analysis suggests that, although the influence of German monetary policies on monetary conditions in the other EMS countries has been pervasive, this influence is not one way. Other countries' monetary policies have occasionally also influenced German monetary conditions. For evidence, see Fratianni and von Hagen (1990) and De Grauwe (1991).

3.3 Symmetric and asymmetric systems compared

An asymmetric system has a number of important advantages, together with disadvantages. Let us analyse the advantages first. One important advantage of this system is that it imposes a lot of discipline on the peripheral country. Suppose the latter should decide to increase its money stock. This would immediately lead to a drain on the international reserves of the central bank of the peripheral country, because residents would seek a riskless higher rate of return in the centre country. The peripheral country would be forced almost instantaneously to lower its money stock again.

It should be noted here that in the asymmetric arrangement the flow of liquidity from the periphery to the centre country does not affect the money stock in the latter country. In this asymmetric system, the centre country automatically sterilizes the liquidity inflow by reverse open market operations. If it did not do so, the monetary expansion engineered by the peripheral country would lead to an increase of the money stock in the centre country. That country would then also lose its function of an anchor for the whole system.

There are other features of the asymmetric system, however, that make it less attractive. These have to do with the way unsynchronized business cycles affect the money markets. In order to show this, we suppose that the peripheral country experiences a recession. We represent this effect in the money markets of the two countries in Fig. 5.5. The recession in the peripheral country shifts the demand for money downwards as shown in Fig. 5.5. This has the effect of reducing the interest rate in the peripheral country. However, interest parity (and assuming that no future devaluations are expected) makes it impossible for the interest rate to decline below

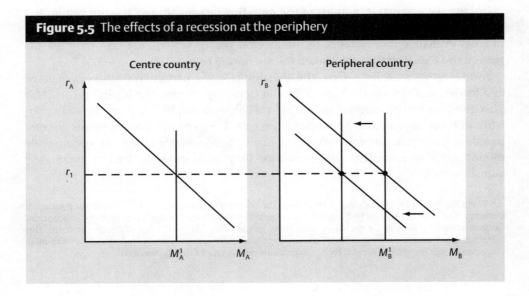

Figure 5.5 The effects of a recession at the periphery

the centre country's interest rate. Since in the centre country no change in the money demand occurs, and its authorities continue to fix the domestic money supply, the interest rate in the centre country cannot change. The result is that the money supply in the peripheral country must automatically decline. This comes about as follows. The downward pressure on the peripheral country's interest rate leads to an outflow of capital to the centre country. This reduces the money stock in the peripheral country, and would increase the money stock in the centre country. However, as the authorities of that country are committed to fix their supply of money, they automatically sterilize the reserve inflow by open market sales of securities.

The less attractive feature of this adjustment mechanism is that a recession which originates in the peripheral country is made worse by a contraction of the country's money stock. The opposite occurs when a boom originates in the peripheral country. In that case the boom is automatically accommodated by an increase in the money stock of the peripheral country, because the upward pressure on its interest rate leads to a capital inflow. (The reader can work out this case for herself/himself using the model of Fig. 5.5.) The result is that the business cycles in the peripheral country are likely to be made more intense by the procyclical movements of the money stock of the periphery.

It is clear that this asymmetric system of monetary control is not very efficient at dealing with asymmetric shocks such as unsynchronized business cycles. The problem is that while the centre country tries to stabilize its money stock without regard to what happens in the rest of the system, it helps to make the money stock volatile in the peripheral country. In this system, there is no one responsible for the money stock of the whole system.

The previous analysis also makes clear that the asymmetric system in which the centre country rigidly fixes its money supply does not guarantee that the money stock will be stable in the system as a whole when asymmetric shocks occur. The symmetric system of monetary control would be more successful in stabilizing the system's money stock when unsynchronized business cycles occur. In order to show this, we take the case of a recession in the peripheral country again. We now assume that the central banks of the centre and the periphery co-operate to stabilize the whole system's money stock. They can achieve this as follows. The peripheral country reduces its money stock, and the centre country increases its money stock. We show this case in Fig. 5.6.

The effect of this co-ordinated approach is that the total money supply is kept unchanged. Note that this result will come about automatically if the centre country does not sterilize the inflows of reserves that are triggered by the decline in the interest rate of the peripheral country.

The problems of monetary control that arise in an asymmetric system when asymmetric shocks occur are likely to lead to conflicts about the kind of monetary policy to be followed for the whole system. For example, during a recession originating in the peripheral countries, these will find that the monetary policies they have to endure are inappropriate. Pressures on the centre country will certainly be exerted. These conflicts of interests will have to be dealt with in one way or another.

The preceding discussion also suggests that an asymmetric system may not survive

Figure 5.6 A recession at the periphery in a symmetric system

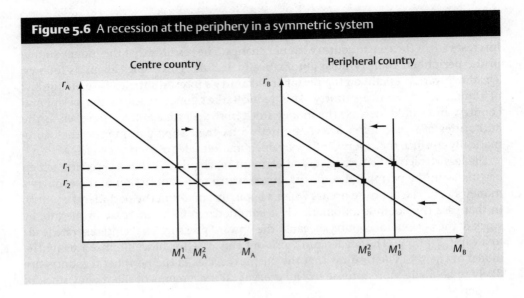

in the long run. Too much conflict will exist about the appropriate monetary policies for the system as a whole. Peripheral countries, especially if they are similar in size to the centre country (as was the case in the EMS), may not be willing to subject their national interests to the survival of the system. In the end, more explicit co-operative arrangements may be necessary.

3.4 The choice of a leader in the EMS

In the previous sections it was argued that asymmetric arrangements are often used to 'anchor' the money stock in a fixed exchange rate system. In this section we analyse the question of why fixed exchange rate systems tend to end up with one leader and many followers. In addition, we determine the factors that decide who becomes the leader. In order to do so, we return to the Barro–Gordon model of two countries. Let us call these two countries Germany and Italy again.

We take as a starting point Fig. 2.14 (Chapter 2). Suppose, as before, that Germany and Italy have decided to fix their exchange rate. In principle, this arrangement can work with any level of the common inflation rate. This could be the German inflation rate. It could also be the Italian inflation rate, or any other inflation rate, as long as it is the same one for both countries. This requirement follows from the purchasing power parity condition which we have imposed.

Which inflation rate will be most beneficial for the two countries? It can easily be shown that this is the lower (German) inflation rate. In order to see this, suppose first that Italy decides to accept the German inflation rate, and suppose that the fixing of the exchange rate can be made credible. Then the welfare gain for Italy will be given

Figure 5.7 The selection of a leader in the EMS

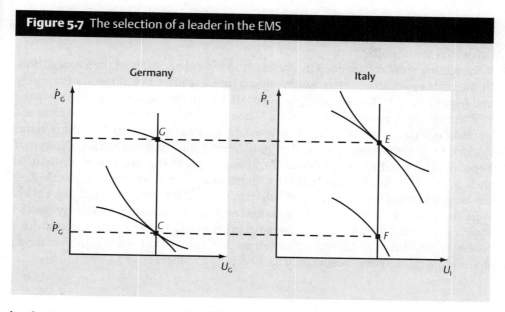

by the movement of the inflation rate from *E* to *F* (see Fig. 5.7). Italy has now a lower inflation rate at no cost in terms of unemployment.[5]

Consider now the alternative. Germany would accept the Italian inflation rate. The inflation equilibrium would now be given by point *G*. This is a clear loss of welfare in Germany, without any gain in Italy. There is no reason to assume that Germany would be willing to strike a deal which would make it worse off, and which would not make Italy any better off. In fact, it can also be seen that Germany has no incentive at all to accept any other inflation rate than the one it had prior to the establishment of the fixed exchange rate. Conversely, Italy has an incentive to aim for the lower German inflation rate. Under those conditions, it is quite easy to understand that Italy will be glad to accept the leadership of Germany in determining the system-wide inflation rate. This is an arrangement that maximizes welfare in Italy without reducing welfare in Germany.

The previous analysis stresses that the leadership position of a country depends on its reputation in maintaining a low inflation equilibrium. Reputations can change, however. For example, political and institutional changes may affect the preferences of the centre country's authorities, leading to a higher inflation equilibrium. Similarly, an increase in the natural unemployment rate may bring about a higher inflation equilibrium. These changes are likely to jeopardize the leadership position of the centre country, as other countries may decide to stop pegging their exchange rates to that country, and to look for another low-inflation country to take up the role of the leader.

Such changes in leadership positions are likely to lead to great disturbances. They can also endanger the stablility of the system, and may lead to its downfall. This is

---

[5] We abstract from the possible short-run losses when Italy disinflates and unemployment increases temporarily.

what happened in the Bretton Woods system when the USA stopped being the low-inflation country of the system. Other countries lost their incentives to peg their currencies to the dollar.

Something similar happened in the newly independent states of the former USSR. In the early 1990s Russia increasingly moved into a situation of monetary instability and hyperinflation. The newly independent states had the choice either to stay in the rouble area, and thus to import hyperinflation, or to drop out of the rouble zone and to introduce their own currency which would float against the rouble. Many states decided to do the latter. At the end of 1993 Azerbaijan, Estonia, Georgia, the Kyrgyz Republic, Latvia, Lithuania, Moldova, Turkmenistan, and Ukraine had all introduced their own currencies. In some of these countries this step was successful in shielding the economy from the Russian hyperinflation (the Baltic states, for example). Others were not successful, and in fact experienced even worse monetary instability than in Russia (Ukraine, for example). Those who experienced success were the countries where legislation was introduced ensuring that the central bank could refuse to finance the government budget deficits by printing money.

4 The EMS during the 1980s

THE surprising fact about the EMS is that it lasted for more than a decade before it succumbed to the problems we identified in the previous sections. Thus, before we study the reasons why the system disintegrated in 1992–3, it will be helpful first to understand why it took thirteen years before it finally happened. What were the factors that helped the system temporarily to overcome the problems discussed in the previous sections? We identify two features of the early EMS, the bands of fluctuation and the existence of capital controls.

4.1 Bands of fluctuation

First, there was the existence of *bands of fluctuation*. Contrary to the Bretton Woods system, where they were relatively narrow (1% above and below the parities), in the EMS the bands were fixed at 2.25% above and below the official parities (central rates). This allowed exchange rates to move by (at most) 4.5%. For some countries (Italy until July 1990, Portugal, Spain, and the UK) the bands of fluctuation were even set at 6% below and above central rates, allowing a maximal range of fluctuation of 12%. These relatively large bands of fluctuation were quite important in stabilizing the system in the following way.

The existence of relatively wide bands made it possible for the authorities of high-inflation countries to change the exchange rate regularly by small amounts without having to face large speculative crises prior to each expected realignment. A country with high inflation (e.g. Italy which faced a band of 12%) could devalue its currency by, say, 8% per year to offset the larger inflation rate. Given the fact that the bands of fluctuations were 12%, after each realignment the new central rate would always fall between the previously prevailing upper and lower limits. As a result, after the realignment the market exchange rate most often would not change, and could even decline. We show this feature in Fig. 5.8. We suppose that prior to the realignment date, at t_1, the exchange rate (the price of the German mark in units of lira) hits the upper limit. At t_1 the lira is devalued against the mark (the official price of the mark increases) by 8% to reflect a higher inflation of 8% in Italy as compared to Germany. One day later the previous market rate will fall between the new limits. The change that occurs on that day will usually be small. Quite often the market exchange rate will fall the day after the realignment, as speculators take their profits.

   This feature of the working of the EMS was quite different from the Bretton Woods system, where the total band of fluctuation was only 2%. We show the contrast in Fig. 5.9. Suppose again that Italy experiences a rate of inflation that is 8% higher than in the USA. At time t_1 Italy decides to devalue by 8%. The day after, the new market rate will necessarily have to jump up by at least 6%. This feature creates huge profit opportunities. Speculators expecting the devaluation to occur on t_1 will be willing to bet very large amounts of money (i.e. to buy large amounts of dollars against lira) to profit from the expected gain. These speculations have a typically asymmetric feature: if the devaluation occurs on t_1 speculators make a large gain; if the devaluation does not happen they make only a small loss. The loss then arises from the fact that the interest rate on dollar assets (which have been bought) is usually smaller than the interest rate on lira assets (which have been sold). As these speculative movements

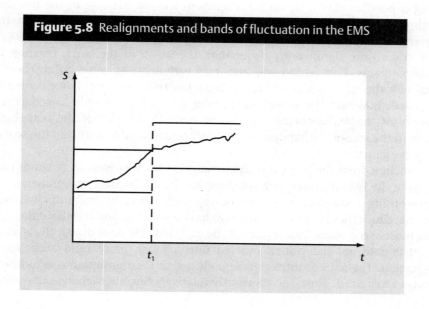

Figure 5.8 Realignments and bands of fluctuation in the EMS

Figure 5.9 Realignments and bands of fluctuation in the Bretton Woods system

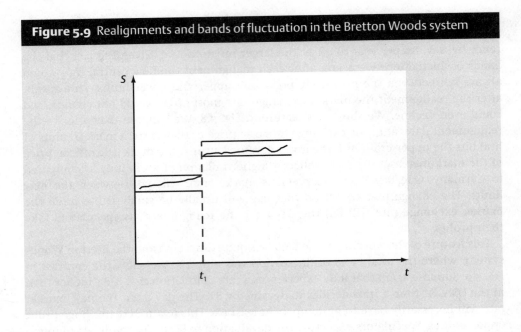

are short term, this loss is very small. This one-way bet feature of speculation was very prevalent during the Bretton Woods system. It was most often absent in the EMS during the 1980s, mainly because monetary authorities were able to keep the size of the realignments small compared to the size of the bands of fluctuation. We show evidence for this in Fig. 5.10, which presents the realignments of the lira and the French franc together with the bands of fluctuation. It can be seen that during the 1980s all the realignments of the lira were smaller than the size of the band, making it possible that after each realignment the market rate of the lira moved smoothly, without jumps. This was not always the case with the French franc, however. We observe that during the period 1982–3, the three realignments of the French franc were significantly larger than the width of the band, creating large speculative gains. This period was also very turbulent. At some point, there was serious talk that the EMS would not survive the frequent speculative crises. After that period, however, the French authorities succeeded not only in reducing the frequency of the realignments but also in limiting the size of the realignments (relative to the size of the band). This certainly contributed to reducing the scope for speculative gains.

We conclude from the preceding discussion that the relatively large bands of fluctuations in the EMS together with relatively small and frequent realignments, while not preventing some countries from having larger rates of inflation than others, helped to reduce the size of speculative capital movements and stabilized the system during most of the 1980s. This feature of the early EMS changed drastically after 1987. From that date on, the system evolved into a much more rigid exchange rate arrangement. The EMS countries made it clear that their ambition was to keep the exchange rates fixed. Thus, the previously relatively flexible exchange rate arrange-

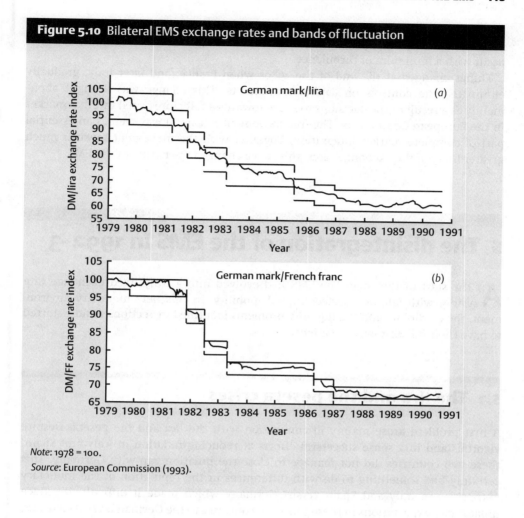

Figure 5.10 Bilateral EMS exchange rates and bands of fluctuation

Note: 1978 = 100.

Source: European Commission (1993).

ment evolved into a truly fixed exchange rate system. In this new environment, the problems identified in the previous section started playing an increasing role.

4.2 Capital controls

The early EMS was also characterized by the existence of capital controls. In particular, France and Italy maintained such controls during most of the 1980s.[6] These controls tended to reduce the size of funds that could be mobilized for attacking a currency. In so doing, they gave the authorities some time to organize an orderly realignment of the exchange rates. Thus, the function of capital controls was not to

---

[6] Belgium had a system of dual exchange markets, separating the current and capital transactions.

maintain unrealistic exchange rates. Rather it was a mechanism that, in conjunction with the willingness frequently to realign the exchange rates, allowed this process to occur with a minimum of turbulence.

Things changed at the end of the 1980s when France, and later Italy, gradually eliminated the controls on capital movements. This change was brought about mainly as a result of the decisions to move towards a fully integrated internal market in the European Community. The free movement of capital was seen as an essential part of complete market integration. Together with the movement towards much greater fixity of the exchange rates, this move changed the nature of the EMS.

5 The disintegration of the EMS in 1992–3

A⊤ the start of the 1990s the EMS had evolved into a truly fixed exchange rate system with (almost) perfect capital mobility. In this new monetary environment, the credibility and the liquidity problems identified in Sections 1 and 2 started to have their full destabilizing effects.

5.1 The lira and the peseta crises

A first problem arose mainly in connection with the lira and the peseta. Despite vigorous and in a sense successful efforts at reducing inflation in Italy and Spain, these two countries did not manage to close the inflation gap with Germany. This certainly had something to do with differences in the reputation of the monetary authorities in Italy and Spain versus Germany which made it difficult to reduce inflationary expectations in these southern countries to the German level. As a result, actual inflation rates in these countries failed to move to the German level. We show the evidence for Italy and Spain in Fig. 5.11. We observe that since the early 1980s the inflation rates of Italy and Spain converged on the German one without, however, moving towards equality with it.

This situation led to a credibility problem. As the Italian and Spanish inflation rates remained above the German one for many years, the price *levels* of Italy and Spain tended to diverge continuously from the German one. Since there were no realignments after 1987 to compensate for these divergent price trends, a continuous loss of competitiveness of the Italian and the Spanish industries occurred.

We present the evidence for Italy and Spain in Fig. 5.12, which shows the Italian and Spanish price indices relative to the German one (expressed in common currency). It can be seen that during the 1980s Italian prices (after correction for the devaluations of the lira) increased by close to 30% relative to German prices. A somewhat smaller increase is noted in the Spanish case. This divergent trend in price levels jeopardized

Figure 5.11 Inflation rates of Italy, Spain, and Germany

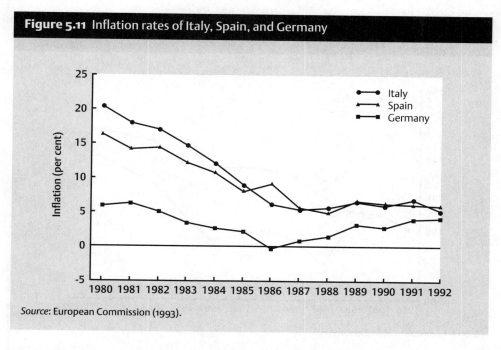

Source: European Commission (1993).

the competitiveness of the Italian and the Spanish industries. In the end this became unsustainable.

5.2 The sterling and French franc crises

The problems that arose with the pound sterling and the French franc were different in nature. The most striking feature of these crises is that there was very little evidence of divergent trends in prices and competitiveness of France or the UK relative to Germany. In fact, when comparing 'fundamental' economic variables of France and the UK with those of Germany (the current accounts of the balances of payment, for example), the former two countries scored as well as Germany. What then triggered the speculative crises?

Some continental European observers and politicians have claimed that the speculation against the pound sterling and especially against the French franc was irrational and driven by an 'Anglo-Saxon plot' against the process of monetary unification in Europe. Such explanations based on irrational motives cannot easily be disproved. One should be suspicious about these explanations, however. In general speculators want to make money, and do not care about the colour of the money they expect to earn.

A better explanation is available. It is based on a combination of the adjustment and the $n-1$ problems of fixed exchange rate regimes. At the start of the 1990s, and especially after 1992, Europe was hit by a severe recession. Very quickly this created a

Figure 5.12 Price index in Italy and Spain relative to Germany (expressed in common currency)

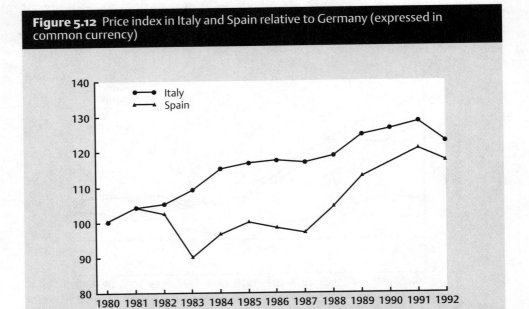

Source: European Commission (1993).

conflict between Germany on the one hand, and Britain and France on the other hand, about the appropriate interest rate policy to be followed in the system as a whole.

Things were complicated by the fact that the German unification of 1990 had led to large increases in government spending in Germany which created inflationary pressures in that country. As a result, the Bundesbank gave complete priority to combating inflation by a restrictive monetary policy. The recession in the UK and France, however, demanded a looser monetary policy. A conflict arose because the Bundesbank maintained a restrictive monetary policy. The UK and France increasingly felt that this policy stance was hurting their economies, and pressured the German authorities to relax their monetary policies and to reduce the interest rates.

This policy conflict did not remain unnoticed by the speculators. These realized that the UK and French authorities were tempted to cut their links with the mark so as to be able to follow more expansionary monetary policies. Influential economists in fact openly urged the authorities to do exactly that. Thus, speculators had good reasons to start speculating against the pound sterling and the French franc. This happened first in September 1992 and led to the withdrawal of the pound sterling from the exchange rate mechanism of the EMS. From then on, as the speculators had expected, the UK authorities engaged in a policy of monetary expansion, and the pound sterling depreciated sharply in the foreign exchange markets.

One year later a new speculative crisis erupted involving mainly the French franc (but also the peseta, the Belgian franc, and the Danish kronor). The underlying reason was the same as in September 1992. The intensity of the recession in France during 1993 and the increase in unemployment were so great that many observers were convinced that the French government would have to stimulate the economy by lowering French interest rates. All this led to speculation of such a magnitude that the EC ministers of finance decided on 2 August to change the rules of the game. The margins of fluctuations were increased to + 15% and – 15%. This implied that the EMS currencies would be able to fluctuate in a band of 30%, transforming the system into a quasi-floating exchange rate regime.

5.3 The self-fulfilling nature of speculation

One of the interesting features of the speculative crises of 1992–3 is their self-fulfilling character. Speculators observe that the authorities had an incentive to change their policies. They also knew that this could be done only by dropping out of the EMS. They then expected that this would happen and they started a speculation. In so doing, they forced the authorities to drop out of the system. This feature has been analysed in theoretical models, and should not have come as a surprise.[7] It has, however, led many people to think that the speculators were to blame for the collapse of the EMS. For it appears that, without objective reasons, they forced the authorities to drop out of the system. The next step to some sinister plot by 'Anglo-Saxon' speculators is a short one.

The self-fulfilling nature of speculation has also led some economists to propose the reintroduction of capital controls, thereby reducing the amount of funds that can be mobilized by speculators.[8] It is doubtful that capital controls are able to sustain a fixed exchange rate, or that they would have prevented the disintegration of the EMS. As was argued earlier, a fundamental reason for the emergence of problems was the fact that the EMS evolved into a system of rigidly fixed exchange rates after 1987. The absence of capital controls certainly affected the timing and the dynamics of the disintegration of the EMS, but it did not fundamentally alter its instability, which resulted from the adjustment and the $n-1$ problems of rigidly fixed exchange rate systems. After all, the Bretton Woods system collapsed for essentially the same reason, despite the fact that capital controls existed at the time of its collapse.

5.4 The role of Germany

It is sometimes said that one of the reasons for the collapse of the EMS was the fact that speculators could mobilize a vast amount of liquid funds, whereas the monetary authorities had only a limited amount of international reserves at their disposal. In this view, the monetary authorities were at the mercy of speculators, who possessed superior weaponry. No wonder that the monetary authorities fought a losing battle.

This view is wrong. Against the large amount of speculative money there is an

---

[7] See e.g. Obstfeld (1986).
[8] An example of such a proposal is Eichengreen and Wyplosz (1993).

equally large amount of money the authorities can throw into the battle. In order to see this, it is useful to return to the two-country money market model of Section 3 (Fig. 5.3). When speculators start selling French francs, they buy German marks. The latter are sold by the Banque de France. As long as the Bundesbank is willing to supply marks to the Banque de France, there is no limit to the size of the interventions by the Banque de France. This has a simple reason. The Bundesbank creates the marks that it supplies to the Banque de France. In principle, it can create an unlimited amount of marks. Therefore, the monetary authorities can always win the battle against the speculators.

Why then did they lose? The answer is that the German authorities refused to continue supplying the French authorities with German marks. This refusal came about because the unlimited supply of German marks would have led to large increases in the German money stock. In other words, when the Bundesbank was supplying marks to the Banque de France, these marks increased the German money stock. As pointed out earlier, the Bundesbank was routinely sterilizing these increases of the supply of marks by reverse operations in the domestic money markets. The size of the interventions was, however, so high that the Bundesbank was not capable of completely sterilizing them. Thus, a massive support of the French franc would have forced the Bundesbank to relax its monetary policy stance. This the Bundesbank was unwilling to do.

Thus, the reason why the speculators won the battle was not that they had more weapons at their disposal than the monetary authorities. Rather, the reason is to be found in the fact that the monetary authorities, and in particular Germany, refused to throw all their weapons into the battle. This refusal was motivated by the fact that the unconditional defence of the French franc would have forced the German monetary authorities to change their policy stance. Therefore, as noted earlier, the fundamental reason for the disintegration of the EMS can be said to be the conflict about the appropriate monetary policy in the system and the refusal of Germany to follow a more expansionary monetary policy.

6 Credibility of the EMS: a formal analysis

THE trends in the credibility of the EMS can be analysed in a formal way. In a number of papers Svensson has proposed several tests to find out whether the existing EMS parities were considered credible by foreign exchange market participants (see e.g. Svensson (1992)). The simplest test can be constructed as follows.[9] In efficient markets the forward exchange rate quoted today reflects the expectations that prevail about the future spot rate. Thus, if we take the one-year forward rate, for example, we have information about the expectations market participants have con-

---

[9] There are more complicated tests also. These give broadly the same results as the simple one explained here. See Rose and Svensson (1993).

cerning the spot exchange rate in one year. Note that this test makes abstraction from the existence of risk premia. Some of the issues relating to risk premia are discussed in Box 8.

We can now find out whether market participants expect a realignment in the following way. The band of fluctuation defines the limits within which the exchange rates must remain if no realignment occurs. Thus, if the forward rate exceeds the upper limit, this is an indication that market participants expect the future spot rate (say, in one year) to be above the upper limit. In other words, they expect a revaluation of the foreign currency (a devaluation of the domestic currency). The opposite occurs if the forward rate is below the lower limit of the band of fluctuation.

In Fig. 5.13 we show the one-year and the five-year forward rates of the German mark relative to the French franc, together with the upper and lower limits as defined by the permissible band of fluctuation.[10] The spot exchange rates have been normalized to 1, so that we measure the forward rate as a percentage deviation from the spot rate. For example, a number of 1.1 means that the forward rate is 10% above the spot rate. Note also that we do not show the realignments. The latter imply that the band of fluctuation shifts up (or down).

Several observations can be made from Fig. 5.13. First, the five-year forward rate exceeds the upper limit much more than the one-year forward rate. This has to do with the fact that when agents expect a devaluation of, say, 5% per year, this cumulates to (more than) 25% over a five-year period. As a result, the five-year forward rate will be (more than) 25% above the spot rate. The one-year forward rate will only be 5% above the spot rate. Note that these expectations also show up in interest differentials. In Box 8 we make the link between the forward rates and interest differentials using the interest parity theory, and we show that the credibility tests can also be performed using these interest differentials.

Second, the one-year forward rate is more often within the band of fluctuation than the five-year forward rate. Except for a brief period in 1991, the latter was always outside the band. This suggests that whereas economic agents were quite often confident that a devaluation would not occur *during the next year*, they almost always perceived a devalution risk over a five-year period. Thus, one can conclude from this that the permanent fixity of the mark/franc rate was almost never credible during the EMS period.

Third, the credibility of the fixity of the mark/franc rate improved continuously during the period. As mentioned earlier, during the early 1990s the fixity of the mark/franc rate came close to full credibility (especially during 1991).

For most other EMS currencies we observe similar phenomena. We show the evidence in Fig. 5.14 for the lira and the Belgian franc. Note that in the Italian case the margins of fluctuation were narrowed from +6% and −6% to +2.25% and −2.25% in 1990. We observe that the five-year forward rates of these two currencies stayed outside the credibility limits all the time, suggesting that economic agents never believed that

---

[10] These forward rates are not quoted rates. They were computed by using the interest parity condition. In Box 8 we explain how this can be done.

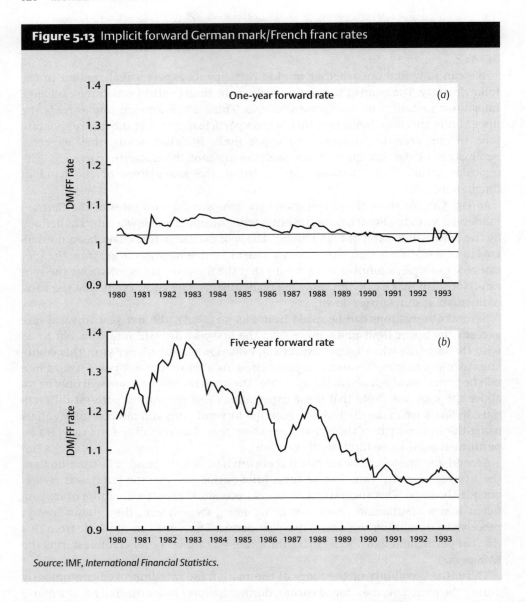

Figure 5.13 Implicit forward German mark/French franc rates

Source: IMF, *International Financial Statistics*.

these exchange rates would remain permanently fixed. We also observe a significant decline of the devaluation risk over time.

The mark/guilder rate is the only exchange rate in the EMS which appears to have been credibly fixed (in the sense that the five-year forward rate remained within its credibility limits). This is seen in Fig. 5.14, which shows that, at least after the middle of the 1980s, the five-year forward rate stayed within its credibility limits during most of the time.

The empirical evidence of the trends in credibility of the EMS raises a number of questions and puzzles. The first one is the following. During the first part of the 1980s

Box 8. Interest parity and EMS credibility

The previous analysis of the credibility of the EMS can also be performed using interest rates. In order to do so, we introduce the interest parity theory, which we write as follows:

$$1 + r_F = \frac{F}{S}(1 + r_G) \tag{B8.1}$$

where r_F is the French (one-year) interest rate, r_G is the German (one-year) interest rate, F is the forward mark/franc rate for contracts expiring in one year, S is the spot mark/franc rate.

The left-hand side is the return of an investment of one franc in a French franc asset. The right-hand side is the return of an investment of one franc in a German mark asset, whereby the German mark is bought spot and sold forward. The latter operation (sometimes also called a swap) ensures that the investment in mark assets is really equivalent (in terms of risk) to the investment in franc assets. This is also the reason why the two returns must be equal. Equation (B8.1) is called the 'closed' interest parity condition and is a very basic relation in international finance.

Things are a little more complicated if the maturity of the investment is different from one year. We can generalize the interest parity equation as follows:

$$(1 + r_F)^{m/12} = \frac{F_m}{S}(1 + r_G)^{m/12} \tag{B8.2}$$

where F_m is the forward rate of a contract expiring in m months. We now have added the exponent m/12 to the interest rates. An example makes clear why. Take a two-year forward contract (m = 24). The investment period is then two years, so that the interest rate return must be compounded over two years. The exponent is 2 (24/12). When the investment period is less than one year, the compounding factor is less than one. For example, if the investment period is three months, the compounding factor becomes 1/4 (3/12).

The next step in the analysis consists in postulating that the forward rate, F, reflects the prevailing expectations about the future spot exchange rate, i.e.

$$F_m = E(S_m) \tag{B8.3}$$

where $E(S_m)$ is the expectation today about the spot exchange rate in m months. Replacing F_m by $E(S_m)$ in equation (B8.2) yields the 'open' interest parity conditions.[11]

Equation (B8.3) assumes absence of risk premia. The consensus today is that these risk premia are real. However, the empirical evidence indicates that these risk premia are extremely variable, and that they cannot be explained very well. In fact, it is fair to say that attempts to find systematic movements in these premia have failed. This is also the reason why we abstract from these risk premia here.

---

[11] The relation with the open interest parity formula used in Section 3 can be seen as follows. In order to simplify the notation we use the one-year interest parity condition. Substitute (B 8.3) into (B 8.I):

$(1 + r_F) = (E(S)/S)(1 + r_G)$.

Subtract $(1 + r_G)$ from both sides and rearrange. This yields

$(r_F - r_G)/(1 + r_G) = (E(S) - S)/S$ or

$(r_F - r_G)/(1 + r_G) = \mu$.

Thus, the open interest parity formula used in Sect. 3 differs from the formula derived here by the term $(1 + r_G)$. If the interest rates are not too high, this is a number close to 1, so that the formula used in Sect. 3 is approximately correct.

The credibility test referred to earlier consists in checking whether

$$S_L < F_m = E(S_m) < S_U \tag{B8.4}$$

where S_L is the lower limit of the permissible band of fluctuation and S_U is the upper limit of the permissible band of fluctuation. Note that in the credibility tests reported in Section 6, we computed F_m using equation B8.2.

It can now easily be seen that the same credibility test can be interpreted by focusing on the interest rates. The limits imposed on F_m defined by equation (B8.4) also place limits on r_F in equation (B8.2). Using (B8.4), these limits can now be written as

$$\left(\frac{S_L}{S}\right)^{12/m} (1 + r_G) - 1 < r_F < \left(\frac{S_U}{S}\right)^{12/m} (1 + r_G) - 1. \tag{B8.5}$$

If the French interest rate remains within the limits defined by (B8.5), we can say that market participants had confidence that the mark/franc rate would not be officially devalued or revalued in the future.

A failure of credibility to hold can now be interpreted in terms of interest rates. When market participants expect a devaluation of the franc, they want to be compensated by an excess return on investments in francs. This then shows up in French interest rates which exceed the upper limit defined in equation (B8.5). If confidence in the French franc increases, the excess return declines. This also has the effect of bringing the French interest rates progressively closer to the German interest rate. Thus, a narrowing of the interest differentials can be interpreted as an increase in the credibility of the fixed exchange rates.

Note that with an increase in the maturity of the investments the band within which the interest rate must stay becomes progressively narrower. The reason is that, when a depreciation of, say, 1% per year is expected, during ten years this will accumulate to an expected devaluation of 10%. The interest rate on a *ten-year* French bond will then be 1% above the German bond. Thus, a 1% interest differential on ten-year bonds indicates that the market expects a 10% devaluation of the franc to occur during the next ten years. The same 1% interest differential on a one-year bond implies that agents expect a depreciation of 1% of the franc next year. Since this keeps the franc within the band of fluctuation, this 1% interest differential does not mean that a realignment is expected next year.

we observe large deviations of the forward rate from the credibility limits, suggesting expectations of large realignments. In the early 1990s these deviations had declined significantly, suggesting much smaller expectations of devaluations. Why is it that the large expected devaluations of the early 1980s did not lead to a collapse of the EMS, whereas much smaller ones triggered the disintegration of the system? In order to answer this question we have to return to the discussion of the change in the nature of the EMS after 1987. Prior to that date there was an understanding in the market that small but frequent realignments were a routine matter. As a result, expectations of devaluation of, say, 5% per year could easily be accommodated without triggering unsustainable speculative crises (see the discussion in Section 4.1). Only

Figure 5.14 Implicit forward five-year rates

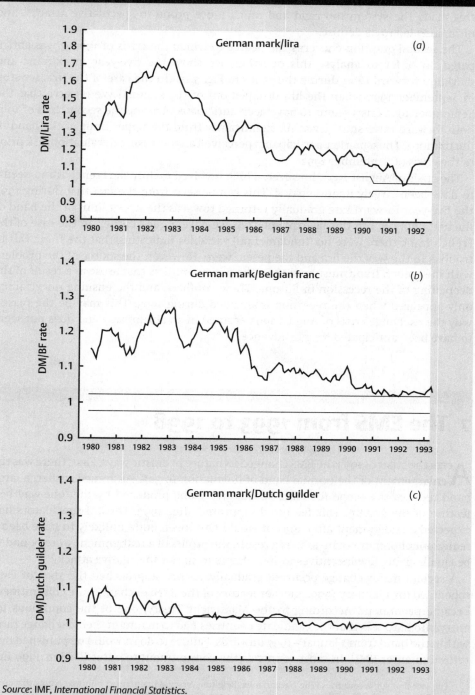

Source: IMF, *International Financial Statistics*.

during 1982–3 was the system close to a collapse. After 1987 it became the objective of the EMS countries to move to a truly fixed exchange rate system. As discussed earlier, this made the system too rigid and much more prone to speculative attacks, and ultimately led to its demise.

The second question concerns the degree to which the crisis of 1992–3 was anticipated. In order to analyse this question, we show the five-year mark/franc and mark/lira forward rates during the 1990s in Fig. 5.15. (In the case of the lira, we stop in September 1992 when the lira dropped out of the system.) We observe that the September 1992 crisis seems to have been anticipated. During the second half of 1991 both forward rates start deviating significantly from the upper limit of the band of fluctuations. Thus, market participants perceived an increasing devaluation risk prior to the crisis of September 1992.

The crisis of August 1993, however, which involved mainly the French franc, seems to have been largely unanticipated. This can be seen from the fact that during 1993 the five-year forward rate gradually returned towards the upper limit of the band of fluctuation. How can this be explained? As we have argued earlier, in the case of the French franc there were no 'fundamental' variables indicating that the franc was in trouble, in the way the lira and the peseta were. However, the source of the problem with the French franc must be seen in the policy conflicts that arose as a result of the deepening of the recession in Europe. These conflicts, and the ensuing uncertainty, only appeared when the recession intensified during 1993. This may be the reason why the exchange crisis of August 1993 erupted in an abrupt way and does not seem to have been anticipated long in advance.

7 The EMS from 1993 to 1998

AFTER the crisis of 1993 the EMS changed its nature in drastic ways. First, there was the enlargement of the normal band of fluctuation to 30%. As argued earlier, a large band reduces the scope for large speculative gains produced by the 'one-way bet' feature of the system. This feature disappeared after 1993. Thus, if speculators had expected a realignment after 1993, it would have been quite unlikely to have been a realignment of more than 30%. As a result, the profits of a realignment were bound to be small, giving few incentives to speculators to start a speculative attack.[12]

A second major change occurred gradually. As one approached the start of EMU scheduled for 1 January 1999, another feature of the fixed exchange rate commitment became prominent. According to the Maastricht Treaty, one of the conditions for entry into EMU was that the candidate countries had to maintain their exchange rates within the band from 1 January 1997 onwards. Failure to do so would be punished by a refusal to enter EMU. In most countries the commitment to enter EMU in 1999 had

---

[12] The fact that some countries (The Netherlands, Belgium, Austria) maintained informal bands that were narrower than the 30% official band of fluctuation does not affect this conclusion.

Figure 5.15 Implicit forward five-year rates during the 1990s

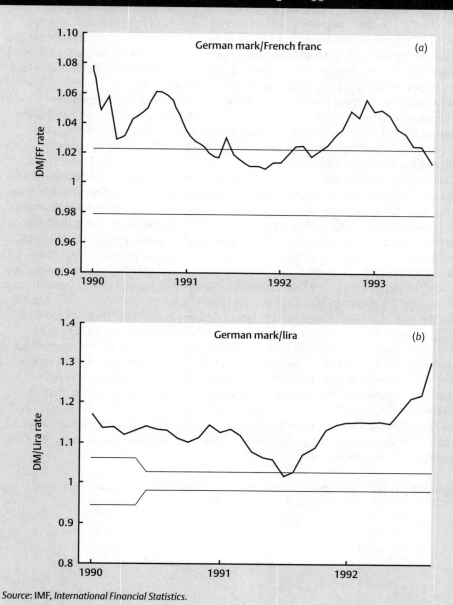

Source: IMF, *International Financial Statistics*.

Box 9 Target-zone models and the European Monetary System

The exchange rate mechanism of the EMS operates with a band within which the exchange rate can move freely. Once the edges of the band are reached, however, the monetary authorities are committed to intervene so as to prevent the exchange rate from moving outside the band. This feature of the system had led theorists to speculate about the behaviour of the exchange rate in such a system. This has led to the so-called target-zone models pioneered by Krugman (1989) and developed further by (among others) Svensson (1990) and Bertola and Svensson (1993).

The basic idea of these models is strikingly simple (although the mathematics is not). Suppose speculators are fully confident that the exchange rate will not go beyond the limits of the band because they are convinced that the monetary authorities will successfully defend these limits. Assume in addition that there are stochastic disturbances in the fundamental variables that determine the exchange rate. These fundamentals could be the money stock, the price level, etc. How is the relationship between these fundamentals and the exchange rate going to look? The answer is given in Fig. B9.1. On the vertical axis we show the exchange rate (S_t), on the horizontal axis the fundamental variable (f_t) The two horizontal lines (S_U and S_L) represent the limits between which the exchange rate will fluctuate. The fluctuations of the fundamental variable lead to fluctuations of the exchange rate. In a world of rational expectations, the exchange rate must lie on the S-shaped curve. That is, as the exchange rate comes close to, say, the upper limit of the band, speculators know that the authorities' commitment will prevent the exchange rate from moving beyond the limit. Therefore, the probability that the exchange rate increases in the future declines as we move closer to the limit, and the probability of a decline increases. Speculators will find it advantageous to sell foreign exchange, thereby pushing the exchange rate downwards. Speculation will be stabilizing, and the authorities will not have to intervene. This result only holds if the credibility of the band is very strong. If this is not the case, speculation will not be stabilizing. Speculators then will test the resolve of the authorities, forcing them to intervene in the market. The model has been extended by Bertola and Svensson (1993) to this case where speculators expect a devaluation. They show that if the devaluation risk is strong enough, the exchange rate will not follow an S-shaped curve as in Fig. B9.1, but may actually cross the margins.

Figure B9.1 The exchange rate and the fundamental variable in a target-zone model

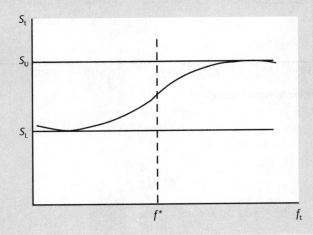

become a major political objective. Failure to achieve this objective was seen as a major political setback. As a result, the cost of a devaluation was raised considerably in all the countries that had decided that they wanted to be a member of EMU in 1999.

We can interpret the effect of this on the credibility of the fixed exchange rate commitment in terms of the model of Figs. 5.1 and 5.2. The cost of a devaluation was raised far above the distance AB (Fig. 5.1). As a result, countries, which in the early 1990s could not credibly fix their exchange rates, were now able to do so. In addition, the cost of devaluation became large enough compared to the cost of defending the exchange rate in the face of an unfavourable economic disturbance (Fig. 5.2). All this stabilized the fixed exchange rate mechanism in the transition towards EMU. (We will come back to some other aspects of the transition period, in Chapter 6, where we will analyse the importance of fixing the final conversion rate.)

8 Conclusion

IN this chapter we have analysed the workings of the European Monetary System. We argued that after 1987, when the system evolved into a truly fixed exchange rate regime, it was unable to cope with the problems that have plagued every fixed exchange rate arrangement of the past. Its downfall in 1992–3 therefore did not come as a surprise and had been predicted by many economists.

Although the disintegration of the EMS was, and could be predicted, the particular way it happened, of course, could not be foreseen. In this chapter, great emphasis was put on the recession in Europe of 1992–3 as an explanation of the downfall of the system. This recession exacerbated the conflicts between the major EMS countries about the appropriate monetary policy response. The inability to resolve this policy conflict lies at the root of the loss of confidence of economic agents in the fixity of the exchange rates, and in the ensuing speculative crises.

The fact that in the second half of the 1990s the fixed exchange rate commitment among potential EMU-member countries gained increasing credibility should not blind us to believe that fixed exchange rate arrangements can be made to work after all. Much of this success came about as a result of the transition to a full monetary union. Because the Maastricht Treaty mandated the candidate countries to keep their exchange rates within a fixed band, or they would not be allowed to enter EMU, the political cost of a devaluation was raised considerably. As a result, the credibility of the fixed exchange rate was increased significantly.

What we learn from this episode of fixing exchange rates in Europe is that this can only work as a transitory device towards full monetary union. As a permanent monetary regime a fixed exchange rate system is too fragile. Countries, therefore, have the choice between more flexible exchange rate arrangements or a full monetary union.

Chapter 6
The Transition to a Monetary Union

Introduction

IN December 1991 the heads of state of the European Union signed a historic treaty in the Dutch city of Maastricht. The Maastricht Treaty went well beyond purely monetary affairs. Nevertheless it is best known for the blueprint it provided for progress towards monetary unification in Europe.

The Maastricht Treaty strategy for moving towards monetary union in Europe was based on two principles.[1] First, the transition towards monetary union in Europe was seen as a gradual one, extending over a period of many years. Second, entry into the union was made conditional on satisfying convergence criteria. In this chapter we analyse this Maastricht strategy. This strategy remains relevant since it will have to be pursued by those EU-countries willing to join EMU in the future.

It is important to be aware that the Maastricht strategy was not the only one available. In fact, throughout history monetary unification has quite often been organized in a very different way. Take as an example the German monetary unification, which happened on 1 July 1990. The characteristic feature of the German monetary union was its speed and the absence of any convergence requirement. The decision to go ahead with monetary union was taken at the end of 1989, and six months later the German monetary union was a reality. As will be seen in the next section it will have taken the European Union at least ten years to do the same. In addition, East Germany was allowed into the West German monetary area without any conditions attached. Surely, had Maastricht-type convergence requirements been imposed on East Germany, the German monetary union would not have occurred. All this shows that a monetary union *can* be established quickly and without prior

---

[1] In this the Treaty was very much influenced by the Delors Committee Report, which was issued in 1989. See Committee on the Study of Economic and Monetary Union (1989).

conditions. It does not show, of course, that this was the desirable way to organize a monetary union in Europe.

1 The Maastricht Treaty

THE approach set out in the Treaty was based on principles of gradualism and convergence. Let us analyse the details of this approach. The Treaty defines three stages in the process towards monetary union.

In the first stage (which had already started on 1 July 1990, prior to the signing of the Treaty), the EMS countries abolished all remaining capital controls. The degree of monetary co-operation among the EMS central banks was strengthened. During the first stage, which lasted until 31 December 1993, realignments remained possible.

The second stage started on 1 January 1994. A new institution, the European Monetary Institute (EMI), was created. It operated only during this second stage, and was in a sense the precursor of the European Central Bank (ECB). Its functions were limited, and were geared mainly towards strengthening monetary co-operation between national central banks.

At the start of the third and final stage, January 1999, the exchange rates between the national currencies were irrevocably fixed. In addition, the European Central Bank started its operations. The ECB issued the euro, which is a currency in its own right. The transition to this final stage of monetary union, however, was made conditional on a number of 'convergence criteria'. A country can join the union only if:

(1) its inflation rate is not more than 1.5% higher than the average of the three lowest inflation rates in the EMS;
(2) its long-term interest rate is not more than 2% higher than the average observed in the three low-inflation countries;
(3) it has joined the exchange rate mechanism of the EMS and has not experienced a devaluation during the two years preceding the entrance into the union;
(4) its government budget deficit is not higher than 3% of its GDP (if it is, it should be declining continuously and substantially and come close to the 3% norm, or alternatively, the deviation from the reference value (3%) 'should be exceptional and temporary and remain close to the reference value', art. 104c(a));
(5) its government debt should not exceed 60% of GDP (if it does it should 'diminish sufficiently and approach the reference value (60%) at a satisfactory pace', art. 104c(b)).

It was decided in May 1998 that eleven EU-countries (Austria, Belgium, Finland, France, Germany, Ireland, Italy, Luxembourg, The Netherlands, Portugal, and Spain) satisfied these convergence criteria. As will be shown later, some number juggling was necessary to come to this conclusion. Greece did not satisfy these criteria but is likely to do so quickly so that it could possibly join before 2002. Three countries (Denmark,

Sweden, the UK) decided to stay out of Euroland despite the fact that they satisfied the convergence criteria. The UK obtained the right to opt out, and Denmark to subject its entry to a national referendum. Sweden decided not to join and used a loophole in the treaty, i.e. it refused to enter the exchange rate mechanism of the EMS before the start of the third stage thereby deliberately failing to satisfy one of the entry conditions.

At the Summit Meeting of the heads of state in Madrid, December 1995, additional agreements were made concerning the nature of the third stage. First, it was decided to call the new currency the euro. Second, the third stage was itself divided into three substages as follows:

■ From 1 January 1999 until 31 December 2001, the national currencies continue to be in circulation alongside the euro, albeit at irrevocably fixed exchange rates. However, commercial banks use the euro for all their interbank dealings. Private individuals have the choice of using their national currency or opening an account in euros. (Note that during this period the euro does not exist in the form of banknotes and coins.) In addition, all transactions between the European Central Bank and the commercial banks are in euros. Finally, *new* issues of government bonds are made in euros and not in national currencies.

■ During the period 1 January to 1 July 2002 the euro will replace the national currencies, which will lose their legal-tender status. Thus, during this period a monetary reform will be organized.

■ From 1 July 2002 on, a true monetary union will come into existence in which the euro will be the single currency managed by one central bank, the European Central Bank (ECB).

It should be noted that the national central banks have not disappeared since 1999, nor will they after 2002. They are part of what is called the Eurosystem. These national banks, however, do not make decisions about monetary and exchange rate policies any more. They are there to implement the decisions taken by the ECB. In this respect the Eurosystem resembles the US Federal Reserve System. It should be noted, however, that national central banks maintain their decision-making powers in the important field of banking supervision.[2] (We will return to some issues relating to the operation of the Eurosystem in Chapters 7 and 8.)

2 Why convergence requirements?

W^E noted earlier that past transitions to monetary unions were usually organized in a different way than in the Maastricht Treaty, i.e. once the decision was taken to have a monetary union, this was done quickly without any of the Maastricht-

---

[2] In some countries the responsibility for banking supervision is not vested in the national central bank but in a separate agency. In these countries the national bank will have few responsibilities left over.

type convergence requirements being imposed on the prospective members. What is more, the theory of optimum currency areas, which we discussed in previous chapters, is silent about Maastricht-type convergence criteria. Instead the OCA theory stresses the need to have labour market flexibility and labour mobility as important requirements for a successful monetary union. According to this theory, if these conditions are satisfied, there is no need to wait more than ten years to do it. Why then did the designers of the Treaty stress so much *macro*-economic convergence (inflation, interest rates, budgetary policies) prior to the start of EMU while the theory stresses *micro*-economic conditions for a successful monetary union?

2.1 Inflation convergence

The answer has to do with the fear that the future monetary union would have an inflationary bias. In order to understand this concern it is useful to go back to the Barro–Gordon model which we developed in Chapter 3, and which we now represent in Fig. 6.1. We assume two countries, called Germany and Italy. The two countries are assumed to be identical except for the preferences of the authorities. (We do not really need this assumption. We do this only to be able to put both countries in the same figure.) The German authorities give a high weight to reducing inflation, the Italian authorities a low weight. This is shown by flat indifference curves for the German authorities and steep ones for the Italian authorities. The natural unemployment rate, u_N, is the same in the two countries, and so is the target unemployment rate of the authorities, u^*. Inflation equilibrium is achieved at E_G in Germany and E_I in Italy. Thus, inflation is on average higher in Italy than in Germany without any gain in unemployment for Italy.

A monetary union between the two countries implies that a common central bank takes over. Two propositions can now easily be established. First, the low-inflation country (Germany) reduces its welfare by forming a monetary union with the high-inflation country. This is so because the union's central bank is likely to reflect the average preferences of the participating countries. As a result, the union inflation rate increases and will be located between E_G and E_I. (There are of course other sources of gains of a monetary union, e.g. lower transaction costs, lower risk, etc. which we discussed in Chapter 4, and which are outside the model of Fig. 6.1. These efficiency gains must then be compared with the welfare losses resulting from higher inflation. If the latter exceed the former, Germany will not want to join in a monetary union with Italy.)

The second proposition follows from the first one: since the low-inflation country, Germany, loses when it joins the union with Italy, it will not want to do so unless it can impose conditions. It follows from the analysis of Fig. 6.1 that this condition must be that the union's central bank should have the same preferences as the German central bank. This can be achieved in two ways. One is that the future European central bank should be a close copy of the Bundesbank. What this means will be analysed in the next chapter.

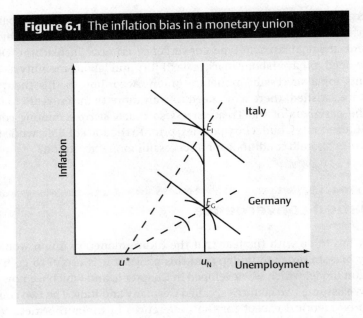

Figure 6.1 The inflation bias in a monetary union

This condition, however, may not be sufficient from the point of view of Germany, because the European Central Bank will be composed of representatives of the participating countries. Even if the ECB is made a close copy of the Bundesbank, these representatives may still have different inflation preferences. Majority voting in the Board may then put the German representative in a minority position, so that the equilibrium inflation rate in the union would exceed the German one. In order to avoid this outcome Germany will want to control entry into the union, so that only those countries with the same preferences join the union (see Morales and Padilla (1994)).

The Maastricht entry conditions can now be interpreted in this perspective. Before the union started, the candidate member countries were asked to provide evidence that they cared about a low inflation rate in the same way as Germany did. This they did, by bringing down their inflation rate to the German level. During this dis-inflationary process, a temporary increase in the unemployment rate was inevitable (a movement along the short-term Phillips curve). This self-imposed suffering was added evidence for Germany that countries like Italy were serious about fighting inflation. Once the proof was given, these countries could be let in safely.

2.2 Budgetary convergence

Can the budgetary convergence requirements (3% norm for the budget deficit and 60% norm for the government debt) be rationalized in a way similar to the inflation convergence requirement? The answer is positive. Let us take again the case of Italy and Germany. Italy has a high debt-to-GDP ratio (more than 100% during the 1990s). A high government debt creates incentives for the Italian government to engineer a surprise inflation. The reason is that some of the Italian government bonds are long-term. The interest rate on these bonds was fixed in a previous period based on the then prevailing expectations of inflation. If the government now creates an unexpectedly higher inflation the real value of these bonds will be eroded and the bondholders will obtain insufficient compensation because the interest rate on their bonds does not reflect this inflation upsurge. Bondholders lose. The Italian government gains. (Obviously, if the bondholders are rational, they will not be willing to invest in Italian bonds any more unless they obtain an extra risk premium on these bonds. Thus, the systematic use of surprise inflation by the Italian authorities may become quite costly in the long run. Rational governments, therefore, will not systematically produce surprise inflation. The problem here is that the political system may create a very short-term outlook for politicians, who will continue to be tempted to create inflation surprises.)

From the preceding analysis, it follows that a monetary union between Germany and Italy creates a problem for Germany. In the union, the German authorities will be confronted with a partner who will have a tendency to push for more inflation. This may happen even if the German and Italian authorities have the same preferences regarding inflation. As long as Italy has a higher debt-to-GDP ratio it will have an incentive to create surprise inflation. As a result, Germany stands to lose and will insist that Italy's debt-to-GDP ratio be reduced prior to entry into the monetary union. In order to achieve this, Italy must reduce its government budget deficit. Once this is achieved the incentives for Italy to produce surprise inflation disappear, and Italy can safely be allowed into the union.[3]

Note again that the argument for debt and deficit reduction prior to entry into EMU is made not because countries with high debt and deficits cannot form a monetary union, but because allowing these countries into the union increases the risk of more inflation in the future EMU.

Other arguments have been developed to justify deficit and debt reductions as conditions for entry into the union. One is that the authorities with a large debt face a higher default risk. If they are allowed into the union, this will increase the pressure for a bailout in the event of a default crisis. The fear that this may happen also explains the *no-bailout* clause which was incorporated into the Maastricht Treaty, i.e. the clause that says that neither national governments nor the European Central Bank can be forced to bail out other member countries. In Chapter 9, where we discuss fiscal policies in monetary unions, we will return to this issue.

Whereas serious arguments can be found to justify the requirements that countries should reduce their government debts and deficits prior to entry the numerical precision with which these requirements have been formulated is much more difficult to rationalize. This has led many economists to criticize the 3% and the 60% norms as

---

[3] It can be argued that if the Italian authorities reduce the maturity of their debt, the incentives to create surprise inflation are reduced. Thus as a substitute for a debt reduction, one could ask the Italian authorities to reduce the maturity of their debt prior to entry into the EMU. The problem with this is that when the maturity of the debt shortens, it becomes more vulnerable to changes in the interest rate, which may lead to liquidity crises as the authorities find it difficult to roll over their debt.

arbitrary, or worse as some form of voodoo economics.[4] But let us at least find some rational grounds for imposing the budgetary numbers of 3% and 60%.

The 3% and 60% budgetary norms seem to have been derived from the well-known formula determining the budget deficit needed to stabilize the government debt:[5]

$$d = gb \qquad\qquad (6.1)$$

where b is the (steady state) level at which the government debt is to be stabilized (in per cent of GDP), g is the growth rate of nominal GDP, and d is the government budget deficit (in per cent of GDP).

The formula shows that in order to stabilize the government debt at 60% of GDP the budget deficit must be brought to 3% of GDP if and only if the nominal growth rate of GDP is 5% ($0.03 = 0.05 \times 0.6$).

The rule is quite arbitrary on two counts. First, it is unclear why the debt should be stabilized at 60%. Other numbers, e.g. 70% or 50%, would do as well. In that case, the deficit to be aimed at should also be different, i.e. 3.5% and 2.5%, respectively. The only reason why 60% seems to have been chosen at Maastricht was that at that time this was the average debt-to-GDP ratio in the European Union. Second, the rule is conditioned on the future nominal growth rate of GDP. If the nominal growth of GDP increases above (declines below) 5%, the budget deficit that stabilizes the government debt at 60% increases above (declines below) 3%.

We have focused on the inflation and budgetary convergence requirements in the preceding paragraphs. Let us briefly discuss the rationale of the other convergence rules, i.e. the no-devaluation rule and the interest rate convergence requirement.

2.3 Exchange rate convergence (no-devaluation requirement)

The main motivation for requiring countries not to have devalued during the two years prior to their entry into the EMU is straightforward. It prevented countries from manipulating their exchange rates so as to force entry at a more favourable exchange rate (a depreciated one, which would increase their competitive position). The stringency of this requirement, however, was reduced considerably since the Treaty of Maastricht was signed. This has to do with the peculiar way the no-devaluation

---

[4] See Buiter *et al.* (1993) and Wickens (1993) among others.
[5] This is confirmed in Bini-Smaghi *et al.* (1993). The formula is derived as follows. The budget deficit (D) is financed by issuing new debt:

$\dot{B} = D$

(where B is the government debt and a dot above a variable signifies a rate of increase per unit of time). By definition one can write

$\dot{B} = bY + b\dot{Y}$

(where $b = B/Y$ and Y is GDP). Combining the two expressions yields

$D = bY + b\dot{Y}$ or $D/Y = b + b\dot{Y}/Y$

which is rewritten as follows

$b = d - gb$ (where $d = D/Y$, $g = \dot{Y}/Y$).

In the steady state $\dot{b} = 0$ which implies that $d = gb$.

condition is formulated in the Treaty. According to the Treaty, countries should maintain their exchange rates within the 'normal' band of fluctuation (without changing that band) during the two years preceding their entry into the EMU. At the moment of the signing of the Treaty, the normal band was $2 \times 2.25\%$. Since August 1993, the 'normal' band within the EMS was $2 \times 15\%$, a considerably larger band of fluctuation.

2.4 Interest rate convergence

We come finally to the interest rate convergence requirement. The justification of this rule is that excessively large differences in the interest rates prior to entry could have led to large capital gains and losses at the moment the EMU took effect. Suppose, for example, that the long-term bond rate in Germany was 5% whereas in France it was 7% just prior to the start of EMU. When EMU started the exchange rate between the DM and the FF was irrevocably fixed. As a result, it would have been quite attractive for bondholders to arbitrage, i.e. to sell low-yield DM bonds and to buy high-yield FF bonds. Since the exchange rate was irrevocably fixed there was no exchange risk involved in such an arbitrage. As a result, it would have gone on until the return on DM and FF bonds was equalized. This would have led to a drop in the price of DM bonds and an increase in the price of FF bonds, until the yields were equal. Thus, economic agents (mainly German financial institutions) holding DM bonds prior to the start of EMU would have made capital losses, and economic agents holding FF bonds (mainly French financial institutions) would have made capital gains. These capital gains and losses would have increased with the size of the interest differential. When they were large enough they could have created large disturbances in national capital markets. In order to limit these disturbances the interest differential had to be reduced prior to the start of EMU.

The peculiarity of this rule is its self-fulfilling nature. The rule says that the long-term government bond rate of a prospective member should not exceed the interest rate level (+ 2%) of the three countries with the lowest rates of inflation. Consider now a country that was strongly expected to be a member of EMU after 1999. It can easily be seen that the long-term bond rate had to be automatically equalized prior to the start of EMU. Note also that the capital gains and losses (which were inevitable) were borne long before the start of the union. At the start of the union, these capital gains and losses were very small. The upshot of all this was that the interest rate convergence criterion was redundant. As soon as countries were expected to satisfy the other criteria, market forces made sure that the interest rates quickly converged.

3 Problems with the Maastricht strategy

IN our analysis of the problems of the Maastricht strategy we will concentrate mainly on the inflation and budgetary convergence requirements. We ask the question whether the Maastricht strategy may not have imposed undue deflationary forces on the European Union, which in turn have made the budgetary norms more difficult to achieve.

A striking fact is that during the 1990s economic growth in the group of countries that had declared their intention to follow the Maastricht transition strategy was low compared to the previous decade and compared to the industrial countries not involved in the Maastricht strategy. In Table 6.1 we show the evidence. We contrast the average growth rate in the EU and the US. Whereas during the 1980s the growth rate of GDP was approximately the same in the EU and the US, this was not the case any more during the 1990s when the EU growth rate dropped significantly below the US level.

All this, of course, could be due to coincidence.[6] There are, however, reasons to believe that the Maastricht strategy was at least partially responsible for the lacklustre economic growth observed during the 1990s. The main problem of the Maastricht convergence criteria was that they imposed a policy mix of budgetary *and* monetary restriction. Countries were asked to reduce their government debts and deficits, while at the same time they had to reduce their inflation rates. Applied by many countries at the same time, this led to strong deflationary forces. First, when all countries reduced their budget deficits by reducing spending and/or increasing taxes the negative effects on aggregate demand in one country spilled over to the other countries.[7] As a result, economic activity in these countries reduced, thereby increasing the budget deficits in the same countries and forcing the authorities to intensify their attempts to reduce budget deficits. Thus, the simultaneous application of the same restrictive budgetary policies may have contributed to the low-growth environment in the European Union, which in turn made budget cutting exercises less effective.

---

[6] In comparing the growth performance of the EU with the US during the 1990s it is important to take into account the fact that the EU and the US experienced a different timing in their business cycles during the 1990s. We find that the US experienced a recession during 1990–1, whereas the recession in the EU occurred during 1992–3. We can conclude that the different timing of the recessions in the 1990s should not affect the difference in the average growth rates during that period observed between the US and the EU.

[7] Giavazzi and Pagano (1990) provide evidence that policies of budgetary restriction do not have to lead to a reduction of aggregate demand. In particular, in countries with a high government debt, forceful policies of cutting budget deficits may create favourable expectational effects that lead to a significant reduction of the domestic interest rate. This may then compensate for the unfavourable Keynesian demand effect of restrictive fiscal policies. These exceptional effects were probably small for most EU-countries, for two reasons. First, the expectational effect works best in countries with a high initial government debt (e.g. Belgium, Italy). In countries with relatively low initial debt (France, Germany) this effect is likely to be small. Second, the expectational effect works well if the budget cutting exercise is done all at once, and not in a gradual way. Political factors explain why most governments chose the gradual approach, thereby very much limiting the favourable effects of expectations.

Table 6.1 Average growth rates of GDP in the EU and the US (1980s and 1990s)

	EU	US
1981–90	2.4%	2.6%
1991–98	1.8%	2.4%

Source: European Commission, *European Economy*.

Second, the inflation convergence requirement forced monetary policies in all countries participating in the Maastricht strategy to be restrictive. This was especially the case during the recession of 1992–3 when most EU-countries kept their short-term real interest rates at record high levels of 5% or more. The contrast with the US was sharp. The US monetary authorities allowed the short-term real interest rates to drop to close to zero during the US recession of the early 1990s. We show the evidence in Fig. 6.2. Together with the restrictive budgetary policies, the restrictive European monetary policies of the first half of the 1990s reinforced the deflationary dynamics in the Maastricht countries.

The most striking effect of these deflationary macroeconomic policies in the EU-countries can be seen in the unemployment evolution. We show these in Fig. 6.3 where we contrast the unemployment rate of the EU-11 with the US. We observe that the unemployment rate in the EU-11 increased dramatically in just three years (1991–3) and stayed at about the same high level during the rest of the decade. In the US there was a significant but less pronounced increase in the early 1990s, which was however completely reversed during the rest of the decade. Our interpretation of these trends is the following. The strongly deflationary European demand policies of the early 1990s contributed to the strong increase of the unemployment rate during those years. The inability of the unemployment rate to decline later on must be attributable to the rigidities in the European labour markets, which make it difficult for workers having lost their jobs to find a new occupation. One can conclude that the Maastricht-induced macroeconomic policies in Europe contributed to the build-up of unemployment and that structural rigidities kept unemployment high.

These policies paradoxically also led to a build-up of government debt. We show the evolution of the government debt in Fig. 6.4. We observe that the EU-11 government debt was close to 75% just prior to the start of EMU coming from 58% when the Treaty was signed, an increase of close to 40%. In the US the government debt was at the same level at the end of the 1990s as at the start.

This strong difference in the trends of government debt between the EU-11 and the US is undoubtedly related to the differences in the policy mix during the 1990s. The EU-11 policy mix of monetary and budgetary restriction led to a situation in which the budget cutting policies were performed in an environment of low growth of GDP and increasing unemployment. This made budget cutting very difficult. Remember that the debt ratio is the ratio of government debt to GDP. Thus the difficulties in reducing

Figure 6.2 GDP growth rates and short-term real interest rates in EU-11 and the USA

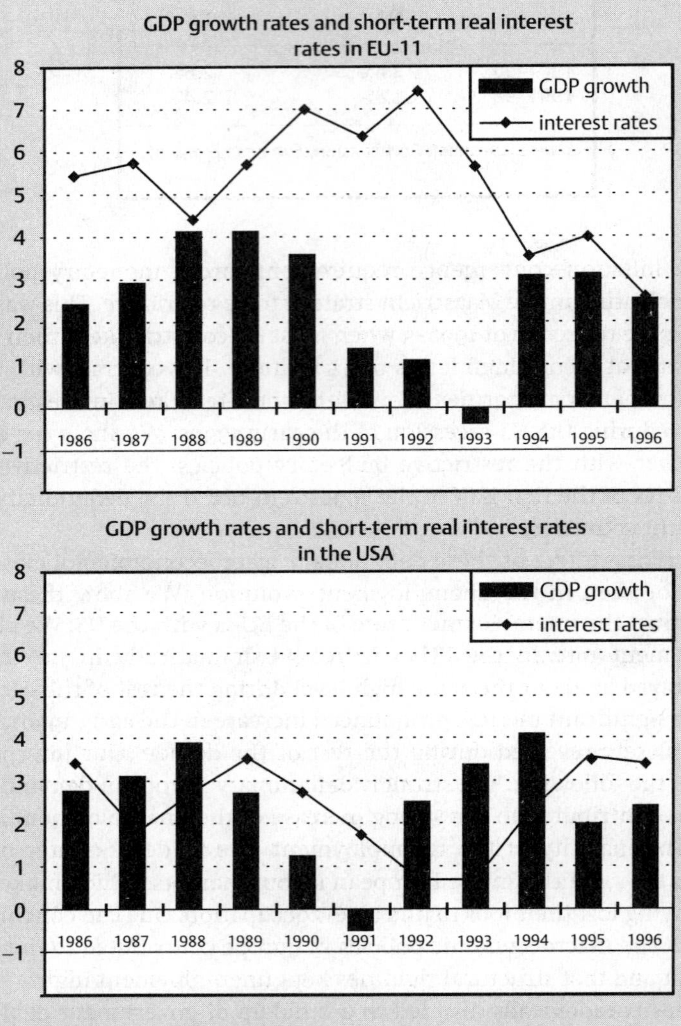

GDP growth rates and short-term real interest rates in EU-11

GDP growth rates and short-term real interest rates in the USA

Source: European Commission, *European Economy*.

the budget deficits made it difficult to reduce the growth rate of the numerator (the debt). At the same time the deflationary policy mix reduced the growth rate of the denominator (the GDP). The latter effect more than compensated for the former, leading to an increasing debt ratio in the EU-11.

Conversely, the US success in stabilizing its debt ratio was certainly helped by the fact that the US policy mix was quite different. The budgetary restriction was applied together with monetary ease. This contributed to stronger economic

Figure 6.3 Unemployment in EU-11 and USA

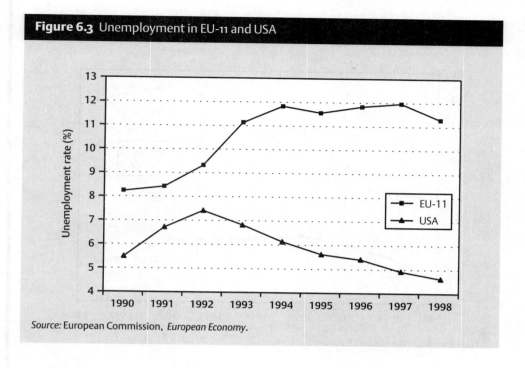

Source: European Commission, *European Economy*.

growth than in the EU-11, which encouraged the implementation of restrictive budgetary policies.

The strange implication of this Maastricht-induced debt build-up is that in 1997 a large number of EMU-candidate countries failed to satisfy the Maastricht debt criterion. We show this in Fig. 6.5. (We take 1997, because this was the year which counted for deciding whether countries could join EMU.) We observe that nine of the eleven EMU-candidates had a debt ratio exceeding 60% in 1997. The Treaty stipulates that when a country had a debt ratio above 60% this should have been declining ('at a satisfactory pace'). Six of the nine countries with a debt ratio above 60% had experienced an increase in that ratio. In May 1998 it was decided that this Treaty provision would not be applied so that all eleven countries could safely join.

4 Technical problems during the transition

THE transition to EMU created a number of technical problems. These problems were mastered quite skilfully. In this section, we discuss the choice of the conversion rates of the national currencies into the euro, and some of the problems of the 1999–2002 transitional stage.

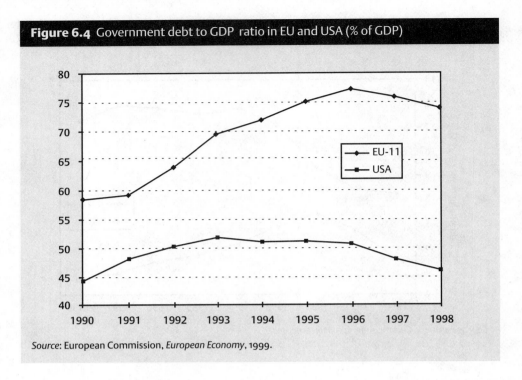

Figure 6.4 Government debt to GDP ratio in EU and USA (% of GDP)

Source: European Commission, *European Economy*, 1999.

4.1 How to fix the conversion rates?

On 1 January 1999 the exchange rates of the national currencies into the euro were fixed irrevocably. This happened remarkably smoothly. How could this be done? The problem faced prior to conversion time was the following. The Treaty together with a decision taken at the Madrid Council of 1995 implied that on 1 January 1999 one ECU would be converted into one euro. At the same time the conversion rates of the national currencies into the euro had to be equal to the market rates of these currencies against the ECU at the close of the market on 31 December 1998. The latter condition was introduced to make sure that the start of EMU would not be accompanied by jumps in the exchange value of the currencies, thereby creating large capital gains and losses.

These conditions created a potential for self-fulfilling speculative movements of the exchange rates prior to 31 December 1998. The reason can be explained as follows. (In Box 10 we go into this problem in a more technical way.) Since the authorities had announced that the market rates of the last day prior to EMU would be used as the conversion rates to be fixed forever on the next day, any movement on the last day would be self-validating. Thus, if on that last day some Soros of this world would drive up the value of, say, the German mark relative to the French franc, this higher DM/FF exchange rate would then be irrevocably fixed the next day. In other words, there was

Figure 6.5 Debt to GDP ratio in EU-11 in 1993 and 1997 (% of GDP)

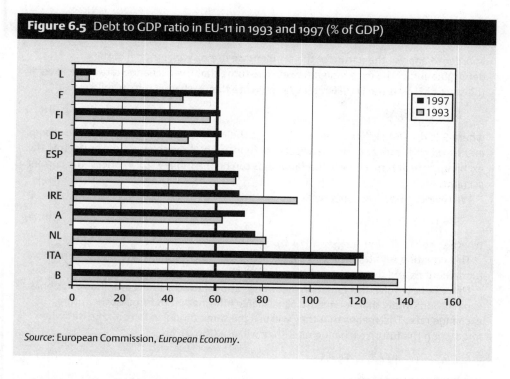

Source: European Commission, *European Economy*.

nothing to anchor the beliefs of the market, so that the exchange rates could drift in any direction as one approached the conversion time.

Such a result had to be avoided. For it could lead to permanently fixing the wrong values of the exchange rates, creating a situation in which some currencies would be undervalued and others overvalued almost permanently. A number of academic researchers solved this problem by proposing that the authorities announce long enough in advance the fixed values at which the currencies would be converted into each other at the start of EMU.[8] If these announcements were credible, then the market would smoothly drive the market rates towards the announced fixed conversion rates.

This is exactly what happened. The authorities announced the fixed bilateral conversion rates in May 1998. They chose the central rates of these currencies in the EMS. This announcement was made credible by also announcing that the central banks of the EMU-candidate countries would closely co-operate to set monetary policies. They also made it clear that they would be willing to intervene in unlimited amounts to make sure that the market rates would be driven towards the announced fixed conversion rates. In fact, very little intervention was necessary. Market participants were very confident that these announced rates would also be the conversion rates. As a result, speculation became stabilizing. As we moved closer and closer to conversion time the market rates converged closer and closer to the fixed conversion rates. In addition the variability of these market exchange rates declined progressively as we moved closer to 31 December 1998. (In Box 10 we show why this had to happen.) All

[8] De Grauwe and Spaventa (1997) and Begg *et al.* (1997) made such a proposal.

Box 10 How to fix conversion rates?

In order to analyse the nature of the problem we use a simple model of the determination of the exchange rate. Let us assume that the exchange rate to be fixed at the start of EMU is the DM/FF rate. We can write that exchange rate as follows:

$$S_t = Z_t + b\,E_t\,\Delta S_{t+1} \tag{B10.1}$$

where S_t is the DM/FF rate at time t, $E_t\,\Delta S_{t+1}$ is the expectation held at t about the *change* in the exchange rate at t + 1; Z_t is a vector of fundamental variables at time t affecting the exchange rate at time t. These fundamentals can be the money stock, prices, the current account, etc.

We rewrite (B10. 1) as follows:

$$S_t = (1-\beta)\,Z_t + \beta\,E_t S_{t+1} \tag{B10.2}$$

where $\beta = b/(1+b)$ and $(1-\beta) = 1/(1+b)$.

This equation says that the current exchange rate is a weighted average of current fundamentals and the expected future *level* of the exchange rate.

One can now solve this equation assuming rational expectations as follows. Rational expectations imply that agents use all available information to forecast the future exchange rate. This means that they will use the same model as in (B10.2). Thus when forecasting the future exchange rate, they will use (B10.2), i.e.

$$E_t S_{t+1} = (1-\beta)\,E_t Z_{t+1} + \beta\,E_t S_{t+2} \tag{B10.3}$$

Substituting (B10.3) into (B10.2) yields

$$S_t = (1-\beta)\,Z_t + \beta[(1-\beta)\,E_t Z_{t+1} + \beta\,E_t S_{t+2}] \tag{B10.4}$$

When forecasting S_{t+2} rational agents will proceed in exactly the same way, i.e. using (B10.2). Continuing this process of forecasting future exchange rates yields:

$$S_t = (1-\beta)\,[Z_t + \beta\,E_t Z_{t+1} + \beta^2\,E_t Z_{t+2} + \ldots + \beta^{T-t-1}\,E_t Z_{T-1}] + \beta^{T-t}\,E_t S_T \tag{B10.5}$$

where T is the time of the start of EMU (conversion time). Thus the exchange rate at time t is a weighted average of the fundamental variables that agents forecast until the start of EMU (at time T) and their forecast of the conversion rate that will be applied. As time moves forward more and more terms in the brackets drop out and so do the weights attached to the fundamentals. Note also that β can be considered as a discount factor, so that as we move closer and closer to T, β converges to 1. Thus, in the limit as we have moved arbitrarily close to T we obtain

$$S_t = E_t\,S_T$$

which becomes $S_t = S_T$ when t = T.

This result illustrates the indeterminacy of the exchange rate when the authorities announced that the conversion rate at time T would be equal to the market rate obtained just prior to conversion time. In that case any expectation that the market has about the conversion rate would be self-validating. In other words, there are infinitely many exchange rates that satisfy this condition.[9]

[9] For more detail see De Grauwe *et al.* (1999).

In order to anchor the market's expectations it was necessary to announce in advance what the conversion rate would be. This is what the authorities did in May 1998. Let us call the announced DM/FF rate S^* (a fixed number). The DM/FF exchange rate then becomes

$$S_t = (1 - \beta) \left[Z_t + \beta\, E_t Z_{t+1} + \beta^2\, E_t Z_{t+2} + \ldots + \beta^{T-t-1} E_t Z_{T-1} \right] + \beta^{T-t} S^* \qquad (B10.6)$$

As we move closer to T the exchange rate must smoothly converge towards the fixed number S^*.

Note also that the variance of S_t can be written as the sum of the variances and covariances of the present and future fundamentals. As we move closer to T, more and more fundamentals between the brackets drop out and so do their variances and covariances. In addition the weight of the final conversion rate increases. Since the final conversion rate is a fixed number, its variance is zero. Thus, as we move closer to T the variance of S_t also converges to zero. All this, of course, assumes that the announced conversion rate S^* is fully credible.

The prediction of this simple model came out beautifully. We illustrate this in the following graph. This shows a number of exchange rates against the DM. We observe the smooth convergence towards the announced conversion rate (normalized at 100). We also observe that as we moved towards conversion time the variability declines.

Figure B10.1 Market exchange rates of DM in 1998 relative to conversion rates

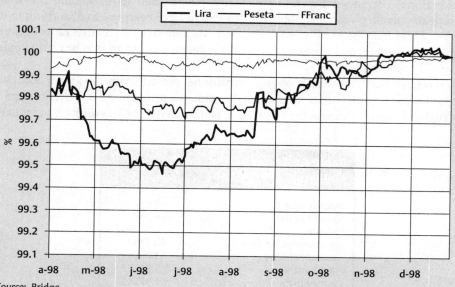

Source: Bridge

Note that the model we have used here is an application of a well-known exchange rate model introduced by Mussa (1979). In normal exchange markets that are not assumed to disappear at some final date (as we have assumed here), the last term in (B10.5) disappears, i.e. as $T \Rightarrow \infty$, $\beta^{T-t} E_t S_T \Rightarrow 0$ since $|\beta| < 1$ (assuming that S_T does not go to infinity).

this happened while the world was hit by major financial crises during the second half of 1998 (South East Asia, Russia).

It should be noted that the authorities could not announce in advance the conversion rates of the national currencies into the euro. The reason is that the euro was linked to the ECU. The latter was defined as a basket of national EU-currencies, which included currencies not participating in EMU (e.g. the pound sterling). As the latter continued to fluctuate the ECU-rates of the currencies participating in EMU could not be fixed in advance. In the end this did not matter much because the basket weight of the currencies not participating in EMU was very low, so that the fluctuations of the ECU *vis-à-vis* the EMU-currencies remained very low. The euro conversion rates were irrevocably fixed on 31 December 1998. They are shown in Table 6.2.

4.2 How to make irrevocably fixed exchange rates credible?

To the outsider it may seem quite surprising that the European leaders decided to start EMU on 1 January 1999 without a true monetary reform, i.e. without replacing the national currencies by the euro, which would then have become the single European currency with legal tender. This would have been the logical thing to do. There would have been no need to have irrevocably fixed exchange rates between national currencies and the euro during three years: a situation that has led to many practical problems.

It has been said that this three-year transitional period, from 1999 until 2002, was necessary for technical reasons, i.e. it takes time to print the new currency, and to make the necessary changes in the national banking systems. It is difficult to take this

Table 6.2 Conversion rates of EMU currencies into the euro	
Belgian franc	40.3399
Spanish peseta	166.386
Irish punt	0.787564
Luxembourgish franc	40.3399
Austrian schilling	13.7603
Finnish marka	5.94573
German mark	1.95583
French franc	6.55957
Italian lire	1936.27
Dutch guilder	2.20371
Portuguese escudo	200.482

Note: the numbers are the amounts of national currency for one euro.

argument seriously, however. After all, the Treaty was signed in 1991 leaving plenty of time (eight years) to prepare the technical changes.

A more plausible explanation is that the commitment to monetary union in a number of countries was quite weak, at least initially. Thus, the additional three years of transition and the maintenance of the national currencies during that period provided a last chance of opting out if 'things would get out of hand'. This would not have been possible if on 1 January 1999 the national currencies had disappeared.

Whatever the truth in this matter, the overriding question today is whether the transitional regime during which national currencies will circulate side by side with the euro, albeit with irrevocably fixed exchange rates, can be made trouble-free. This is the same as asking the question whether the fixity of the exchange rates can be made fully credible. Fortunately, the institutional set-up that is in place since 1 January 1999 (and which was devised by the drafters of the Maastricht Treaty) should, in principle, solve this credibility issue. Let us look at the different ingredients of this institutional structure. We can distinguish three important credibility-enhancing features.

(1) There has been one central bank since 1999, the ECB, responsible for the monetary policy of the union as a whole. This central bank, therefore, targets *union-wide* variables, e.g. the total money stock in the union. It does not care about, say, the money stock in Germany or in France. In addition, the ECB uses the euro to implement these policies, e.g. it buys and sells euros to influence the interest rate, or to target the money stock in the union.

(2) The Eurosystem (ECB and the national central banks) is ready to convert one member currency into another member currency on demand. Thus, if say French residents desire to get rid of their French francs and to hold euros (or even German marks) the Eurosystem will be ready to convert these French francs into euros (or German marks). There is no limit to the conversion capacity of the Eurosystem, because it can 'manufacture' the euro (and the German mark). Thus, speculators cannot expect that the Eurosystem could 'run out of money' to organize the conversion. It is precisely the expectation that the central bank will 'run out of money' that triggers speculative attacks. In addition, there is no danger that this intervention will increase the total money stock in the system. The creation of German marks exactly offsets the destruction of French francs.

(3) The conversion of one member currency into the euro, or into another currency, occurs at a fixed rate without a fluctuation band. This is possible because there is no foreign exchange market in which these currencies are traded. Commercial banks are converting these currencies at the fixed conversion rate. Of course, banks will charge a fee for this service, very much in the same way as they charge fees to a customer who 'converts' a cheque into cash, or who uses his credit card. The absence of a band of fluctuation is important. The existence of such a band and the movements of the exchange rates within the band has often triggered speculative pressure.

These three features are quite essential in providing the basis for the full credibility of the transitional monetary regime during 1999–2002. In order to illustrate this further we use the two-country monetary model developed in the chapter on the EMS. This will also allow us to contrast the transitional regime between 1999 and 2002 with the EMS, which suffered so much from credibility problems.

We represent the model in Fig. 6.6 and we assume that the two countries are France and Germany.[10] Let us assume that output declines in France. As a result, the money demand function in France shifts to the left because French residents now have a lesser need to hold money for transaction purposes. The ECB is the sole monetary authority and targets the money stock of the Euro-area as a whole. Initially this money stock was $M^*_E = M^1_G + M^1_F$. Thus, after the shock in France, the ECB continues to target the same money stock M^*_E. This means that a redistribution of the money stock between France and Germany will have to come about. The excess supply that now exists in France at the initial interest rate spills over into Germany. The money stock in France declines to M^2_F and the money stock in Germany increases to M^2_G. As a result, the total Euro-money stock remains unchanged. Note that the shock in France reduces the demand for money in the system as a whole. Since the ECB targets the Euro-money stock this must lead to a decline in the Euro-interest rate. This, in turn, increases the demand for money in both Germany and France (we move down along the money demand functions). At the end of this process, there will be more money in Germany and less in France. Note, however, that because of the decline in the interest rate, the stock of money held in France will have declined less than if the interest rate had remained unchanged. We have seen that the latter is precisely what happened in the EMS when Germany was the leader and was targeting its own money stock. In that case the money stock in France had to decline more, exacerbating the recession, and leading to tensions between the two countries.

Figure 6.6 Asymmetric shocks during the transitional period

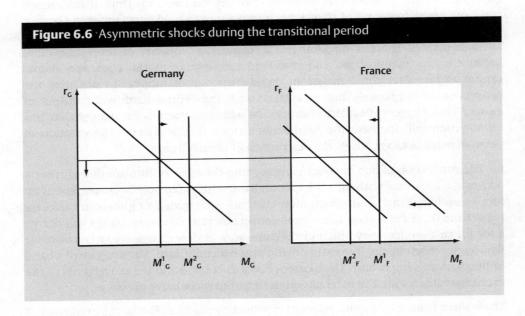

[10] Alternatively Germany could be considered as the rest of the union.

In practice the redistribution of money between France and Germany will be realized automatically through the banking system without the ECB having to intervene in the foreign exchange market (which will not exist between the currencies involved). This automatic redistribution of money can be described as follows. As the French economy is going through a recession, the French demand for bank loans declines. French banks find themselves with excess funds that they will invest in the inter-bank market. As a result, there will be excess supply in that market, part of which will flow into Germany. At the same time, the excess supply in the inter-bank market reduces the inter-bank interest rate (and probably also the other short-term interest rates linked to that market). This increases the willingness of German banks to borrow funds in that market. Thus, there will be a redistribution of liquidity towards Germany, which will increase the money stock in that country.[11]

This automatic redistribution of liquidity through the banking system can only work satisfactorily if two conditions are satisfied. First, there must be a full integration of the inter-bank markets in the system. In order to achieve this, a new payment system (called TARGET) was set up on 1 January 1999, which makes it possible for banks in the EMU to transfer funds to other banks in the EMU (almost) instantaneously. Second, there must be full confidence in the absolute rigidity of the exchange rate. This also implies that there should be no bands of fluctuation. For, if the latter were the case, banks would carry some risk when making transfers to another country, i.e. they would never be completely sure about the exchange rate they would have to pay when making the transfer (or the exchange rate they would receive when obtaining a payment). When large shifts occur, this would limit the willingness of banks to take large open positions in the currencies involved, making it necessary that the ECB itself would intervene. The existence of a band of fluctuation would also lead to differences in the interest rates in the different currencies as the riskiness of these currencies would not be evaluated in the same way.

Can one conclude that there is no risk of a collapse of the 'irrevocably fixed' exchange rate arrangement during 1999–2002? A traditional speculative attack like the one that destroyed the EMS in 1993 cannot occur. The only risk is political. The period 1999–2002 leaves a very small window open for countries to pull out before their currencies are taken out of circulation. Although this risk is very small, it is not zero either.

---

[11] Asymmetries in the size of countries matter here. If Germany is large relative to France, the increase in the German money stock will be small in relative terms.

5 How to organize relations between the 'ins' and the 'outs'

E_{MU} has started with eleven out of fifteen EU-countries. How should the exchange rate relations be organized between these two groups of countries? The main issue that arises here is the exchange rate regime that should be set up between the euro and the currencies of the 'outs'.

The principles that should guide the exchange rate relationships between the 'ins' and the 'outs' were agreed upon at an ECOFIN meeting in June 1996. The main principles are the following. A new exchange rate mechanism (the so-called ERM-II) has replaced the old ERM since 1 January 1999. Adherence to the mechanism is voluntary. (This principle was accepted much to the chagrin of the French authorities at the insistence of the UK government). Its operating procedures are determined in agreement between the ECB and the central banks of the 'outs'. The new mechanism is based on central rates around which margins of fluctuations are set. The latter are relatively wide, such as the ones in the old ERM, but can be decided by the countries concerned. Thus, countries may choose different margins. The anchor of the system is the euro. When the exchange rates reach the limit of the fluctuation margin, intervention in principle is obligatory. This obligation, however, will be dropped if the interventions conflict with the objectives of price stability in the EMU-countries or in the outside country. The ECB has the power to initiate a procedure aimed at changing the central rates.

Up to now, only two countries, Denmark and Greece, have adhered to the ERM-II. The UK, the most prominent outsider, has made it clear that it does not want to be constrained by an ERM-type of arrangement, even when the band of fluctuation is relatively wide. There is thus very little choice but to have a floating sterling/euro exchange rate, until (and if) the UK decides to join EMU. This may create problems if in the future this exchange rate fluctuates a lot and creates large movements in the competitive position of the UK economy relative to the EMU economy. It is, therefore, also unclear whether such a free floating exchange rate arrangement can be maintained in the long run. The only conceivable constraint that could exist for the UK while it stays outside EMU, is given by Article 109m of the Treaty. This says that member states that do not participate in EMU should 'treat their exchange rate policies as a matter of common interest and it is accordingly agreed that exchange rates should be monitored and assessed at the Community level with a view, in particular, to avoiding any distortion in the single market'.

The second country which has not adhered to the ERM-II, is Sweden. As will be remembered, Sweden decided to stay out of EMU by not joining the ERM prior to 1999. Since the political will to enter EMU is rather weak in Sweden, it is possible that this country will continue to stay out of ERM-II. Entering this exchange rate arrangement would legally bind Sweden also to enter EMU (provided the other convergence criteria are satisfied).

Finally, there is the issue of the intervention commitment of the ECB. The principles agreed upon today stipulate that the ECB should stand ready for unlimited intervention when, say, the Greek drachma drops below the lower limit of the band, except if this intervention would jeopardize price stability in the EMU. This may seem to seriously reduce the intervention commitment of the ECB. However, it is very unlikely that the ECB interventions can destabilize the price level in Euroland. First of all, the outside countries are small relative to the whole of the EMU-area so that the intervention activities of the ECB will have a small quantitative impact in the EMU money market. In addition, the ECB is likely to sterilize these interventions so that they will not affect the EMU money markets. It is therefore reasonable to conclude that if the ECB is committed to intervene, it can do so without jeopardizing price stability in the EMU.

To conclude, it should be stressed that the ERM-II arrangement only makes sense in the framework of a temporary regime that facilitates the quick convergence and acceptance of the 'outs' into EMU. If the prospects for a quick entry of the 'outs' are weak then an ERM-II arrangement may be undesirable. It may then quickly face similar problems to those the EMS experienced in 1992–3 with speculative crises and a collapse of the arrangement.

6 Conclusion

THE Maastricht strategy followed by the EU-countries was successful in bringing about EMU in Europe. Few observers had expected this success in the early 1990s. This success, however, was achieved at a price. The deflationary demand policies that the EMU-candidate countries initiated in the first half of the 1990s contributed to the significant build-up in the rate of unemployment in Europe. Europe's supply rigidities then ensured that this (demand induced) increase in the rate of unemployment acquired a quasi-permanent character.

In addition, and quite paradoxically, the Maastricht strategy ultimately led to a situation in which EMU was started with a significantly higher debt level than when the Treaty was signed. This means that budgetary policies in Euroland will have to continue to be restrictive for years to come. One can only hope that the ECB will be willing to perform sufficiently stimulatory policies so that Euroland does not repeat the mistakes of the past in applying a policy mix of budgetary and monetary restriction.

The technical problems associated with the start of EMU were solved remarkably well. In particular the decision to announce fixed conversion rates in May 1998 stabilized the exchange markets in Europe. This stability was maintained despite the world financial upheavals in the second half of 1998.

Chapter 7
The European Central Bank

1 The design of the ECB: The Maastricht Treaty

IN the post-war period, two models of central banking have evolved. One can be called the *Anglo-French model*, the other the *German model*. These two models differed from each other on two counts. One of them was concerned with the objectives a central bank should pursue, the other related to the institutional design of the central bank.

■ *The objectives of the central bank*

In the Anglo-French model, the central bank pursues several objectives e.g. price stability, stabilization of the business cycle, the maintenance of high employment, financial stability. In this model, price stability is only one of the objectives and does not receive any privileged treatment. This is very different in the German model, where price stability is considered to be the primary objective of the central bank. And, although the central bank can pursue other objectives, this is always conditional on the requirement that their pursuit does not endanger price stability.

■ *The institutional design of the central bank*

The Anglo-French model is characterized by the political dependence of the central bank, i.e. the monetary policy decisions are subject to the government's (the minister of finance's) approval. Thus, in this model the decision to raise or to lower the interest rate is taken by the minister of finance.

Things are very different in the German model, where the guiding principle is political independence. Decisions about the interest rate are taken by the central bank without interference of political authorities. This principle is enshrined in the statutes of the central bank and jealously guarded by the central bank authorities.[1]

When the European countries negotiated the Maastricht Treaty a choice between these two models had to be made. It can now be said that the Anglo-French model was discarded as a guide for the design of the European Central Bank, and that the German model prevailed. This is made clear by analysing the statutes of the ECB, which are enshrined in the Maastricht Treaty.

On the objectives of the ECB, the Treaty is very clear. According to article 105, the primary objective of the ECB is the maintenance of price stability. The same article adds:

Without prejudice to the objective of price stability, the ECB shall support the general economic policies in the Community with a view to contributing to the achievement of the Community as laid down in article 2. (Article 105(1).)

Article 2 of the Treaty defines these objectives, which include 'a high level of employment'. Thus, the Treaty recognizes the need for the ECB to pursue other objectives. However, these objectives are seen as secondary, i.e. they should not interfere with the primary objective of price stability.

In a similar vein the Treaty is very clear on political independence. This principle is formulated in very strong language in article 107:

When exercising the powers and carrying out the tasks and duties conferred upon Them by this Treaty [. . .] . . . neither the ECB nor a national central bank, nor any member of their decision-making bodies shall seek or take instructions from Community institutions or bodies, from any Government of a Member State or from any other body.

In addition, the Treaty recognizes that political independence is a necessary condition for ensuring price stability. For, in the absence of political independence, the central bank can be forced to print money to finance government budget deficits. This is the surest way to inflation. In order to exclude this the following sentence was included in the Treaty:

Overdraft facilities or any other type of credit facility with the European Central Bank or with the national central banks of the Member States [. . .] with Community institutions or bodies, central governments, regional or local authorities, public authorities [. . .] shall be prohibited, as shall the purchase directly from them by the ECB or national central banks of debt instruments. (Article 104(1).)

One can conclude that the Bundesbank has been the role model for the ECB. In fact, the language used by the drafters of the statutes of the ECB is tougher on inflation and political independence than the statutes of the Bundesbank. The political independence of the ECB is certainly greater than that of the Bundesbank. The reason is that a simple majority in the German parliament can change the statutes of the Bundesbank. Changes in the statutes of the ECB are much more difficult. They can only occur by a revision of the Maastricht Treaty, requiring unanimity among all

---

[1] In the German model there is some ambiguity about who is responsible for the exchange rate policy, the central bank or the government. We return to this issue at a later stage.

EU-member states, including those that are not members of EMU. (This feature has in fact led some to criticize the ECB for absence of democratic accountability. We will come back to this issue).

2 Why has a German model prevailed?

THE success of the German model of central banking is an intriguing phenomenon. After all, when the EU-countries negotiated the Maastricht Treaty the Anglo-French model of central banking prevailed in almost all the EU-member states. Why, then, was this model rejected in favour of the German one? Two reasons can be identified. One has to do with an intellectual development, i.e. the 'monetarist counter-revolution'; the other with the strategic position of Germany in the process towards EMU.

During the 1950s and 1960s, Keynesianism triumphed. High economic growth and low unemployment were seen as objectives for which monetary and fiscal authorities were responsible. Expansionary monetary and fiscal policies were seen as instruments to reach these objectives. The 1970s were a watershed. Backed by increasing evidence that these policies had produced an inflationary bias, monetarism as a counter-revolution erupted. In the monetarist view, which is very well synthesized by the Barro–Gordon model, monetary authorities cannot systematically lower the unemployment rate below its natural level. They can only lower unemployment temporarily. If they target the unemployment rate below the natural one, they will do this at a price, i.e. they will create a systematic inflation bias. The only way to lower unemployment permanently is by lowering the natural unemployment rate. This can only be achieved by 'structural policies', i.e. by introducing more flexibility in the labour market and by lowering labour taxes. Conversely, the central bank must occupy itself only with what it can control, namely the price level.[2]

This monetarist view also led to a new view about the nature of the relations between the central bank and the government. Since the pressures to follow expansionary monetary policies aimed at stimulating the economy typically come from politicians who pursue short-term electoral gains, the central bank should be protected from these political pressures by making it independent.

These theoretical prescriptions were given a strong empirical backing by a series of econometric studies that appeared during the 1980s and early 1990s (see Box 11 for a brief overview). These demonstrate that countries in which central banks were politically independent had managed their economies better. These countries had maintained lower inflation on average without experiencing costs in terms of higher unemployment or lower economic growth. We discuss some of the issues relating to these empirical models in Box 11. We also show there that there are some problems of

---

[2] This view was first formulated by Friedman (1968) in his celebrated presidential address to the American Economic Association.

interpretation of the results. The main one is that political independence and inflation are jointly determined by deeper social and political factors. Therefore, it is not
obvious that imposing independence in the statutes of the central banks will automatically lead to lower inflation. In order for political independence to lead to the
desired price stability, it must be backed by a social and political consensus favouring
price stability.

Despite these recent criticisms, there is a general consensus that political
independence, although not sufficient to guarantee price stability, is necessary to
achieve and to maintain it.

It is no exaggeration to state that since the 1980s the monetarist paradigm has
become the prevailing one, especially among central bankers. In annual reports
and countless speeches of central bank officials, the monetarist analysis and prescriptions have become the dominant intellectual framework.

It is no surprise, therefore, that when the central bankers drafted the Delors report
(which provided the intellectual framework for the Treaty) they were willing to take
the Bundesbank as their model. By stressing price stability as the primary objective
and political independence as the instrument to achieve it, the Bundesbank appeared
as the living embodiment of the new monetarist paradigm.

The second reason why the Bundesbank was taken as the role model for the ECB
has to do with the particular strategic position of Germany during the run-up towards
monetary union. (We used the Barro–Gordon model to analyse this problem in
Chapter 6, Section 2.1.) The German authorities faced the risk of having to accept
higher inflation when they entered monetary union. In order to reduce this risk,
they insisted on creating a central bank that would be even more 'hard-nosed' about
inflation than they were themselves. Put differently, in order to accept EMU, the
German monetary authorities insisted on having an ECB that gives an even higher
weight to price stability than the Bundesbank did. Our analysis of the statutes of the
ECB confirms that the German monetary authorities succeeded in achieving this
objective. This victory was greatly facilitated by the fact that most central bankers
had been converted to monetarism.

3 The ECB: a 'conservative' central bank

THE monetarist counter-revolution and the German strategic position have led to
the creation of a European central bank with a strong mandate for price stability
and a weak responsibility for stabilizing output and employment fluctuations. In this
sense one can say that the ECB is a 'conservative' central banker, i.e. an institution
that attaches greater weight to price stability and lesser weight to output and
employment stabilization than the rest of society.

In a famous article Rogoff (1958b) argued that this is precisely what should be done
to eliminate the inflation bias. By appointing a conservative central banker the

Box 11 The case for independence: the empirical evidence

The idea that political independence will lead to less inflation has been subjected to much empirical analysis. There have been studies by Bade and Parkin (1985), Demopoulos, Katsimbris, and Miller (1987), Grilli, Masciandro, and Tabellini (1991), Cukierman (1992), Alesina and Summers (1993), and Eijffinger and Schaling (1995) showing that central banks that are politically independent tend to produce less inflation than central banks that have to take orders from the government. In Figure B11.1 we show an example of such an empirical test. On the vertical axis the average yearly rate of inflation of industrial countries (1972–91) is represented. On the horizontal axis an index of political independence of the central banks as computed by Cukierman (1992) is represented. We observe that there is a negative relationship, i.e. countries where the central banks have a great deal of political independence enjoy a lower rate of inflation, on average.[3]

Of course, many problems arise in testing this hypothesis. One concerns the measurement of political independence. It must be said that much careful analysis has been performed using alternative measures of political independence. On the whole the empirical results remain robust for these alternative measures.

An important aspect of these empirical studies is that they also reveal that on average and in the long run political independence does not lead to more unemployment or to a lower growth rate of the economy. All this seems to suggest that the basic Barro–Gordon paradigm is the correct way to view reality, and that political independence is a desirable institutional feature of the ECB.

Figure B11.1 Average annual inflation and political independence (1972–91)

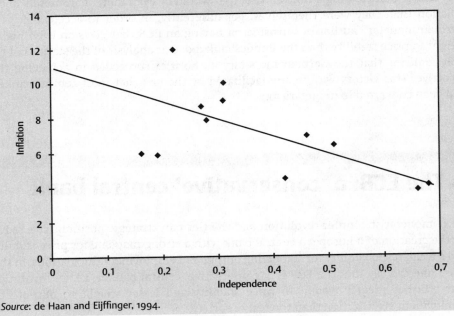

Source: de Haan and Eijffinger, 1994.

[3] A regression exercise involving twenty-one industrial countries confirms this conclusion (*t*-statistics in parentheses): inflation = 11.2 − 9.4 independence R^2 = 0.88.
(8.7) (−2.9)

An important question that arises here is whether the explicit recognition in the statutes of the ECB of political independence is sufficient to guarantee price stability. One can express doubts about this. In this connection, Posen (1994) has performed very interesting research about the link between political independence and inflation. His main conclusion is that both political independence and inflation are the result of deeper social and economic interests. Some countries have strong pressure groups against inflation (e.g. financial institutions). In these countries we observe that the central bank tends to be politically independent *and* that inflation is low. In other countries the major pressure groups are less opposed to inflation. In these countries central banks will be less independent and inflation will be higher. This research teaches us that central banks' behaviour is very much influenced by the underlying social and economic forces, so that a mere change of the statutes of the central bank will not by itself change behaviour.[4]

One should, however, not go too far in a neo-Marxian interpretation of the issue. In this interpretation economic forces drive the institutions. A more balanced view recognizes that institutions (and incentives) can also change behaviour. Thus, the incorporation in the statutes of the central banks of political independence as a means to guarantee price stability can help in influencing behaviour and in changing society's view about the role of monetary policy. In addition, there is scope for the strengthening of these institutions so that the risk of inflation is reduced.

credibility of low inflation policies can be achieved and maintained. In this section we analyse the problems that this solution leads to.[5]

We analyse the problem using the Barro–Gordon model of the previous chapters, which we reproduce here in Fig. 7.1. We showed that the inflation equilibrium is obtained in point A, where unemployment is at its natural level and where at the same time the short-term Phillips curve is tangent to the authorities' indifference curve. The latter ensures that the authorities have no incentive any more to create surprise inflation. In our previous discussions of the Barro–Gordon model we did not study how the central bank reacts to shocks in the short-term Phillips curve. We do this now. The upward sloping dotted line in Fig. 7.1 is the collection of all points for which the short-term Phillips curve is tangent to an indifference curve. It can be interpreted as the optimal stabilization line. The following example clarifies this. Suppose a positive (and temporary) shock occurs in the short-term Phillips curve, moving it from U to U′. Point B then defines the optimal response of the monetary authorities (given their preferences as represented by the indifference curves). Thus, the monetary authorities will react to the temporary increase in unemployment by expansionary monetary policies, which raise inflation to π_1. This expansionary policy will limit the increase in unemployment to U_1. If the authorities would not react by expansionary monetary policies unemployment would increase to U_2.

The slope of the optimal stabilization line is determined by the weight the authorities attach to the stabilization of unemployment. If the weight is high (we observe steep indifference curves) then the stabilization line will also be steep. For any given shock

---

[4] See Hayo (1998) for an interesting analysis.
[5] For a more formal analysis see Walsh (1998).

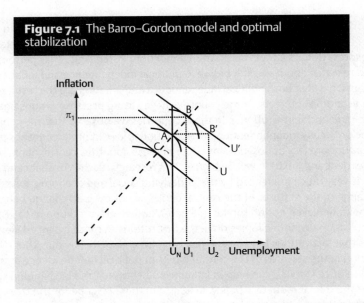

Figure 7.1 The Barro–Gordon model and optimal stabilization

in unemployment they will react by strongly expansionary monetary policies. The price the authorities pay is that the equilibrium inflation rate will be high. There will be a strong inflation bias. (In the Appendix we derive the exact expression of the slope of the stabilization line. We show that it is equal to the weight given to the stabilization of unemployment times the slope of the short-term Phillips curve.)

A similar reasoning leads to the conclusion that when there is an unexpected and temporary decline in unemployment the authorities will react by contractionary monetary policies bringing us to point C.

How can the inflation bias, which results from the active stabilization policies pursued by the monetary authorities, be eliminated? Rogoff showed that this can be done by appointing a conservative central bank, which he defined to be a central bank attaching less weight to unemployment stabilization than the rest of society. We show this in Fig. 7.2. The steep stabilization line is the same one as in Fig. 7.1 and represents the preferences of society. The flatter stabilization line is the one of the conservative central bank which has been appointed to run monetary policies. We will call this central bank, the ECB.

We observe that *on average* Euroland gains from having appointed a conservative central banker. On average, it will have lower inflation without any loss in employment. In hard times, however, this may not be the case. In Fig. 7.2 we show the case of an unexpected recession which increases unemployment. This is shown by a displacement of the short-term Phillips curve. True to its reputation, the ECB does relatively little to accommodate for it by expansionary policies. At least it does less than what society, which has appointed the ECB, would like it to do. This leads to a potential for conflict between the ECB and elected politicians who represent society's desires closer than the ECB. Of course, the latter will claim that it is precisely this greater reluctance to accommodate temporary shocks in unemployment that gives them the reputation and thus that creates the average superiority of a

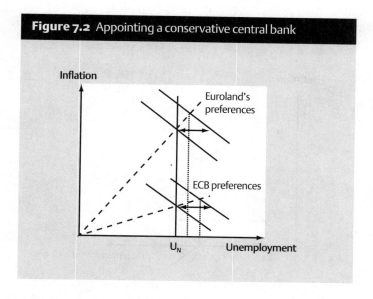

Figure 7.2 Appointing a conservative central bank

system that shields the ECB from political pressure. We return to these issues in Section 4, when we study the relation between independence and accountability of the ECB.

4 How to solve conflicts: first best solution

IN the previous section we showed that the appointment of a conservative ECB leads to a trade-off between credibility and stabilization. If we want a credible central bank capable of keeping inflation low, this central bank will not do much to stabilize the economy. This is an uncomfortable situation that will often lead to conflicts.

Can this trade-off be made more comfortable? It is important to realize here that the fundamental reason why there is an inflation bias is the fact that the monetary authorities pursue a target for unemployment which is lower than the natural unemployment rate. This can be seen in our graphical representation of the Barro–Gordon model (Fig. 7.1) by noticing that the optimal stabilization line starts from the origin. This implicitly assumes that the authorities target a zero unemployment rate and a zero inflation rate.[6]

Suppose, however, that the authorities would set their target for the unemployment rate equal to the natural unemployment. In other words they stop having an ambition permanently to lower the unemployment rate below the natural rate. The effect of this is shown in Fig. 7.3. The optimal stabilization line now shifts to the

[6] Note that we could re-label the origin and call it the point π^*, U^*, representing target values of inflation and unemployment that are different from zero.

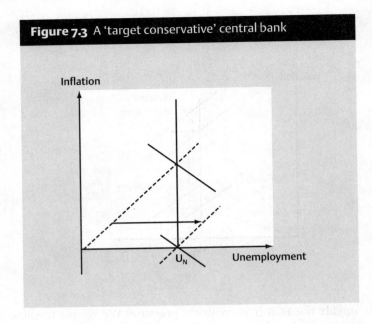

Figure 7.3 A 'target conservative' central bank

right and intersects with the natural unemployment point on the horizontal axis. The result is quite dramatic: the inflation bias disappears. At the same time the authorities are now capable of stabilizing unemployment in the same way as society desires. This can be seen by the fact that the optimal stabilization line going through U_N has the same slope as the one going through the origin (which represented society's preferences).

This solution to the problem amounts to appointing a central banker who is 'target conservative', in contrast to the 'weight conservative' central banker proposed by Rogoff.

From the policy statements of the ECB-officials it is clear that the ECB considers itself to be a 'target conservative' central bank. This is made very clear in the ECB's 'Monetary Policy Strategy' which was published in the ECB Monthly Report in January 1999 (for a discussion of this policy statement see Section 2 of Chapter 8). In unambiguous terms the ECB states that its only responsibility is price stability, and that unemployment is a structural phenomenon that cannot be alleviated by monetary policies. Put differently, for the ECB monetary policies should not be used to lower unemployment below the natural unemployment. The corollary is that the politicians are responsible for the lowering of the natural unemployment rate by structural policies, such as introducing flexibility in the labour market and reducing taxes on labour. These policies of reducing distortions in the labour market will then also have the effect of reducing the pressure on the ECB to tackle a problem that it is not equipped to solve.

The problems arising from an uncomfortable trade-off between credibility and stabilization seem to be resolved in Euroland. The ECB is a truly 'target-conservative' bank so that there is no danger of an inflationary bias. In addition, within this con-

straint imposed by target conservatism, the ECB can still pursue the kind of stabilization that society desires. Several issues remain though.

■ The ECB may still be a 'weight conservative' central banker and do too little
  stabilization. It may do this out of a fear that too much emphasis on stabilization
  may undermine its credibility. The future will show whether this will happen. In
  any case the incentive to attach a low weight to stabilization declines when the
  correct unemployment target is selected.

■ A second more important issue has to do with a new type of conservatism which
  can arise if the ECB systematically estimates the *natural* unemployment rate to
  coincide with the *observed* unemployment rate. This may lead to a situation in
  which the ECB stabilizes too little. This problem is illustrated in the Fig. 7.4. Suppose that initially the natural unemployment rate is given by U_N and that the
  observed unemployment rate coincides with the natural unemployment rate. The
  ECB targets the unemployment rate at its natural level. Therefore, there is no
  inflation bias. Suppose there is now a temporary increase in unemployment. We
  show this by a displacement of the short-term Phillips curve. The ECB observes this
  increase and interprets it as an increase in the natural unemployment rate. It will
  then also increase its target unemployment rate. This shifts the optimal stabilization path to the right: the ECB will not attempt any stabilization. It behaves as if it
  were super-conservative by attaching a zero weight to unemployment stabilization.

  Is there a risk that the ECB will react in the way we just described? The risk is
real. In the policy statements of the ECB the observed levels of unemployment have
systematically been associated with structural unemployment. All movements in
the unemployment rate are routinely interpreted as coming from structural factors. In so doing, the ECB clears itself from all responsibilities for unemployment.
This creates the risk that in a future recession, the ECB will tend to interpret

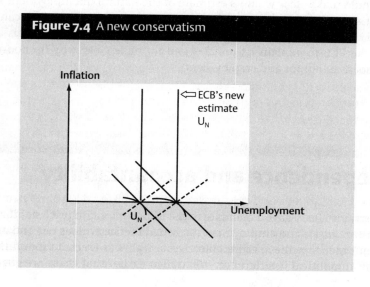

Figure 7.4 A new conservatism

increases in unemployment as being structural in nature. As a result, it may decide to do nothing (or too little). This possibility leads to a third problem.

■ The third problem arises from the existence of hysteresis in unemployment in Euroland. We discussed some of these issues in Chapter 6. Hysteresis is the phenomenon whereby a temporary shock in unemployment, due to say a temporary recession, is transformed into a permanent one. This phenomenon has been observed in Europe mainly because the rigidities in the labour markets prevent workers who have lost their job during a recession from finding a new job when the economy turns around.

If the ECB behaves as the 'super-conservative' bank as described in the previous section, there is a real danger that it will aggravate this problem of hysteresis. In that case, it will apply too little stabilization, so that the temporary increase in unemployment will be unduly large. This in turn will lead to a level of permanent unemployment that is larger than in the case where some stabilization is applied.

The recent economic history in the European Union shows us the danger of this scenario. In the previous chapter, we showed the evolution of the unemployment rate in the countries of Euroland during the 1990s (see Fig. 6.3). It is striking to find that almost the whole of the increase in unemployment that these countries experienced during the 1990s occurred during only two years, i.e. 1992 and 1993. As we argued in the previous chapter, the European authorities failed to apply macroeconomic stabilization during these years. Structural rigidities then ensured that much of the temporary increase in unemployment became permanent. At the end of the 1990s the authorities could rightly claim that much, if not most, of the European unemployment was structural in nature. They forgot to tell, however, that the origin of this structural problem was a failure to react to a demand shock that occurred in 1992–3.

The previous analysis has some policy implications. The most important one is that the ECB should make clear what its estimate of the natural unemployment rate is. In addition, it should make public the method it uses to obtain it. This can then be confronted with the estimates of other institutions (e.g. the OECD). This approach will force the ECB to explain its policies and to make clear why it chooses not to stabilize shocks in output and employment.

5 Independence and accountability

THE Maastricht Treaty gave a mandate to the ECB to maintain price stability but also to stabilize output and employment (provided the latter does not endanger price stability). In order to achieve these objectives a wall was erected around the ECB to protect it from political interference. We argued earlier that there are good reasons for ensuring the political independence of the central bank. However, there are also problems. These have to do with the lack of accountability of the ECB.

The ECB has to fulfil its mandate. It can, however, like any other institution, make systematic mistakes. It can also be led to do things that go against its mandate. For example, we have shown in the previous section that the ECB could systematically make wrong estimates of the natural unemployment rate and therefore fail to stabilize output and employment while it could do so without endangering price stability. Errors in the other direction are also possible. The ECB could just fail to provide for price stability.

It is, therefore, important that there should exist a mechanism to check whether the ECB fulfils its mandate, and if this is not the case, that sanctions should be applied. This is nothing but the application of a general democratic principle. In a democracy, citizens delegate power to politicians. The politicians exert this power until they face the electorate again. Thus, the delegation of power to the politicians has two stages. The first one starts when the politicians are vested with power. During this stage they exert this power independently of the electorate. The second stage is the accountability stage, when the electorate evaluates and sanctions the record of the politicians.

Much of what politicians do is to further delegate power to specialized institutions. This secondary delegation must have the same two stages. In the first stage, the politicians delegate power to the institution in the form of a contract in which the objectives and the means to achieve them are specified. In the second stage the politicians evaluate the performance of the institution. The first stage can be called the stage in which some form of independence is granted, the second one is the stage in which control is exerted (accountability). These two stages are inextricably linked. The politician who is accountable to the electorate cannot afford to delegate power to an institution (make it independent) except if he can also exert control over that institution.

The more the politician delegates power, the better the control must be organized about how this power is used. If there is little delegation, there is little need for control. Thus (applying these principles to the central bank), if the government decides about the interest rate then there is no need for having explicit accountability of the central bank. If, however, the government delegates a lot of power to the central bank there is a corresponding need to have a lot of accountability. The reason is that the government maintains its full accountability towards the voter, and therefore cannot afford to delegate power without maintaining control over the use of this power. Thus independence and accountability are part of the same process of delegation.

These ideas are given a graphical interpretation in Fig. 7.5. We represent the degree of independence granted to the central bank on the vertical axis. On the horizontal axis we set out the degree of accountability of the central bank. The upward sloping line represents the optimal combinations of independence and accountability from the politician's point of view. The more independence he grants the more risk he takes and therefore the more he wants to hedge his risks by organizing a system of control over the performance of the central bank.

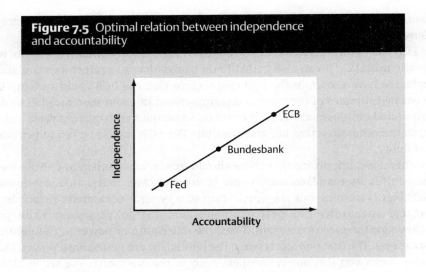

Figure 7.5 Optimal relation between independence and accountability

In Fig. 7.5, the empirical evidence about the degree of independence of three central banks, the Federal Reserve, the Bundesbank, and the ECB, is used. This evidence is based on Cukierman (1992) and a recent update by Bini-Smaghi and Gros (1999). Using several indicators of independence (e.g. who sets the targets? Who formulates the policy? What are the limitations on lending to governments? What is the length of the terms of office?) Bini-Smaghi and Gros conclude that the ECB is the most independent central bank followed by the Bundesbank and the Federal Reserve.[7]

Can it also be concluded that the ECB has the strongest degree of accountability? This does not seem to be the case. On the contrary, the evidence suggests that the degree of accountability of the ECB is less well developed, at least compared to the Federal Reserve (see Buiter (1999) and Eijffinger and de Haan (1999) on this issue). Although the presidents of both central banks have to appear regularly before the parliament, the implications are very different. When the chairman of the Federal Reserve appears before Congress he faces an institution which can change the statutes of the Federal Reserve by a simple majority. He therefore cannot afford systematically to disregard the opinions of the Congressmen. When the president of the ECB appears before the European Parliament, he faces an institution that has no power whatsoever to change the statutes of the ECB. These can be changed only by changing the Treaty, requiring unanimity of all EU-member states (including those that do not participate in EMU). As a result, the balance of power is very much tilted in favour of the ECB.

Thus, the ECB is an institution that was granted a lot of independence compared with the other major central banks, while the degree of accountability it is subjected to appears to be weaker than in these central banks. This goes against the theory developed here, stressing that accountability should be increased together with the degree of independence.

There is an additional problem in the way power was delegated to the ECB. Delega-

---

[7] See also Eijffinger and de Haan (1999) who come to the same conclusion.

tion of power implies the writing of a contract in which the objectives to be pursued are defined, together with the method to achieve them.

A crucial issue is the precision with which the objectives are described.[8] If objectives are left vague, it will be difficult to monitor the behaviour of the central bank. Accountability will be weak. The more precise the definition of the objectives is, the easier it is to monitor the central bank. How does ECB compare here with other central banks?

As pointed out earlier, the Maastricht Treaty has singled out price stability as the primary objective of the ECB. At the same time the Treaty mandates the ECB to support the general economic policies of the Community provided this does not interfere with price stability. Two issues arise here. First, the concept of price stability has not been given a precise content in the Treaty. This has made it possible for the ECB to fill the void and to define this concept itself (see Section 6 of Chapter 8, which describes the Monetary Policy Strategy of the ECB). Thus, in a sense the ECB has filled out itself the fine print of the contract it has with the politicians.

Second, the other objectives the ECB should pursue (provided price stability is guaranteed) have been left very vague in the Treaty: so vague, that it is unclear what these other objectives are. This state of affairs has made it possible for the ECB to develop its own interpretation of the objectives it should pursue. This interpretation has been made public in the ECB's Monetary Policy Strategy (see Chapter 8, Section 6). Something remarkable has happened. Given the vagueness of the Treaty about the other objectives besides price stability, the ECB has interpreted this to mean that it has to pursue only price stability. All reference to other objectives has been dropped. As a result, the ECB has drastically restricted the domain of responsibilities about which it can be called to account. If the ECB's interpretation of the Treaty is left unchallenged, the ECB will be able to claim that its only responsibility is inflation, and that it cannot be made responsible for business cycle developments and movements in employment. This strategy, if successful, will make the ECB accountable only for the its performance in the area of inflation.

The contrast with other central banks is great. The Federal Reserve, for example, has been made responsible by law for movements in employment. There is no way it could decide on its own that the employment objective is none of its business, contrary to what the ECB has done. As a result, the area of responsibilities about which the Federal Reserve is accountable is much broader than the ECB's.

To summarize, the accountability of the ECB is weak for two reasons. First, there is an absence of strong political institutions in Europe capable of exerting control over the performance of the ECB. Second, as a result of the Treaty's vagueness in defining the objectives of the ECB (apart from price stability), the ECB has effectively restricted its area of responsibility to inflation, so that it will only be accountable for its anti-inflation performance.

This state of affairs creates a long-term problem for the political support of the ECB. Modern central banks have a wider responsibility than simply price stability. Their responsibility extends to macroeconomic stability in general i.e. reducing business

---

[8] There are other issues, e.g. how detailed the contract should be; how to design the right incentives for the agent. We do not discuss these issues here. (See Walsh (1998).)

cycle fluctuations, avoiding deflation, and maintaining financial stability. It is difficult to see how European politicians will continue to support an institution to which great power has been delegated and over which they have so little control. Conflicts between the ECB and the European governments will arise when the ECB is perceived to act too little to avoid recessions and escalating unemployment.

The ECB could do a lot to defuse these conflicts. First, in order to compensate for the lack of formal accountability, it could enhance informal accountability. This can be achieved by greater transparency. This means, for example, that the ECB informs the public about its objectives and the way it wants to achieve them. It also requires openness in the decision-making process so that the public is aware of why the ECB is making certain decisions. Put differently, the ECB can compensate for the lack of formal accountability by volunteering information about its policies. Given its high degree of independence, the ECB should in fact do more of this volunteering than other central banks. It must be recognized that the ECB has gone some way in this direction. It publishes a Monthly Report in which it explains its policies in detail. In addition, after every meeting of the Governing Council, the ECB President explains to the press what has been decided and why.

Accountability can be improved indirectly by other means. Some economists (e.g Svensson) have argued that inflation targeting promotes informal accountability. The reason is that by announcing a particular target for inflation the central bank is forced to explain to the public why it misses the target subsequently (if it does).[9] Similarly, as we argued in the previous section, the ECB could announce its estimate of the natural unemployment rate. If the observed unemployment rate exceeds the natural unemployment, the ECB would be expected to do something about it. If it does not want to stimulate the economy, it would have to explain why it does not want to do this. All of these measures would promote informal accountability.

In this connection, the issue arises of whether or not the ECB should publish the minutes of the meetings of the Governing Council. Some central banks, e.g. the Federal Reserve, do this, including the voting record of the members of the Board. The advantage of such a publication is that it informs the public better about the process through which the central bank has gone to make a decision. This tends to improve accountability. The ECB has not been willing to do this up to now. It claims that it is forbidden by the Treaty to do so. Indeed, article 10.4 of the Statutes can be interpreted to mean that the publication of the minutes and the votes is prohibited.[10]

Finally, the ECB should broaden its area of responsibility and recognize that there are objectives other than price stability. A central bank that neglects its stabilizing role is soon going to encounter stiff political resistance. This problem may be even more pronounced for the ECB because of the occurrence of asymmetric shocks. We discuss this in the next section.

---

[9] We shall return to inflation targeting when we analyse it more technically.
[10] For a dissenting interpretation see Buiter (1999) who comes out very strongly in favour of the publication of the minutes and the votes.

Box 12   How to make the ECB pay for mistakes

Economists have proposed various penalty schemes aimed at ensuring some accountability of the central bank.[11] An interesting one was proposed by Walsh in 1995. It consists of a linear penalty for every percentage point of inflation above the target rate. Thus, if the inflation exceeds the target by 1% the central bank would pay a fine equal to a fixed amount of euros (dollars).

The interesting aspect of this proposal is that it can be shown to lead the central bank to behave exactly like the 'target-conservative' central banker. We illustrate this in figure B12.1. Without the penalty, the country experiences an inflation bias equal to the difference between $E(\pi)$ and π^* (the latter is the inflation rate desired by society). The penalty is now computed as a fixed euro (dollar) value times the inflation bias. This penalty will induce the central bank to exactly eliminate the inflation bias. Graphically, the optimal stabilization line shifts downwards. Comparing this result with the one obtained under target conservatism we observe that the outcome is identical. Whether such a penalty scheme can be applied in practice is another question.

Recently, Svensson has shown that the linear penalty scheme and inflation targeting also are equivalent. If we set the target that the central bank should pursue equal to π^t, the central bank will behave exactly in the same way as when it faces a linear penalty à la Walsh. Since the latter is equivalent to target conservatism we find that the three schemes are equivalent.[12]

Figure B12.1 Penalty schemes and inflation targeting

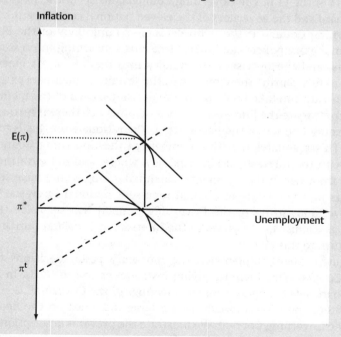

---

[11] Examples are Vaubel (1989), Neumann (1990), Bade and Parkin (1978).
[12] See also Lippi (1999) on these issues.

6 The ECB: institutional framework

THE continuing importance of nation-states in the European Union made it neces-sary to construct monetary institutions for Euroland that are sufficiently decentralized and yet maintain unity in the conduct of monetary policy. The result has been an institutional framework that is quite unique in the world. We first describe this institutional framework and then ask the question of whether it is not too decentralized.

6.1 The institutions of Euroland: the Eurosystem [13]

The institutions of Euroland were established in the Maastricht Treaty. Monetary policy is entrusted to the Eurosystem. This consists of the European Central Bank (ECB) and the national central banks (NCBs) of the EU-countries that have joined EMU. Today (in 2000) there are eleven such NCBs.

The governing bodies of the Eurosystem are the Executive Board and the Governing Council. The Executive Board consists of the President, the Vice-President, and the four Directors of the ECB. The Governing Council consists of the six members of the Executive Board and the governors of the eleven national central banks.

The Governing Council is the main decision-making body of the Eurosystem. It formulates monetary policies and takes decisions concerning interest rates, reserve requirements, and the provision of liquidity into the system. It meets every two weeks in Frankfurt. During these meetings, the seventeen members of the Governing Council deliberate and take the appropriate decisions. Each of the members has one vote. Thus, contrary to the European Council of Ministers, there is no qualified voting in the Governing Council of the Eurosystem. The rationale for this is to be found in the Treaty. This mandates that the members of the Governing Council should be concerned with the interests of Euroland as a whole, and not with the interests of the country from which they originate. Qualified voting would have suggested that the members of the Governing Council represent national interests. Whether the national governors sitting in the Governing Council will set aside their national interests so as exclusively to promote the interests of Euroland remains to be seen. We shall return to this matter.

The Executive Board implements the monetary policy decisions taken by the Governing Council. This includes giving instructions to the NCBs. In addition, the Executive Board sets the agenda for the meetings of the Governing Council. As such, it has a strategic position and can have a large influence on the decision-making process in the Governing Council. We illustrate the previous description of the organ-

---

[13] For a good description and discussion, see Gros and Tabellini (1998).

izational structure of Euroland's monetary institutions in the form of a flow chart in Fig. 7.6.

This whole decision-making structure is called the Eurosystem. The ECB is only a part of this system, and cannot take decisions on its own about monetary policies in Euroland. Nevertheless we shall continue to use the label ECB as a synonym for the Eurosystem, mainly because this has become common practice. The reader should, however, keep in mind that the label ECB then refers to a broader concept than its legal definition.

6.2 Is the Eurosystem too decentralized?

The organizational structure we just described combines unity of decision-making with decentralization in structure and in implementation of the decisions. This can also be seen from Fig. 7.6. This shows that the national central banks are fully involved in the decision-making process within the Governing Council. The decisions of the Governing Council are then implemented by the ECB. Following the instructions of the ECB, the NCBs carry out these decisions in their own national money markets.

The question arises here of whether this system is not too decentralized. Put differently, is the influence of the NCBs in the Governing Council not too great so that national interests will tend to prevail at the expense of the system-wide interests? We analyse this question here.

Some observers have argued that the system is indeed too decentralized.[14] The governors of the national central banks have a clear majority (eleven out of seventeen members) in the Governing Council. This contrasts with other decentralized central banks. For example, the US Federal Reserve System's decision-making body is the Board of Governors. It consists of twelve members, five of whom are presidents of regional banks. The other seven members are appointed by Congress and are representing the interests of the System as a whole. Thus, the regional banks' presidents who could be said to represent regional interests, are always in a minority position. The US Federal Reserve System used to be more decentralized during the 1920s and 1930s than today. In their famous book 'The Monetary History of the United States', Milton Friedman and Anna Schwartz (1963) argued that in the early 1930s the Federal Reserve Board failed to take decisive action to avert the banking crisis because the Board was torn by opposing regional interests. There was no authority in the Board looking at the system-wide interests and strong enough to overcome divergent regional interests. This exacerbated the depression according to Friedman and Schwartz.[15]

This criticism of an excessive influence of the NCBs in the decision-making process is given additional substance by considering the size of the NCBs in relation to the ECB. We show the number of employees in the NCBs and in the ECB in Table 7.1. The

[14] See Begg *et al.* (1998) and Gros and Tabellini (1998).
[15] Friedman and Schwartz (1963). See also Eichengreen (1992) on this issue.

Figure 7.6 Organizational framework of Eurosystem

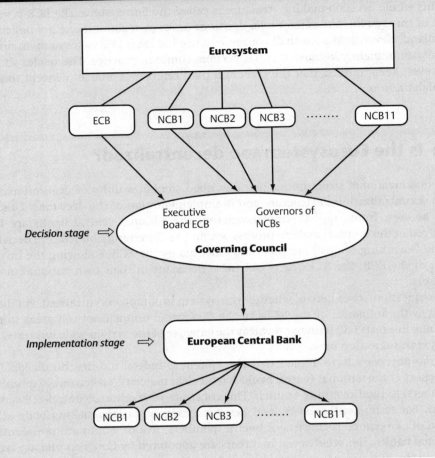

Table 7.1 Staff at ECB and NCBs

	Total staff	In analytical functions (research, statistics, economics)
ECB	600	100–150
Bundesbank	17,632	360
Banque de France	16,917	750
Banca d'Italia	9,307	300
Banco de España	3,269	350
Nederlandsche Bank	1,721	165

Source: Gros and Tabellini (1998). Data for NCBs refer to 1995.

differences are striking. The staff of the ECB is only a small fraction of the total staff of the NCBs. The latter amounts to approximately 60,000 employees (in all the NCBs). Of course, many of these NCBs' staff members are engaged in operational tasks that are necessary to implement monetary policies. But even the staff engaged in analysis and policy formulation is much larger in the NCBs than in the ECB. These large national staffs are not likely to sit idle. They will brief their governors about the desirable monetary policy actions to be taken by the Governing Council in Frankfurt. As a result of such strong national analysis and scrutiny, it is not far-fetched to believe that the national governors will have a definite national outlook on what is desirable.

Despite the risks, one should not exaggerate the problem. In a recent paper, De Grauwe *et al.* (1999) analysed this problem in the following way. They first constructed stylized models of the eleven Euroland countries, and allowed asymmetric shocks to hit these economies. They then assumed that all the governors derive the interest rate that is optimal for their own countries (given the shock they are subjected to). The Executive Board, however, takes a Euroland perspective and derives the optimal interest rate for Euroland as a whole. Governors and Executive Board then meet in the Governing Council and decide, by majority voting, about the interest rate to apply for Euroland. De Grauwe *et al.* (1999) found that if the Executive Board votes in unison, its desires about the interest rate are almost always fulfilled. Thus, even if all governors think nationalistically, the Executive Board (provided it takes a Euroland-wide perspective) would still determine the outcome most of the time.

This may seem surprising given the fact that the Executive Board has a minority position in the Governing Council. In fact it is not really surprising. When there are asymmetric shocks, the national governors want different things. Some like an increase in the interest rate, others prefer a lower interest rate, still others no change. The Executive Board, however, uses Euroland aggregates to derive the best possible interest rate. This will be very close to the interest rate desired by the 'median governor', i.e. the governor who happens to be in the middle of the distribution of nationally desired interest rates. As a result, with majority voting, the actual outcome will be very close to the desires of the Executive Board. Thus, despite its minority position, the Executive Board will have a strong influence on the Governing Council's decision at least if it acts in unison.

Complications could arise, however, if the shocks that hit the Euroland countries are not symmetrically distributed. We show this in Fig. 7.7. The left panel shows the distribution of the interest rates desired by the national governors when the shocks are symmetrically distributed. In this case the governors wishing a high interest rate are matched by those that wish a lower interest rate. The Executive Board, which computes the desired interest rate based on a model for Euroland as a whole, will propose an interest rate which is close to the median. With majority voting the median voter will prevail. This is likely to be the Executive Board.

This result contrasts with the result obtained in the right panel of the figure. Here the distribution of the desired interest rates is asymmetric around the mean. There is a concentration of governors desiring a low interest rate, while a few desire a very high interest rate. The ECB will then come up with a Euroland-wide average

Figure 7.7 Distribution of the desired interest rate

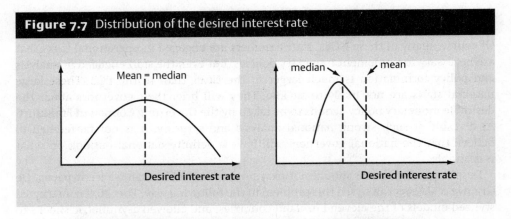

Figure 7.8 Bi-modal distribution of the desired interest rate

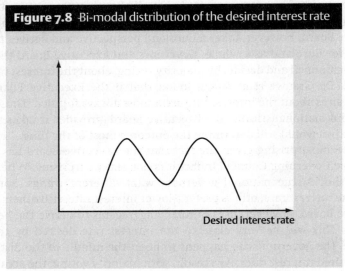

which will be higher than the desired interest rate of the 'median governor'. In this case the Executive Board is likely to be overruled by a coalition of governors desiring a low interest rate. If shocks that hit the Euroland economies are of the type described by the right panel, the decisions about the interest rate would be the result of shifting coalitions among the national central banks. The Executive Board would be powerless much of the time.

The worst possible scenario would be one where the shocks are distributed as in Fig. 7.8. In this case, about half of the governors want a low interest rate, and the other half a high interest rate. This could be due to the fact that half of Euroland experiences a boom and the other half a recession.[16] In this scenario the decision process could

---

[16] Alternatively, this could be due to a split in the preferences of the national governors, some becoming, say, Keynesians, others remaining monetarists.

become unstable (cyclical): some of the time the low interest rate coalition prevails, alternating with periods when the high interest rate coalition wins the battle.

We conclude that if the structure of the asymmetric shocks is of the kind as represented by the right panel of Fig. 7.7 or by Fig. 7.8, the decentralized nature of the decisions of the Eurosystem would present problems. In these cases the decisions would be erratic and unpredictable.

7 Bank supervision and financial stability in Euroland

ONE of the most peculiar features of Euroland's monetary system is the fact that while monetary policy was entrusted to a European institution the responsibility for banking supervision was kept firmly in the hands of nation-states. This peculiar situation could lead to future problems. We analyse them in this section.

The broad principles of bank regulation and supervision have been set out in an EC-Directive (the Second Banking Directive of 1989) prior to the signing of the Maastricht Treaty. These principles can be summarized as follows. The responsibility for the supervision of banks is entrusted to the authorities of the country where the banks have their head office. This is called the principle of *home country control*. For example, the responsibility for supervising Deutsche Bank rests with the German supervisory authority, since Deutsche Bank has its head office in Germany. This also implies that the German authorities are responsible for the supervision of the branches of Deutsche Bank in Belgium, France, Italy, etc.

The second principle states that the host country is responsible for financial stability in its own market. This is called the *host country responsibility*. To give an example, the French monetary authorities are responsible for maintaining stability of the banking system operating in France. This implies that the French authorities must care about the soundness of all banks operating in France (including the French branch of Deutsche Bank).

As long as the national banking systems remain pretty much segmented this peculiar distribution of responsibilities should not create major problems. In that case home and host country responsibilities overlap to a large degree. For example, when most banks in France are French banks (i.e. banks with head offices in France) the French authorities that are responsible for banking stability in France obtain their information on the soundness of banks from the same French authorities.

Today, the degree of segmentation of the banking markets is still very large as Table 7.2 illustrates. It shows that most European banks have only a small fraction of their total assets in the form of claims on non-residents. As a result, the present division of responsibilities between home and host country is not problematic.

Things are likely to change, however, when, as should be expected, the banking

Table 7.2 Cross-border assets to non-banks as percentage of total (1998)	
Austria	5.7
Belgium	12.3
France	3.8
Germany	6.8
Italy	13.1
The Netherlands	14.3
Spain	6.6
Source: Danthine *et al.* (1999).	

systems in Euroland become increasingly integrated. In order to analyse the problems that will arise, consider the example of Italy. In a fully integrated banking system, it is quite possible that 50% or more of the banks operating in Italy will be branches of banks with head offices in Germany, the Netherlands, France, etc. The Italian monetary authorities will then face the following problem. Since they are responsible for the stability of the banking system in Italy they will need information on the soundness of the banks operating in Italy so as to be able to set up an early warning system to detect banking problems. A large part of that information, however, will be held by the supervisory institutions in Germany, The Netherlands, France, etc. In principle, these institutions should provide the information to the Italian authorities. But, will they do so in a timely fashion? And will they be willing to disclose all relevant information? The answer is uncertain. Experience shows that institutions tend to guard information jealously. Supervisory institutions also have strong incentives not to disclose information on the soundness (or lack thereof) of individual banks, out of fear that the dissemination of such information may trigger a run on the bank. Thus, it is quite likely that the Italian (and all other national) authorities responsible for maintaining financial stability will be badly informed about large parts of the banks operating in their territory. This will make it difficult to anticipate problems.

The problem will be compounded during crisis situations. Let us assume that a banking crisis erupts in Italy. Typical ingredients of a bank crisis are the failure of a bank with bad loans, a run on other (sound) banks by deposit-holders, threatening to lead to closures of these banks also. The major responsibility of the monetary authorities then consists in preventing sound (solvent) banks from being pulled down because of a lack of liquidity. The famous English economist of the nineteenth century Walter Bagehot defined the principles that central banks should follow to prevent such a crisis. First, the central bank should lend without limits to sound but illiquid banks. This is the lender of last resort principle.[17] Second, the insolvent banks should

---

[17] Bagehot added, however, that this lending should be at penalty rates. This is necessary to avoid moral hazard.

either be allowed to fail or should be restructured, whereby the bad loans are taken out of the failing bank and the remaining sound portfolio is placed in a new and recapitalized bank. Typically, the taxpayer will be asked to foot the bill of such a restructuring.

The problem for the central bank during the crisis is to distinguish banks that are insolvent from banks that are merely illiquid. In order to do so, the central bank, i.e. the Banca d'Italia in our previous example, will need to obtain information quickly from the other EU-country authorities. The emphasis here is on speed, since in a banking crisis every minute counts. It is unclear that the right information will be available quickly.

The lack of information available to the Banca d'Italia will handicap quick rescue operations. For example, the Banca d'Italia may hesitate to lend to a sound bank, e.g. the Italian branch of Credit Lyonnais, because of the uncertainty it faces about the quality of that bank's loan portfolio. If Credit Lyonnais turns out to be insolvent the Banca d'Italia may end up with a worthless loan portfolio after a lender of last resort operation. To avoid having to foot the bill, it may refrain from taking action, thereby precipitating a full-scale crisis.

We conclude that the present distribution of responsibilities for maintaining financial stability in Euroland will become increasingly problematic as the integration of national banking systems in Euroland moves forward. Sooner or later a more rational organization of these responsibilities will be necessary. This will necessarily involve a centralization of the supervisory and regulatory responsibilities at the European level. This centralization means that the ECB should take responsibility for the lender of last resort function. The supervision may or may not be taken over by the ECB. It is also possible that a new European authority may be created that would centralize the supervisory functions. Failure to move in this direction would subject Euroland to unnecessary upheavals when banking crises erupt.[18]

8 Conclusion

THE Eurosystem is a remarkable construction, unique in history. In designing the Eurosystem, it was necessary to take into account existing national sensitivities, and the desire of national banks to keep some power in the formulation and the implementation of monetary policies. At the same time a clear and unified decision-making process was needed to make the monetary union work. What has come out is a fine compromise that balances these opposing desires.

There are a number of shortcomings in the design, however, that we discussed in this chapter. One is the lack of clear accountability. The strong degree of independence that the ECB has obtained (a positive thing) is not matched by an equally strong procedure to control the performance of the ECB. The only way to compensate for

---

[18] This criticism has been formulated by the IMF (1998). A dissenting view is presented by Padoa-Schioppa (1998). A good survey of the issues in Lannoo (1998).

this shortcoming today is for the ECB to develop a climate of transparency so that its policy actions are well understood and a broad consensus can be developed.

A second major shortcoming has to do with the failure to centralize the supervision of the banking system at the level of Euroland. Although today the need to do so may not yet be apparent because banking systems are still segmented, this is changing quickly. In an integrated Euro banking system, the present structure of supervision and regulatory control will make it difficult to prevent and to manage financial crises. One can only hope that the necessary institutional changes will occur before the next financial crisis.

Box 13 The TARGET payment system

In order for EMU to function efficiently the payment system must be integrated, so that cross-border payments can be handled as smoothly as the payments within the same country. This integration was achieved by the TARGET system. The main features of this system are the following:

✓ It is a real time system. This means that payments reach their destination 'instantaneously', i.e. with a delay of a few seconds or minutes.

✓ It is a gross settlement system. This means that the gross amount of each payment goes though TARGET. This requires the paying banks to provide collateral for each payment. This contrasts with a net settlement system, which is used in most national payments systems. In the latter, banks can accumulate net debtor or creditor positions during the day without having to provide collateral. These positions are settled at the end of the day.

The fact that TARGET is a gross settlement system makes it an expensive one compared to the net settlement systems. As a result, cheaper private payments systems have emerged based on net settlement.

The reason why TARGET was selected is that it eliminates the risks that a bank default will have a domino effect on other banks involved in the payments chain. At the same time, it avoids that the ECB would have to intervene.

✓ TARGET connects existing national payment systems. This contrasts with the US payments system, Fedwire, which is a single unified system. The result of this is that the cross-border payments within EMU are likely to be more expensive than the payments within the same border.

Appendix
The optimal stabilization path in the Barro–Gordon model

In this Appendix we derive the optimal stabilization path used in our analysis of the Barro–Gordon model in this chapter. We start out by specifying the loss function of the central bank as follows:

$$L = (\pi - \pi^*)^2 + b(u - u^*)^2 \qquad (1)$$

where L is the loss of the central bank. This is a function of the difference between observed (π) and target inflation (π^*), and of the difference between observed (u) and target unemployment (u^*); b is the weight attached by the central bank to stabilizing the unemployment around the target. We will assume that target inflation is zero ($\pi^* = 0$). Target unemployment is assumed to be determined by the following expression

$$u^* = \lambda\, u_N$$

where u_N is the natural unemployment rate. We assume that $\lambda < 1$, i.e. the central bank targets an unemployment rate below the natural rate. The usual rationale for this assumption is that distortions in the labour market keep the natural unemployment rate too high. The first best solution would be to remove these distortions. If this first best policy cannot be achieved, the second best policy consists in targeting the unemployment rate below its natural level.

The short term Phillips curve is specified as follows:

$$u = u_N - a(\pi - \pi^e) + \varepsilon \qquad (2)$$

where π^e is expected inflation, and ε is a stochastic disturbance in output. This Phillips curve equation captures the standard assumption that only inflation surprises can affect unemployment. More precisely, an unexpected increase in inflation lowers unemployment relative to its natural level. The parameter a is the elasticity of unemployment with respect to inflation surprises.

The central bank now minimizes its loss function with respect to inflation, given the inflation expectations of agents. We use the conventional assumption that the central bank directly controls inflation. We could alternatively add an equation linking inflation to some policy instrument such as the money stock (see Walsh (1998)). Substituting (2) into (1) yields:

$$L = \pi^2 + b[a(\pi^e - \pi) + (1 - \lambda)\, u_N + \varepsilon]^2 \qquad (3)$$

Taking the derivative of L with respect to π, and solving for π yields the optimal inflation rate for a given expected inflation:

$$\pi = \frac{a^2 b}{1 + a^2 b}\, \pi^e + \frac{ab(1 - \lambda)}{1 + a^2 b}\, u_N + \frac{ab}{1 + a^2 b}\, \varepsilon \qquad (4)$$

In a rational expectations world agents know this optimal rule that the authorities use. They will therefore incorporate this rule in their expectations formation. Thus they set their expectations accordingly, i.e.

$$\pi^e = \frac{a^2 b}{1 + a^2 b}\, \pi^e + \frac{ab(1 - \lambda)}{1 + a^2 b}\, u_N \qquad (5)$$

Note that the expected value of ε is zero. This is why the last term in (4) drops out when we take expectations. We can now solve for π^e. This yields

$$\pi^e = ab(1 - \lambda)\, u_N \qquad (6)$$

We obtain the well-known result of the Barro–Gordon model: in equilibrium the average inflation is positive reflecting an inflation bias. This inflation bias increases with a, b, and u_N

Given that there are shocks in the Phillips curve the observed inflation will deviate from this average inflation, reflecting the fact that the central bank sets the inflation rate so as to reduce the variance of unemployment. Thus

$$\pi = \pi^e + \frac{ab}{1 + a^2 b}\, \varepsilon \qquad (7)$$

or

$$\pi = ab(1 - \lambda)\, u_N + \frac{ab}{1 + a^2 b}\, \varepsilon \qquad (8)$$

We can now substitute (8) into the Phillips curve. This yields the solution for u:

$$u = u_N + \frac{1}{1 + a^2 b} \varepsilon \qquad (9)$$

Equation (9) says that on average $u = u_N$, i.e. the authorities cannot systematically have an unemployment rate below the natural level. The unemployment rate will deviate from this average when there are shocks in the Phillips curve. Consider a positive shock, $\varepsilon > 0$. In this case the effect of the shock on unemployment will be influenced by b, i.e. the stabilization parameter in the loss function of the authorities. The larger is this b, the weaker is the effect of a given shock on unemployment. Note that a high b also produces a high inflation bias. The latter is the price the authorities pay for their stabilization efforts.

We can now derive the optimal stabilization path as follows. Take the derivative of π with respect to ε in equation (7) and the derivative of u with respect to ε in equation (9). This yields

$$\frac{d\pi}{d\varepsilon} = \frac{ab}{1 + a^2 b} \qquad (10)$$

$$\frac{du}{d\varepsilon} = \frac{1}{1 + a^2 b} \qquad (11)$$

Equation (10) tells us how the central bank optimally sets the inflation rate in response to shocks. Equation (11) says how this optimal response to shocks affects the unemployment rate. Taking the ratio of these two expressions yields the slope of the optimal stabilization line, i.e

$$d\pi/du = ab$$

Thus, the optimal stabilization line becomes steeper when the parameters a and b increase.

Chapter 8
Monetary Policy in Euroland

Introduction

IN the previous chapter we discussed fundamental problems relating to the design of the ECB.[1] We identified some flaws in its design. With or without flaws, the ECB is there and working. In this chapter we therefore discuss more practical problems that have to do with the conduct of monetary policies in Euroland.

We first identify the major problem with which the ECB will be confronted, i.e. how to conduct monetary policies in a union where asymmetric shocks occur and where the same shocks are transmitted differently among member-countries. We then shift our focus towards the formulation of ultimate and final targets of monetary policy. In this connection, we will discuss the ECB 'Monetary Policy Strategy'. Finally, we discuss the instruments the ECB uses to achieve these targets.

1 Central banking and asymmetries of shocks

EUROLAND is likely to experience asymmetric shocks. How will the existence of such asymmetries affect policy-making by the ECB? In Figs. 8.1 and 8.2 we analyse this issue by presenting a two-country version of the Barro–Gordon model. We will first analyse the effects of a 'pure' asymmetric shock. We will then contrast it with a 'pure'

---

[1] As mentioned in the previous chapter, we shall use the label ECB in a broad sense indicating the institutions that formulate and implement monetary policies in Euroland (the Eurosystem).

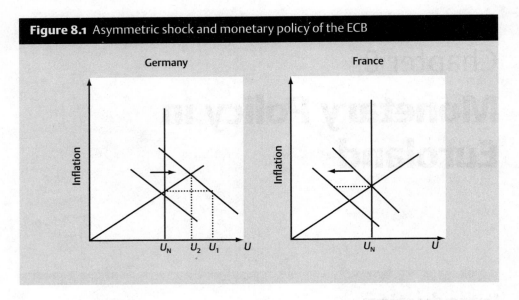

Figure 8.1 Asymmetric shock and monetary policy of the ECB

symmetric shock. In Fig. 8.1 we study asymmetric shocks. We show one country hit by a boom (France), the other by an increase in unemployment (Germany), and assume that the positive shock in one country is exactly offset by the negative shock in the other country. This assumption makes it a pure asymmetric shock. The ECB, which is responsible for maintaining price stability and for stabilizing the economy *in Euroland as a whole* aggregates the numbers. As a result, when observing the economic conditions prevailing in Euroland, it will decide that since inflation and unemployment have remained unchanged, no change in policies is called for. As can be seen from Fig. 8.1, the result is a greater fluctuation in unemployment in the individual countries. In Germany, unemployment increases to U_1, which exceeds the increase one would obtain if the central bank were able to take action to deal with the shock occurring in that country. The opposite holds in France.

In this extreme case of a pure asymmetric shock, the ECB never stabilizes. The ECB is completely paralysed. It behaves as if the weight the ECB attaches to unemployment stabilization is zero. As a result, unemployment (and output) in the individual countries fluctuate not around positive expansion paths but around a horizontal line. In the countries involved, the ECB will be perceived as super conservative.

The symmetric case is shown in Fig. 8.2. We now assume that the shock is exactly the same in both countries, i.e the short-term Phillips curve shifts upwards in both France and Germany. The ECB observes an increase in unemployment in Euroland as a whole. Given its desire to stabilize as expressed by the upward sloping optimal stabilization line, it takes action and follows an expansionary monetary policy. We move to points A and A'. Although from the German point of view, the shock is the same, the ECB is now capable of stimulating the economy in Germany and France, and to reduce the increase in unemployment.

Figure 8.2 Symmetric shock and monetary policy of the ECB

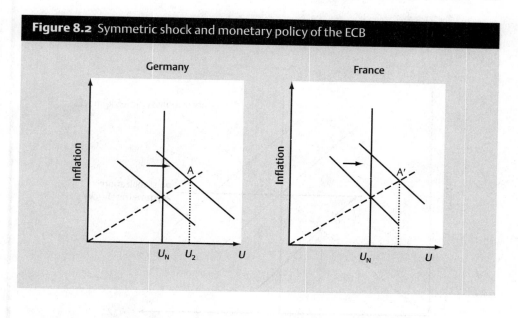

Thus, the effectiveness of the ECB to stabilize output in individual countries depends on whether the shocks are symmetric or asymmetric. In practice, shocks will always be some mixture of symmetric and asymmetric movements. We can derive the following important conclusion. To the extent that there is some asymmetric component in the shocks, the ECB will generally stabilize too little from the point of view of the individual member state. We illustrate this in Fig 8.3, where we show an individual member state. We assume that the short-term Phillips curve moves up and down in an unpredictable way. When these shocks are purely asymmetric, the ECB does nothing so that unemployment varies along the horizontal dotted line. If these shocks in the Phillips curve are purely symmetric, the ECB will stabilize to the extent given by its optimal stabilization line. Unemployment will then fluctuate between the points A and A'. We show the more likely intermediate case where the shock is a combination of symmetry and asymmetry. In this case the stabilization will be given by the line SS which is intermediate between the pure asymmetry and symmetry cases. Unemployment now fluctuates between the points B and B'. Thus, there will always be too little stabilization from the point of view of the individual country. This may lead to conflicts between individual nations and the ECB.

Can this problem of insufficient stabilization be resolved? The answer is negative. The analysis we have performed is just an extension of the analysis we made in the first chapter when we discussed the theory of optimum currency areas. There we found that if countries are subject to asymmetric shocks and, if they lack sufficient flexibility, they will find it costly to be in a monetary union. The analysis of the current chapter gives practical content to this theory. Thus, if countries do form an optimum currency area (in the sense of not being subjected much to asymmetric shocks) the ECB will have a relatively easy time to stabilize shocks, and there will be

Figure 8.3 Monetary policy of the ECB in reality

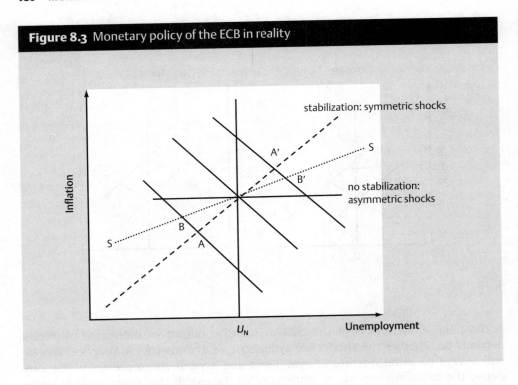

few conflicts between member-states and the ECB. Conversely, if countries do not form an optimum currency area the ECB will have a hard time to stabilize output and employment. There will also be a lot of conflict between member-states and the ECB.

The sixty-four thousand dollar question is how important these asymmetric shocks will be in the future? In Chapter 2 we analysed this question and we came to the conclusion that as Euroland integrates more an increasing amount of shocks are likely to be regional or border-overlapping. As a result, the problem the ECB will face may not be very different from the problem any central bank of a country (that is not too small) faces when regional shocks occur. Such a central bank is equally incapable of using its monetary policy to deal with a regional problem.

2 EMU versus EMS

THE previous analysis revealed a problem of monetary stabilization in a monetary union. One may argue that the way the problem was presented is unfair to EMU, because we compared EMU to an ideal situation in which each country can set monetary policies optimally. In practice, many countries (if not most) do not select an optimal point on their stabilization line because they fear that the exchange rate variations that are implicit in such policies, will introduce new sources of volatility and affect their trade negatively. As a result, many countries peg their exchange rate and abstain from using monetary policies as a stabilizing tool. This was also the case within the EMS, which preceded EMU. During the EMS-period, most EU-countries pegged their exchange rate to the German mark, letting the Bundesbank decide about monetary policies. It may therefore be fairer to EMU to compare the latter regime with the EMS-regime. We do this in Fig. 8.4. We assume that Germany is the leader in the EMS-regime. It sets its monetary policy optimally based on the shocks that occur in Germany. France pegs its currency to the German mark and, therefore, has to accept whatever policy decision Germany takes.

In Fig. 8.4, we suppose as before a pure asymmetric shock. The short-term Phillips curve shifts upwards in Germany and downwards in France. Germany has the freedom to set its monetary policy optimally, and selects point G, i.e. it reacts to the increase in unemployment by expansionary monetary policies, which raise the inflation rate temporarily. Since France has pegged its currency to the German mark, it has to follow this expansionary policy. This brings the French economy to point F.

When we compare this outcome with EMU we find (not surprisingly) that Germany does worse in EMU than in the EMS. In the latter, it can stay on its optimal stabilization line, while in the former it has to accept point E_G which implies less stabilization of the unemployment shock. Exactly the opposite holds in France. EMU is definitely better from the point of view of stabilizing shocks in unemployment. In EMU, the same unemployment shock is better stabilized (point E_F) than in the EMS (point F). Since in EMU there is no stabilization at all (given our assumption of pure asymmetry in shocks), the EMS actually destabilizes unemployment in France. That is, the EMS monetary regime reinforces the unemployment shock in France.

We can construct a 'stabilization' line of France under the EMS-regime (assuming

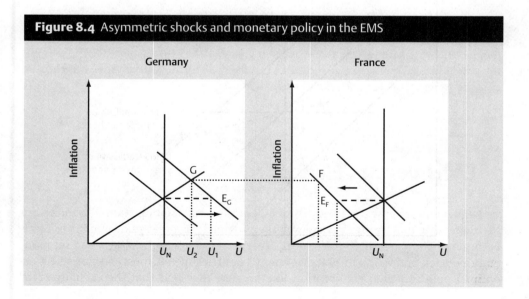

Figure 8.4 Asymmetric shocks and monetary policy in the EMS

that shocks are purely asymmetric) much in the same way as we derived stabilization lines in Fig. 8.3. We show this in Fig. 8.5. Under EMU there is no stabilzation, so that the economy moves along the horizontal line when the Phillips curve shifts up and down. Under the EMS regime these shocks in the Phillips curve are amplified, so that the economy moves along the negatively sloped 'stabilization' line. Thus, when shocks are asymmetric, the EMS destabilizes unemployment. This feature is absent in EMU. We conclude that from the point of view of France EMU is welfare improving because it leads to a less inefficient stabilization than the EMS. Since most countries that are now members of EMU were in the position of France before the start of EMU, the latter can be said to have improved the efficiency of stabilization in these countries. The only loser in this respect is Germany.

Note that the more the shocks become symmetric the closer the stabilization lines under the EMS- and EMU-regimes approach the upward-sloping stabilization line under symmetry. At the limit of pure symmetry in the shocks, the two regimes (EMU and EMS) have the same stabilization properties.

There are, of course, a number of provisos to be added here. First, nation-states are different from regions, and may react differently when they feel that the central bank is not capable of dealing with shocks that hit them more than other countries. Second, as we argued in Chapter 2, the fact that nation-states continue to exist creates the potential for shocks that have a political or social origin. Again, the difficulty of dealing with such a shock in a monetary union may lead politicians to look for a scapegoat in the ECB. Third, as argued in Chapter 2, the existence of different nations

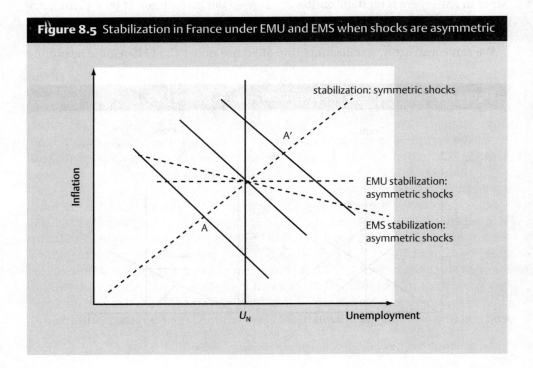

Figure 8.5 Stabilization in France under EMU and EMS when shocks are asymmetric

with their own legal and cultural systems leads to different transmission mechanisms of the policies of the ECB, creating a different view about what exactly the ECB should do. We pursue this question of asymmetric transmission mechanisms in Section 4.

3 Asymmetries in the transmission and optimal monetary policies

IN the preceding sections we analysed how asymmetric shocks affect the monetary policies of the ECB. In this section we take a different perspective. We study symmetric shocks but stress that these can be transmitted in an asymmetric way because economies have different structures and institutions. Recently, exciting new research analysing these differences in institutions within Euroland has been undertaken.[2] These asymmetric transmission processes arise because institutions in labour, products, and financial markets differ. Quite often these differences have a deeper cause that relate to culture, social, and legal systems.

In this section we focus on just one such institutional asymmetry, i.e. the one that exists in the labour markets. We shall assume that there are two countries that differ in the degree of rigidity in their labour markets. One country has a high degree of rigidity, the other has a low degree of rigidity in its labour market. We represent these two countries in Fig. 8.6. The 'flexible' country (left panel) is characterized by a relatively flat short-term Phillips curve, the 'rigid' country (right panel) by a relatively steep one. Put differently, due to rigidities in its labour markets, inflationary surprises have little effect on unemployment in the rigid country.

We now assume that the ECB estimates the euro-wide short-term Phillips curve. This will produce an estimated Phillips curve whose slope is an average of the slopes of the Phillips curves of the individual countries. We represent this euro-Phillips curve by the downward sloping dotted lines. Assuming that the ECB is target conservative (as defined in the previous chapter) it computes the optimal stabilization path for Euroland as a whole based on its estimate of the euro-Phillips curve. This yields the upward sloping optimal stabilization line SS. In the absence of shocks equilibrium is obtained in E and E'.

Let us now analyse the effect of a symmetric shock. We assume this takes the form of an equal displacement of the short-term Phillips curves in the two countries. We present this shock in Fig. 8.7. In both countries the Phillips curve shifts to the right by the same distance $U_N - U_1$. Since the shock is the same, the euro-Phillips curve shifts to the right by the same amount. The ECB now computes the optimal response to the shock and finds the point E, which is located at the intersection of the euro-Phillips curve and its optimal stabilization path SS. Thus the optimal inflation rate for Euroland is π_1. The unemployment rates in the two countries is given by the points F and R.

---

[2] See Dornbusch *et al.* (1998), Cecchetti (1999) and Maclennan *et al.* (1999).

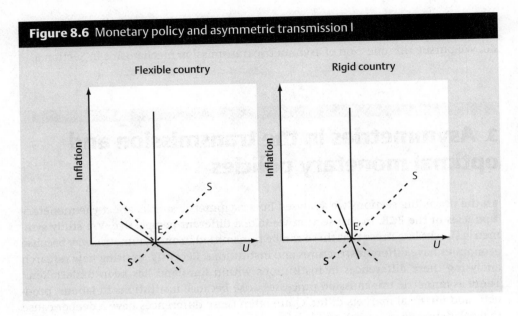

Figure 8.6 Monetary policy and asymmetric transmission I

Not surprisingly, in the flexible country the stabilization done by the ECB is quite effective in limiting the increase in unemployment. This is much less the case in the rigid country. There the stabilization effort of the ECB does very little to reduce the impact of the shock in unemployment.

We conclude that, due to structural differences in the workings of the labour markets, the same policy of the ECB has very different effects on outcomes in different countries.

4 The Monetary Policy Strategy of the ECB: a description

THE ECB has formulated the strategy it will follow to set monetary policies in Euroland. This strategy starts out by defining the ultimate targets (inflation, output) and the intermediate targets. As is well known, the ultimate targets are often affected by central bank actions very indirectly and with long lags. Therefore, central banks select intermediate targets that are known to influence the ultimate targets, and that they can influence more directly. We first describe the ECB-strategy. In the next sections we critically evaluate it.

The first step in the formulation of the Monetary Policy Strategy (MPS) consists in giving a precise definition of price stability. The Governing Council of the ECB has adopted the following definition: 'price stability shall be defined as a year-on-year

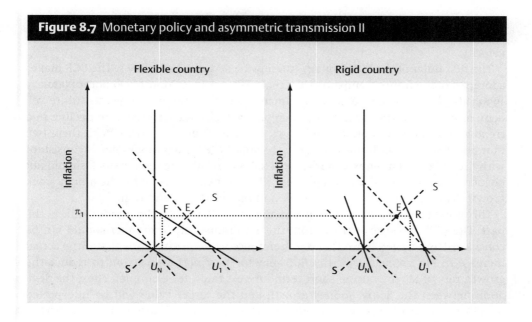

Figure 8.7 Monetary policy and asymmetric transmission II

increase in the Harmonised Index of Consumer Prices (HICP) for the euro area of below 2%' (ECB Monthly Bulletin, January 1999, p. 46).[3] The ECB adds that for all practical purposes this phrasing implies a target range of inflation of 0% to 2%. Price stability according to this definition 'is to be maintained over the medium run'. This means, for example, that if inflation suddenly increases above the target range due to a large disturbance, the ECB will allow for a gradual adjustment back to the target range. The ECB, however, does not define what the 'medium run' is.

Having identified the target of monetary policies the ECB then describes the strategy to achieve it. A 'two-pillar' approach is proposed. The first pillar is the monetary one. Since inflation is ultimately a monetary phenomenon, money should be given a prominent role in this strategy. In order to see this, it is useful to start from the quantity theory equation, which we can write (in log-linear form) as follows:

$$m + v = p + y \tag{8.1}$$

where m is the money stock, v is the velocity of money, p is the price level, and y is real GDP, all in logarithms.

We can also express this equation in first differences. This yields, after rearranging

$$\Delta m = \Delta p + \Delta y - \Delta v \tag{8.2}$$

where Δ is the change from one year to the other. Since we take changes of logarithms these changes should be interpreted as growth rates.[4] Equation (8.2) can

---

[3] The HICP is a price index for Euroland constructed from a harmonized definition of the national price indices.

[4] Note that this is only approximately true.

be interpreted as the growth rate of the money stock that is consistent with a particular target of inflation, given the underlying growth rates of GDP and of velocity.

The first pillar of the ECB strategy can now be described as follows. The ECB makes a forecast of the future trend growth of real GDP (Δy). In its Monthly Report of January 1999 this was estimated to be approximately 2%. Next the ECB forecasts future velocity of money. In the same Monthly Report velocity was estimated to decline in a trendwise fashion by approximately 0.5% per year. Thus $\Delta v = -0.5\%$. With these two numbers fixed, the ECB finds the growth rate of the money stock that is consistent with the inflation target, which is at most 2%. As a result, the money stock should not be increasing by more than 4.5% per year.[5] This is then the target for the money stock growth. The ECB selected M3 as the relevant money stock definition.

This is exactly the same procedure as the one followed by the Bundesbank in the past. The ECB, however, stresses that the 4.5% money stock number should not be considered as a target, but rather as a 'reference value'. This means that if the actual increase in M3 exceeds 4.5%, the ECB may (or may not) take action to reduce the growth rate of M3 (by raising short-term interest rates, for example). Thus, the deviation between the actual money growth and the target value will be interpreted flexibly by the ECB. Although the wording was somewhat different, this was also the attitude of the Bundesbank towards the use of the money growth target.

The second pillar in the Monetary Policy Strategy remains very vague. The ECB will use a wide range of indicators of future price developments. 'These variables include, *inter alia*, wages, the exchange rate, bond prices and the yield curve, various measures of real activity, fiscal policy indicators, price and cost indices and business and consumer surveys' (ECB, Monthly Report, January 1999, p. 49). Thus, if for example wages increase a lot in Euroland, the ECB may deem this to threaten future price stability and may therefore take appropriate action (in this case increase the short-term interest rate, and/or reduce liquidity in the system). Again the ECB has preferred not to tie itself down. The list of potential indicators is open ended. Others may be added, and those on the list may or may not receive much attention.

In a nutshell, the Monetary Policy Strategy of the ECB sets an inflation target of 2% at most. In order to steer actual inflation towards that target, the ECB watches a number of variables that influence future inflation. The most prominent of these variables (the intermediate targets) is the growth rate of M3. In the next section we evaluate this monetary policy strategy.

---

[5] This number could change in the future if the ECB deems that the trend growth of GDP and/or of velocity changes.

5 The Monetary Policy Strategy of the ECB: an evaluation

THE Monetary Policy Strategy (MPS) of the ECB can be criticized on several grounds. We shall concentrate here on the selection of the ultimate target, on the privileged use of the money stock as an intermediate target, and on alternative strategies.

5.1 The selection of the target

The ECB recognizes only one target of monetary policy. This goes counter to the Treaty, which mandates that the ECB should also pursue other targets, if these do not interfere with price stability. We have criticized the ECB for this narrowing of its responsibilities in the previous chapter.

It is useful to point out here that the exclusive targeting of inflation does not necessarily mean that other objectives cannot be realized at the same time. In particular inflation targeting also leads to output stabilization when the source of the shock comes from the demand side (see Bofinger (1999) and Clarida *et al.* (1999) on this issue). This is illustrated in Fig. 8.8.

The left panel shows an economy experiencing a boom, which is the result of a high level of aggregate demand (represented by the dotted AD'-line). As a result,

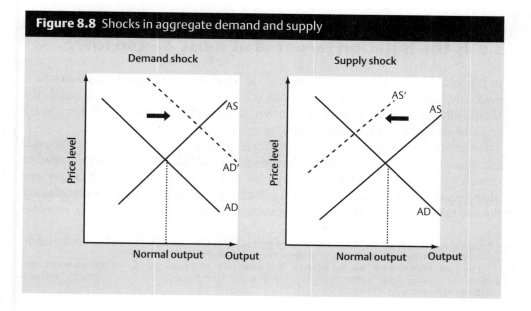

Figure 8.8 Shocks in aggregate demand and supply

output exceeds full capacity level (the normal level). To prevent inflationary pressures the ECB will follow restrictive monetary policies (shown by the arrow, which shifts the AD'-line back to its normal level). This has the effect of stabilizing both the price level and the output level. There is no trade-off between price and output stabilization when shocks in aggregate demand occur.[6]

Things are very different when shocks originate in the supply side of the economy. We show this in the right panel of Fig. 8.8. The economy has experienced a negative supply shock, which lowers output but increases prices. When the ECB targets the price level, it will tend to reduce aggregate demand thereby lowering the price level again at the expense of an even lower output level. In this case there is a trade-off between inflation and output stabilization. (This was also the underlying assumption when we discussed the optimal stabilization in the context of the Barro–Gordon model.) In its official pronouncements, the ECB has made it clear that when there is such a trade-off, it will always pursue price stabilization.

It should be pointed out that the ECB has left the door open for some output stabilization even in this case of a supply shock. As mentioned earlier, the ECB defines price stability over the 'medium run'. Thus, if after a supply shock, prices start to rise, the ECB may apply gradualism in its response. This means that it would not immediately react by contractionary monetary policies aiming at stopping the price increases immediately. Instead it would try to lower the inflationary pressures gradually. In doing so, it would avoid the sharp decline in output.

It should be mentioned that proponents of inflation targeting (e.g. Svensson (1997)) have stressed that the *gradual* transition to the inflation target after a shock is the right approach and allows a central bank to also care about output stabilization. The future actions of the ECB will make it clear whether the ECB is willing to follow this gradualist approach to inflation targeting.

5.2 Is the inflation target of at most 2% too low?

In the 1950s Milton Friedman formulated the view that the optimal inflation rate is zero. The basic reason for this conclusion is that a zero inflation rate maximizes the total utility of holding money. Two other factors, that recently have been much researched, cast doubts on this conclusion.

First, there is evidence that because of rapid technological change the conventional measures of inflation (the rate of change of the consumption price index) tend to overestimate the true inflation rate by 0.5% to 1.5% a year (see Gordon (1996), and Shapiro and Wilcox (1996)). The reason is that the conventional measures of inflation do not take into account quality improvements.[7] As an example, take a personal

---

[6] Note that in this model the ECB stabilizes the price *level* rather than the inflation rate. One can develop the same analysis in terms of inflation rates, however. See Clarida *et al.* (1999).

[7] There are other reasons, too. For example, when the price of a particular commodity increases, consumers will substitute that commodity with a cheaper one. Measurements of inflation typically disregard these substitution effects.

computer in 2000 and compare it to one in 1980. Their price may be approximately the same. However, the computing power of the 2000 version is probably 1,000 times greater, if not more. As a result, the price per unit of computing power in 2000 has dropped to a very small fraction of what it was in 1980. Many similar examples can be given. We conclude that if we observe an inflation rate of 0.5% to 1.5%, the true underlying inflation rate is probably zero.

Second, there are theoretical arguments to be made for a rate of inflation a little higher than 0%. The main one is that sectoral or microeconomic shocks require adjustments in relative real wages. In particular, sometimes a sector or a firm is confronted by a negative shock necessitating a decline in the real wage level. If the rate of inflation is zero, such a decline in the real wage can only come about by a decline in the nominal wage rate. If, however, inflation is positive one can achieve a decline in the real wage by keeping the nominal wage increases below the rate of inflation. There is a lot of evidence that the resistance against nominal wage reductions is high, thereby limiting real wage adjustments when the rate of inflation is zero. Put differently, in a environment of zero inflation, there is likely to be more real wage rigidity making adjustments to asymmetric sectoral shocks more difficult to achieve. Akerlof *et al.* (1996) come to the conclusion that this effect may require the monetary authorities to target an inflation rate close to 2% per year.

The previous analysis then leads to the conclusion that the optimal inflation rate may be of the order of 2.5% to 3.5% per year (0.5% to 1.5% on account of the measurement bias, and 2% on account of the real wage effect).

The ECB has recognized the quality bias problem, although it claims that it is less important in Euroland than in the US. Thus, implicitly the ECB considers the lower bound of the inflation target range to be larger than zero. It has not been willing to put an exact number for this lower bound. The ECB, however, does not accept the real wage flexibility argument.

The above arguments lead to the conclusion that the ECB may have set its inflation target too low for the good of Euroland's economy.

5.3 Excessive reliance on the money stock?

The ECB has singled out the money stock (M3) as a privileged indicator for steering its monetary policy actions. This approach has come under increasing criticism. Most central banks that used it at some point (the Federal Reserve and the Bank of England in the 1980s) have dropped it. The Bundesbank was the only major central bank that used it until 1999 (when it lost its sovereignty). However, there is strong evidence that it was not very successful in its money stock targeting. Half of the time the actual money stock numbers fell outside the targeted range.[8]

The reasons why central banks were not successful in using the money stock as an

---

[8] See Bernanke and Mihov (1997), and Clarida and Gertler (1996). This has led these authors to conclude that the strong reputation of the Bundesbank had nothing to do with money targeting (which the Bundesbank failed to apply successfully). It had everything to do with its success at keeping inflation low.

intermediate target are the following. First, the concept of money stock is very elusive. Should one use M1, M2, or a broader concept of money stock? The ECB has selected a broad concept of M3. Financial innovations can, however, affect these numbers in ways that have nothing to do with signals of future inflation.

Second, as equation (8.2) makes clear, the precision with which targeting the money stock will bring us close to the ultimate inflation target depends on the precision with which output growth and velocity growth can be forecast. Major problems have arisen with forecasting velocity growth. This is due to the fast speed of financial innovation, which has led to unpredictable behaviour of velocity.[9] It is likely that this will go on in the future. The introduction of the euro by itself constitutes a major financial innovation.

The result of all this is that most central banks that attempted to apply money supply targeting have been quite unsuccessful, and have missed their announced targets often, and by wide margins. It also means that the money stock numbers give too many wrong signals about the future course of inflation to be useful as an intermediate target. Whether one calls the money stock the 'reference value' (as the ECB does) or an intermediate target does not change the essence of this criticism. M3 will be pretty much useless as a reference value much of the time.

The ECB seems to have understood this criticism. In the first half of 1999 the growth rate of M3 has consistently been above its reference value of 4.5% and yet the ECB did not act on this signal. It must have judged that M3 was giving wrong signals.

One can understand that the ECB, concerned as it was with building up its reputation, decided to copy the Bundesbank behaviour as closely as possible. This included copying the Bundesbank in its (unsuccessful) attempt of monetary targeting. It is likely that, once the ECB has grown up, it will decide to drop this relic of the past. This means that it will use the money stock as one of the many indicators of future inflation without giving it the privileged position it has now.

5.4 Inflation targeting: a model for the ECB?

Recently, several central banks in the industrialized world (Bank of Canada, Bank of England, Bank of Sweden) have shifted towards inflation targeting. The academic enthusiasm for this strategy has been quite strong.[10]

By inflation targeting is meant here a strategy whereby the central bank not only chooses inflation as its ultimate target, but also uses its inflation forecasts as the intermediate target. It will then typically also announce this inflation forecast. Thus,

---

[9] There is a large literature on the question of whether the European money demand equation is more predictable than the national money demand equations (see Monticelli and Papi (1996)). The evidence indicates that in the past the European money demand was more stable than the national money demand functions. It has been stressed by Arnold and de Vries (1997) that this is due to the fact that the uncorrelated error terms of the national money demand functions tend to offset each other in the aggregation process towards a European money demand function.

[10] For an evalution, see Bernanke *et al.* (1999)

inflation targeting is similar to money stock targeting. Both strategies have as their ultimate target the rate of inflation. Their choice of the intermediate target, however, is different. In the money stock targeting the money stock is used as an intermediate target, in the inflation targeting it is the current forecast of inflation that plays the role of intermediate target. We represent this in Table 8.1. (We assume that in both cases the central bank uses the interest rate as its instrument. See the next section on the use of instruments.)

It has been claimed by the proponents of inflation targeting that this is superior to money stock targeting (see Svensson (1998)). The reason is that in the inflation targeting strategy the central bank uses information of all the variables (including the money stock) that will affect future inflation. The forecast inflation is then the best possible intermediate target. This contrasts with money stock targeting that omits a lot of information and, in addition, uses irrelevant information also (because as we argued earlier, the money stock today can change for reasons that have nothing to do with inflation).

If the current experiments with inflation targeting in a number of central banks turn out to be successful, it is likely that an increasing number of central banks will want to use it, including the ECB.

Table 8.1 Money and inflation targeting compared

	Instrument		Intermediate target		Ultimate target
MS-targeting	interest rate	⇨	money stock	⇨	inflation
Inflation targeting	interest rate	⇨	inflation forecast	⇨	inflation

6 The instruments of monetary policy in Euroland

In the previous sections we discussed the choice of the ultimate and the intermediate targets of the ECB. In this section, we analyse the instruments that the ECB uses to steer the economy towards these targets.

The ECB uses three types of instruments: open market operations, standing facilities (credit lines), and minimum reserve requirements.

6.1 Open market operations

Open market operations are the most important instrument of the monetary policy of the ECB. They imply buying and selling of securities with the aim of increasing or reducing money market liquidity. Open market operations can be performed in many ways. The ECB can do outright buying and selling operations of securities in the 'open market'. These are open market operations in the traditional sense. The main technique the ECB is using, however, is not these outright transactions but reverse transactions using tenders. The ECB calls these its *main refinancing operations*. Let us describe this technique because it also illustrates the role the interest rate plays as an instrument of monetary policy.

The first crucial decision the Governing Council makes is to set the interest rate that will be applied on the main refinancing operations. (From January to April 1999 this was 3%. In April 1999 this rate was lowered to 2.5%. In November 1999 it was raised again to 3%.) The ECB then announces a tender procedure. This can be a fixed rate or a variable rate tender. The interest rate chosen by the Governing Council applies to fixed rate tender procedures. In the latter procedure, private financial institutions are invited to make a bid to obtain a certain amount of liquidity in exchange for delivering collateral. These bids are collected by the NCBs and centralized by the ECB. The ECB decides about the total amount to be allotted, and distributes this to the bidding parties pro rata of the size of the bids. We illustrate this by a numerical example in Table 8.2. The Bid column presents the amounts each bank is bidding. The total amount of the bids is 250 million euros. We assume that the amount the ECB decides to allot is 150 million euros. This is 60% of the total bids. The ECB then applies this 60% to all the individual bids to obtain the individual allotments (last column). In practice this allotment ratio turns out to be very low. During 1999 it was often less than 10%, mainly because banks overbid to obtain the desired amount of liquidity. Note that although the

Table 8.2 Hypothetical example of bids and allotments in a fixed rate tender (million euros)

	Bid	Allotment
Bank 1	30	18
Bank 2	40	24
Bank 3	50	36
Bank 4	60	30
Bank 5	70	42
Total	250	150

Source: EMI, *The Single Monetary Policy in Stage Three*, 1997.

NCBs announce and collect the bids in their own markets, the bids are centralized by the ECB which then determines the individual allotments based on the formula just described.

The ECB can also use variable rate tenders. This implies that banks bid the amounts of liquidity they want to buy at successive interest rates. In that case the interest rate used in the fixed rate tenders will act as a floor, i.e. the ECB will not normally provide liquidity through variable rate tenders at conditions more favourable than through fixed rate tenders. Variable rate tenders add flexibility to the provision of liquidity. Banks in need of liquidity may obtain extra liquidity, at a higher price than through standard fixed rate tenders. In Table 8.3 we provide an example of a variable rate tender.

Suppose the ECB decides to allot 80 million euros, then all bids of 3.05% and more are satisfied. The ECB can use two bidding procedures. In the Dutch auction procedure the interest rate of 3.05% is applied to all the allotments. In the American auction procedure each bidder pays a different interest rate for his successive bids, e.g. Bank 1 receives 5 million euros at 3.06% and 5 million euros at 3.05%.

As indicated earlier, open market operations are the main tools for the ECB to affect monetary conditions. By increasing or reducing the interest rate on its main financing operations it affects the market interest rates. In addition, by changing the size of the allotments it affects the amount of liquidity directly.

6.2 Standing facilities

These facilities aim to provide and absorb overnight liquidity. Banks can use the *marginal lending facility* to obtain overnight liquidity from the NCBs. The Governing Council fixes the marginal lending rate (3.5% in July 1999). Banks can borrow from

Table 8.3 Hypothetical example of variable rate tender (million euros)

Interest rate (%)	Bank 1	Bank 2	Bank 3	Total bids	Cumulative bids
3.10				0	0
3.09		5	5	10	10
3.08		5	5	10	20
3.07		5	5	10	30
3.06	5	5	10	20	50
3.05	5	10	15	30	80
3.04	10	10	15	35	115
3.03	5	5	5	15	130
3.02	5		10	15	145
Total	30	45	70	145	

Source: EMI, *The Single Monetary Policy in Stage Three*, 1997.

this facility without limit provided they present adequate collateral. The marginal lending rate acts as a ceiling for the overnight market interest rate.

Similarly, banks can use the *deposit facility* to make overnight deposits. The Governing Council fixes the interest rate on the deposit facility (1.5% in July 1999). This interest rate acts as a floor for the overnight market interest rate.

These two facilities are administered by the NCBs in a decentralized manner. By changing the interest rate on these two facilities the Governing Council affects the short-end of the interest rate structure.

6.3 Minimum reserves

The third instrument of the monetary policy of the ECB is the imposition of minimum reserves for banks. By manipulating reserve requirements the ECB can affect money market conditions. For example, an increase in the reserve requirements increases the shortage of liquidity, and tends to reduce the money stock.

The use of reserve requirements was very much promoted by the Bundesbank but strongly resisted by commercial banks which felt that this would give them a competitive disadvantage with respect to foreign (e.g. British) banks, not subject to reserve requirements. In order to alleviate this problem it was decided that the ECB would remunerate these minimum reserves.

It is unclear that the use of reserve requirements increases the effectiveness of monetary policy. It is, therefore, possible that in the future the ECB will want to reduce or even abandon its use.

6.4 Conclusion

We conclude that the ECB, like any modern central bank, has quite a large range of instruments at its disposal. In addition, it has been careful to allow some division of labour with the NCBs, without jeopardizing the unity of the Euroland's monetary policy. Some doubt, however, can be expressed whether the present division of labour can be maintained. It is likely that as money markets in Euroland integrate further, the actual interventions in the money markets will increasingly be centralized. One scenario in this centralization process is that one national central bank emerges as the most important one so that most of the money market interventions will be executed by this particular NCB. This is also the scenario that has emerged in the US Federal Reserve System during the twentieth century: the New York Federal Reserve has become the regional bank through which most of the open market operations are executed.

Chapter 9
Fiscal Policies in Monetary Unions

Introduction

THE traditional theory of optimum currency areas, which was discussed in Chapter 1, offers interesting insights about the conduct of national fiscal policies in a monetary union. In this chapter we start out by developing these ideas. We then challenge this theory by introducing issues of credibility and sustainability of fiscal policies.

The analysis of this chapter will allow us to answer questions such as:

- What is the role of fiscal policy in a monetary union?
- How independent can national fiscal policies be?
- Does a monetary union increase or reduce fiscal discipline? What rules, if any, should be used to restrict national fiscal policies? This will lead us into an analysis of the 'stability pact'.

1 Fiscal policies and the theory of optimum currency areas

IN order to analyse what the theory of optimum currency areas has to say about the conduct of fiscal policies, it is useful to start from the example of an asymmetric demand shock as developed in Chapter 1. Suppose again that European consumers shift their demand in favour of German products at the expense of French products.

We reproduce Figure 1.1 from Chapter 1 here (Fig. 9.1). What are the fiscal policy implications of this disturbance?

Suppose first that France and Germany, being members of the same monetary union, have also centralized a substantial part of their national budgets to the central European authority. In particular, let us assume that the social security system is organized at the European level, and that income taxes are also levied by the European government.

It can now be seen that the centralized budget will work as a shock absorber. In France output declines and unemployment tends to increase. This has a double effect on the European budget. The income taxes collected by the European government in France decline, whereas unemployment benefit payments by the European authorities increase. Exactly the opposite occurs in Germany. There, output increases and unemployment declines. As a result, tax revenues collected by the European government in Germany increase, while European government spending in Germany declines. Thus, the centralized European budget automatically redistributes income from Germany to France, thereby softening the social consequences of the demand shift for France.

Consider now what would happen if France and Germany form a monetary union without centralizing their government budgets. It can easily be demonstrated that the negative demand shock in France will lead to an increase in the French government budget deficit, because tax receipts decline while unemployment benefit payments by the French government increase. The French government will have to increase its borrowing. In Germany we have the reverse. The German government budget experiences increasing surpluses (or declining deficits). If capital markets work efficiently, the need for the French government to borrow can easily be accommodated by the increasing supply of savings coming from Germany.

In this case of decentralized budgets, France increases its external debt, which will

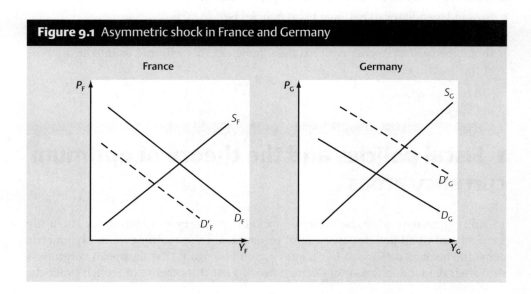

Figure 9.1 Asymmetric shock in France and Germany

have to be serviced in the future. This will reduce the degrees of freedom of future French fiscal policies. This contrasts with the case where the national budgets are centralized: in such a system, France will not have to face such external debt problems, as German residents automatically transfer income to France. They will not necessarily be repaid for their generosity.

It should also be stressed that the size of these budgetary effects very much depends on the degree of wage and price flexibility and/or labour mobility. If these are large, the automatic transfer from Germany (or, in the second case, the French budget deficit) will be low. If, for example, labour mobility between France and Germany is high, there will be little unemployment in France, so that unemployment benefit payments are correspondingly low.

The theory of optimum currency areas leads to the following implications for fiscal policies in monetary unions (see Kenen (1969)). First, it is desirable to centralize a significant part of the national budgets to the European level. A centralized budget allows countries (and regions) that are hit by negative shocks to enjoy automatic transfers, thereby reducing the social costs of a monetary union. This was also a major conclusion of the influential MacDougall Report, published in 1977. The drafters of that report argued that monetary union in Europe would have to be accompanied by a significant centralization of budgetary power in Europe (more precisely a centralization of the unemployment benefit systems). Failure to do so would impose great social strains and endanger monetary union. (In Box 15 we ask the question of how much centralization of national budgets is desirable.)

Secondly, if such a centralization of the national government budgets in a monetary union is not possible (as appears to be the case in the context of European monetary union), national fiscal policies should be used in a flexible way. That is, when countries are hit by negative shocks, they should be allowed to let the budget deficit increase through the built-in (or automatic) budgetary stabilizers (declining government revenues, increasing social outlays).

This requirement that fiscal policies respond flexibly to negative shocks also implies that a substantial autonomy should be reserved for these national fiscal policies. In the logic of the optimum currency area theory, countries lose an instrument of policy (the exchange rate) when they join the union. If there is no centralized budget which automatically redistributes income, countries have no instrument at their disposal to absorb the effects of these negative shocks.[1] The fiscal policy instrument is the only one left.

This theory about how fiscal policies should be conducted in a monetary union has been heavily criticized. This criticism is not directed at the first conclusion, i.e. that it is desirable to centralize a significant part of the national budgets in a monetary union. The criticism has been formulated against the second conclusion, which calls for flexibility and autonomy of national government budgets in monetary unions, when the degree of budgetary centralization is limited. To this criticism we now turn.

---

[1] We assume here that wages are inflexible and that labour mobility is non-existent.

2 Sustainability of government budget deficits

THE major problem with the previous analysis is the underlying assumption that governments can create budget deficits to absorb negative shocks without leading to problems of sustainability of these deficits. As many Western European countries have experienced during the 1980s and the 1990s, however, government budget deficits can lead to such problems.

The sustainability problem can be formulated as follows. A budget deficit leads to an increase in government debt which will have to be serviced in the future. If the interest rate on the government debt exceeds the growth rate of the economy, a debt dynamic is set in motion which leads to an ever-increasing government debt relative to GDP. This becomes unsustainable, requiring corrective action.

This debt dynamics problem can be analysed more formally starting from the definition of the government budget constraint (see Box 14 for more explanation):

$$G - T + rB = dB/dt + dM/dt \qquad (9.1)$$

where G is the level of government spending (excluding interest payments on the government debt), T is the tax revenue, r is the interest rate on the government debt, B, and M is the level of high-powered money (monetary base).

The left-hand side of equation (9.1) is the government budget deficit. It consists of the primary budget deficit $(G - T)$ and the interest payment on the government debt (rB). The right-hand side is the financing side. The budget deficit can be financed by issuing debt (dB/dt) or by issuing high-powered money dM/dt. (In the following we represent the changes per unit of time by putting a dot above a variable, thus $dB/dt = \dot{B}$ and $dM/dt = \dot{M}$.)

As is shown in Box 14, the government budget constraint (9.1) can be rewritten as

$$\dot{b} = (g - t) + (r - x)\, b - \dot{m} \qquad (9.2)$$

where $g = G/Y$, $t = T/Y$, $x = \dot{Y}/Y$ (the growth rate of GDP), and $\dot{m} = \dot{M}/Y$.

Equation (9.2) can be interpreted as follows. When the interest rate on government debt exceeds the growth rate of GDP, the debt-to-GDP ratio will increase without bounds. The dynamics of debt accumulation can only be stopped if the primary budget deficit (as a percentage of GDP) turns into a surplus $((g - t)$ then becomes negative). Alternatively, the debt accumulation can be stopped by a sufficiently large revenue from money creation. The latter is also called seigniorage. It is clear, however, that the systematic use of this source of finance will lead to inflation.

The nature of the government budget constraint can also be made clear as follows: one can ask the question under what condition the debt-to-GDP ratio will stabilize at a constant value. Equation (9.2) gives the answer. Set $\dot{b}$ = zero. This yields

$$(r - x)\, b = (t - g) + \dot{m}. \qquad (9.3)$$

Thus, if the interest rate exceeds the growth rate of the economy, it is necessary that either the primary budget shows a sufficiently high surplus ($t > g$) or that money creation is sufficiently high in order to stabilize the debt–GDP ratio. The latter option has been chosen by many Latin American countries during the 1980s, and more recently by some Eastern European countries. It has also led to hyperinflation in these countries.

The important message here is that, if a country has accumulated sizeable deficits in the past, it will now have to run correspondingly large primary budget surpluses in order to prevent the debt–GDP ratio from increasing automatically. This means that the country will have to reduce spending and/or increase taxes.

It may be interesting here to present a few case-studies of the experience of European countries during 1980–97. We select Belgium, The Netherlands, and Italy. We present data on government budget deficits of these countries during 1979–97 (see Fig. 9.2).

It can be seen that these countries allowed their budget deficits to increase signifi-cantly during the early part of the 1980s. This increase in government budget deficits came mainly as a response to the negative consequences of major recessions in these countries. The rest of the period was characterized by strenuous attempts to contain the explosive debt situation that followed from these earlier policies. We show the evolution of the debt-to-GDP ratios in these countries during 1980–97 in Fig. 9.3. At the end of the 1980s after many years of budgetary restrictions, Belgium and the Netherlands had succeeded in stabilizing the debt-to-GDP ratio. They were able to do so by running substantial surpluses in the primary budget. These are shown in Fig. 9.4. The level at which Belgium achieved this stabilization of the debt-to-GDP ratio, however, was very high. As a result, when the next recession hit the country in 1992–3

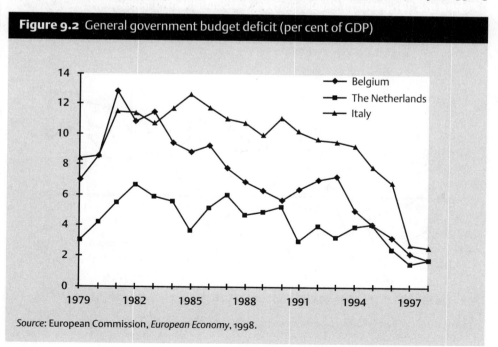

Figure 9.2 General government budget deficit (per cent of GDP)

Source: European Commission, *European Economy*, 1998.

Figure 9.3 Gross public debt (per cent of GDP)

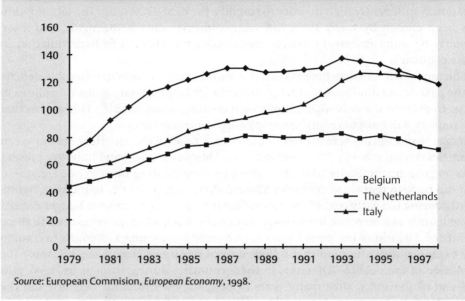

Source: European Commision, *European Economy*, 1998.

Figure 9.4 Government budget surplus, excluding interest payments (per cent of GDP)

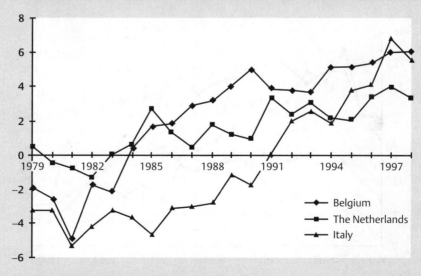

Source: European Commission, *European Economy*, 1998.

it was quite difficult to use fiscal policies in a countercyclical way. On the contrary, Belgium was forced to clamp down on government spending and to increase taxes, thereby exacerbating the recession, without preventing the debt–GDP ratio from increasing again during 1992–3.

Italy did not succeed in stabilizing its debt–GDP ratio during the 1980s because it failed to create the required primary budget surpluses. Only from 1992 on did it manage to produce primary budget surpluses that led to a stabilization of the debt–GDP ratio in 1994–5. Note that this prevented the Italian government from using budgetary policies in a countercyclical way.

These examples vividly demonstrate the limits to the use of fiscal policies to offset negative economic shocks. Such policies cannot be maintained for very long. The experience of these countries shows that large government budget deficits quickly lead to an unsustainable debt dynamics from which countries find it difficult to extricate themselves. The 'success' of Belgium in stabilizing the debt–GDP ratio by running primary budget surpluses during the second half of the 1980s came about after many years of spending cuts and tax increases.

The previous discussion also makes clear that fiscal policies are not the flexible instrument that the optimum currency theory has made us believe. The systematic use of this instrument quickly leads to problems of sustainability, which forces countries to run budget surpluses for a number of years. Put differently, when used once, it will not be possible to use these fiscal policies again until many years later.

This analysis of the sustainability of fiscal policies has led to a completely different view of the desirable fiscal policies of member states in a monetary union. This view found its reflection in the Maastricht Treaty, which defines budgetary rules countries have to satisfy in order to enter EMU (the 3% deficit and the 60% debt norms).[2] It also found expression in the so-called 'stability pact' that the EU heads of state, at the insistence of Germany, agreed would have to be implemented after the start of EMU. This stability pact is quite important as it is likely to guide national fiscal policies in the future EMU. Its main principles are the following. First, countries will have to aim at achieving balanced budgets. Second, countries with a budget deficit exceeding 3% of GDP will be subject to fines. These fines can reach up to 0.5% of GDP. Third, these fines will not be applied if the countries in question experience exceptional circumstances, i.e. a natural disaster or a decline of their GDP of more than 2% during one year. In cases where the drop in GDP is between 0.75 and 2% the application of the fine will be subject to the approval of the EU finance ministers. Countries that experience a drop in their GDP of less than 0.75% have agreed not to invoke exceptional circumstances. The presumption is that in that case they will have to pay a fine, although even in that case the imposition of the fine will require a decision of the Council.[3]

---

[2] The drafters of the Maastricht Treaty were very much influenced by the Delors Report, which was the first to express the need for strict rules on budgetary policies.

[3] The original proposals of the German minister of finance implied the automatic application of fines. This, however, would have been in contradiction to the Maastricht Treaty, which stipulates that fines can only be imposed with a majority of two-thirds of the weighted votes in the Council. This implies that the implementation of the fines foreseen in the stability pact will in any case need a two-thirds majority independent of the question whether or not the excessive deficit came about because of a drop in GDP, and whatever the size of that drop.

Box 14 Debts and deficits

In this box we derive the relation between debts and deficits. Let us start from the government budget constraint:

$$G - T + rB = dB/dt + dM/dt \qquad (B14.1)$$

where G is the level of government spending (excluding interest payments on the government debt), T is the tax revenue, r is the interest rate on the government debt, B, and M is the level of high-powered money (monetary base).

The left-hand side of the equation (B14.1) is the government budget deficit. It consists of the primary budget deficit ($G - T$) and the interest payment on the government debt (rB). The right-hand side is the financing side. The budget deficit can be financed by issuing debt (dB/dt) or by issuing high-powered money dM/dt. We will assume, however, that the monetary financing constitutes such a small part of the financing of the government budget deficit in the European countries that it can safely be disregarded (in this connection see Table 1.2 in Chapter 1 showing how small the monetary financing has become in the EU-countries). In the following we represent the changes per unit of time by putting a dot above a variable, thus $dB/dt = \dot{B}$.

It is convenient to express variables as ratios to GDP. Let us therefore define

$$b = B/Y \qquad (B14.2)$$

where Y is GDP, so that b is the debt to GDP ratio.

This allows us to write

$$\dot{b} = \dot{B}/Y - B\dot{Y}/Y^2 \qquad (B14.3)$$

or using (B14.2) and manipulating

$$\dot{B} = \dot{b}Y + b\dot{Y} \qquad (B14.4)$$

Substituting (B14.4) into (B14.1) yields

$$\dot{b} = (g - t) + (r - x)b \qquad (B14.5)$$

where $g = G/Y$, $t = T/Y$, $x = \dot{Y}/Y$ (the growth rate of GDP).

This equation defines the dynamics of debt. It says that in a world where the nominal interest rate, r, exceeds the nominal growth of the economy, x, then the government must make sure that the primary budget ($g - t$) has a surplus. If not, the debt–GDP ratio will increase without bound. This must surely lead to a default on the government debt. We can therefore impose a necessary condition for solvency, i.e.

$$\dot{b} = 0$$

or $(r - x)\, b = t - g$.

The Maastricht Treaty and the stability pact take the view that fiscal policies in a monetary union should be subjected to rules. Let us evaluate the arguments for rules on government budget deficits in a monetary union.

3 The argument for rules on government budget deficits

THE basic insight of this view is that a country that finds itself on an unsustainable path of increasing government debt creates negative spillover effects for the rest of the monetary union. A country that allows its debt–GDP ratio to increase continuously will have increasing recourse to the capital markets of the union, thereby driving the union interest rate upwards. This increase in the union interest rate in turn increases the burden of the government debts of the other countries. If the governments of these countries choose to stabilize their debt–GDP ratios, they will be forced to follow more restrictive fiscal policies. Thus, the unsustainable increase in the debt of one country forces the other countries to follow more deflationary policies. It will therefore be in the interest of these other countries that a control mechanism should exist restricting the size of budget deficits in the member countries.

There is a second spillover that may appear here. The upward movement of the union interest rate, following the unsustainable fiscal policies of one member country, is likely to put pressure on the ECB. Countries that are hurt by the higher union interest rate may pressure the ECB to relax its monetary policy stance. Thus, unsustainable fiscal policies will interfere with the conduct of the European monetary policy. Again it may be in the interest of the members of the union to prevent such a negative spillover from occurring by imposing limits on the size of government budget deficits.

These arguments based on the spillover effects of fiscal policies appear reasonable. They have, however, been subjected to serious criticism.[4] The criticism has been twofold. One is theoretical and concerns the role of capital markets. The second has to do with the enforceability of such rules.

(a) *The efficiency of private capital markets.* Implicit in the spillover argument, there is an assumption that capital markets do not work properly. Let us now suppose that capital markets work efficiently, and ask the question what will happen when one country, say Italy, is on an unsustainable debt path. Does it mean that the union interest rate will increase, i.e. that the interest rate to be paid by German, Dutch, or French borrowers will equally increase? The answer is negative. If capital markets in the monetary union work efficiently, it will be recognized that the debt problem is an Italian problem. The market will attach a risk premium to Italian government debt.

---

[4] See e.g. Buiter and Kletzer (1990), van der Ploeg (1990), von Hagen (1990), and Wyplosz (1991).

The German government, however, will not be affected by this. It will be able to borrow at a lower interest rate, because the lenders recognize that the risk inherent in German government bonds is lower than the risk involved in buying Italian government debt instruments. Thus, if the capital markets work efficiently, there will be no spillover. Other governments in the union will not suffer from the existence of a high Italian government debt. In addition, it does not make sense to talk about *the* union interest rate. If capital markets are efficient there will be different interest rates in the union, reflecting different risk premia on the government debt of the union members.

This is certainly a powerful argument. There is, however, a possibility that lenders will find it difficult to attach the correct risk premium to the Italian government debt. Let us analyse under what conditions this may happen. Suppose the lenders believe that in case of a serious debt crisis, i.e. an inability of the Italian government to service its debt, the other countries will step in to 'bail out' the Italian government. These countries may have an interest in doing so, because an Italian debt crisis may spill over to the rest of the financial system. For example, financial institutions in other countries may hold Italian government paper. A default by Italy may lead to defaults of these financial institutions, and may create a general debt crisis. To avoid this, the governments of other countries may decide to step in and buy up the Italian government paper. The realization that such an implicit 'bailout' guarantee exists will lower the risk premium on Italian government paper. Thus, the capital market fails to attach the correct price to risky Italian debt instruments.

One way to solve this problem consists in a solemn declaration of the members of the union that they will never bail out other member countries' governments. Such a 'no-bailout' clause was in fact introduced in the Maastricht Treaty. Although such a clause may help to resolve the problem, it is unlikely completely to eliminate it because it may not be fully credible. When an Italian debt crisis occurs, it will be in the interest of the other member countries to bail out the Italian government for the reasons given earlier. Thus, even if they have previously declared their intention not to intervene, they may very well decide to make an exception this time. The realization that this may happen in the future will hamper private lenders in correctly pricing the risk of Italian government debt.

(b) *The enforcement of fiscal policy rules*. A second problem with rules on the size of government budget deficits and debts has to do with the enforceability of these rules. Experience with such rules is that it is very difficult to enforce them. An example of such difficulties is the Gramm–Rudman legislation in the USA. In 1986 the US Congress approved a bill that set out explicit targets for the US Federal budget deficit. If these targets were not met, spending would automatically be cut across the board by a given percentage so as to meet the target. It can now be said that this approach with rules was not very successful. The US executive branch found all kinds of ways of circumventing this legislation. For example, some spending items were put 'off the budget'.

There is also evidence collected by von Hagen (1991) for the American states pointing in the same direction. Von Hagen found that those states that had constitutional limits on their budget deficits or on the level of their debt had frequent recourse to the technique of 'off-budgeting'. As a result, he found that the existence of constitutional rules had very little impact on the size of the states' budget deficits.

To sum up, one can say that some rules on the conduct of fiscal policies by the EMU members are necessary. Given the interdependence in the risk of bonds issued by different governments, financial markets may find it difficult to price these risks correctly. As a result, some form of mutual control is necessary. The question arises, however, whether the stability pact may not have gone too far in stressing rigid rules on the conduct of fiscal policies.

Before coming to a final verdict, it is important to analyse two issues. First, we study the extent to which monetary unions impose additional discipline on national budgetary authorities. If so, the need for additional rules is weakened. Second, we analyse the risk of defaults and bailouts in monetary unions. This risk is often considered to provide the major rationale for additional rules on fiscal policies in a monetary union.

4 Fiscal discipline in monetary unions

A N important issue relating to the need for rules on fiscal policies has to do with the way a monetary union affects the fiscal discipline of national governments in such a union. Proponents of rules have generally argued that a monetary union is likely to reduce the fiscal discipline of national governments. Adversaries of rules have argued the opposite.

In order to see clearly the different, and opposing, arguments it is useful to ask the question of how a monetary union may change the incentives of fiscal policy-makers, and, in so doing, may affect budgetary discipline.

The issue of whether a monetary union increases or reduces the degree of fiscal discipline of countries joining the union has been hotly debated in the literature.[5] Broadly speaking there are two factors that are important here and that can lead to a change in the incentives of countries in regard to the size of their budget deficits when they join the union. The first one leads to less discipline, the second to more discipline.

The phenomenon that leads to incentives for larger budget deficits can be phrased as follows. When a sovereign country issues debt denominated in the domestic currency, the interest rate it will have to pay reflects a risk premium consisting of two components, the risk of default and the risk that the country will devalue its currency in the future. The latter can be completely eliminated by issuing debt in foreign currency. The risk premium then reflects the pure default risk (sometimes also called credit risk). This also happens when a country joins a monetary union: the govern-

---

[5] For a survey see Wyplosz (1991).

ments of the member states have to issue debt in what is equivalent to a 'foreign' currency. As a result, the risk premium (if any) will reflect the probability that the issuing government may not fully service its debt in the future.

As was indicated earlier, however, the lenders may have difficulties in correctly estimating this default risk because of an implicit bailout guarantee that other members of the union extend. The possibility of a bailout then gives an incentive to member states to issue unsustainable amounts of debt. This is a moral hazard problem. A no-bailout provision may not solve this problem because it is not likely to be credible. Even if the European authorities were solemnly to declare never to bail out member states, it is uncertain whether they would stick to this rule if a member country faced the prospect of being unable to service its debt. Thus, the monetary union leads to excessive budget deficits of the member states.

There is a second factor, however, which tends to reduce the incentive of member states of a monetary union to run excessive deficits. Countries which join the union reduce their ability to finance budget deficits by money creation. As a result, the governments of member states of a monetary union face a 'harder' budget constraint than sovereign nations. The latter are confronted with 'softer' budget constraints and therefore have a stronger incentive to run deficits.[6]

Which one of the two effects—the moral hazard or the no-monetization one—prevails is essentially an empirical question in that it depends on institutional features and on the incentives governments face. It is, therefore, useful to analyse the experience of member states in existing monetary unions and to compare this with the experience of sovereign nations. This is done in Table 9.1, where the average budget deficits of member states of existing monetary unions are presented together with the average of the budget deficits of the EC countries.

The most striking feature of Table 9.1 is the fact that the *average* budgetary deficit

Table 9.1 Budget deficits of member states of unions and of EC member countries (as a per cent of revenues)

	Weighted mean	Unweighted mean
USA (1985)	+10.9	+4.6
Australia (1986–7)	−10.1	−9.1
West Germany (1987)	−6.4	−8.2
Canada (1982)	−0.4	−1.4
Switzerland (1986)	−1.3	−0.7
European Community (1988)	−10.1	−11.4

Note: A positive sign is a surplus, a negative sign a deficit. The weighted mean is obtained by weighting the deficits with the share of the member state in the union's GDP.
Source: Lamfalussy (1989: 102–24).

---

[6] For a formalization of the incentives of governments in multi-party systems, see Alesina and Tabellini (1987) and Persson and Svensson (1989). A classic analysis is Buchanan and Tullock (1962).

of the member states in monetary unions tend to be lower than the average deficit of independent countries in the EC.[7] This suggests that on average the existence of a union adds constraints to the size of the budget deficits of the member states. Thus, it appears that the no-monetization constraint is a powerful disincentive to running large budget deficits. It therefore seems that governments of member states of a monetary union face a 'harder' budget constraint than sovereign nations. The latter are confronted with 'softer' budget constraints and therefore have a stronger incentive to run deficits.

It should also be noted that, except in the case of Germany, in none of the monetary unions analysed in Table 9.1 does the federal authority impose restrictions on the budget deficits of the member states. In the Federal Republic the federal government can limit the borrowing requirements of the Länder with the consent of their representatives in the Bundesrat. This provision, however, has been invoked only twice (in 1971 and 1973).[8]

Whereas federally imposed limits are rare, one frequently finds *self-imposed* constitutional limits on state and *Länder* budget deficits. In fact, in the USA the majority of the states have introduced such constitutional limitations. One possible interpretation for the frequency of self-imposed limits is that they may help to improve the reputation and the creditworthiness of the states in the capital markets, and therefore reduce the cost of borrowing.[9]

The evidence of Table 9.1 is of course not conclusive. More research should be carried out to find out whether the difference observed between the average deficits of member states of monetary unions and the average deficits of sovereign nations can be generalized to different time-periods and a larger sample of countries. At the very least, the results of Table 9.1 suggest that the idea that in monetary unions member states have a strong incentive to create excessive levels of government debt is not corroborated by the facts of the 1980s.

Additional indirect evidence for the hypothesis that the size of deficits depends on the 'softness' of the budget constraint is provided by Moesen and Van Rompuy (1990). They classify industrial countries according to the degree of centralization of total government spending. The hypothesis tested is that more centralized governments face a softer budget constraint than decentralized governments. This is so because in centralized countries a larger part of total government spending can potentially be financed by the issue of money. In decentralized countries, however, a larger part of government spending occurs through lower-level authorities who lack the access to monetary financing. Moesen and Van Rompuy find evidence for this hypothesis: during the period 1973–86 the total government deficits in centralized countries increased faster than in decentralized ones. Put differently, during a period when government budgets were negatively affected by supply shocks and economic recession, the countries with more decentralized governments faced a stronger

---

[7] This is also confirmed by Van Rompuy *et al.* (1991).

[8] Van Rompuy *et al.* (1991: 19).

[9] As discussed earlier, von Hagen (1990) has argued that these constitutional limits on the budget deficits have been relatively ineffective. This would then suggest that, if perceived as ineffective in the capital markets, these constitutional restrictions should have a low effect on the risk premium.

pressure to reduce spending and/or increase taxes than countries with more centralization of government functions.[10]

5 Risks of default and bailout in a monetary union

THE discussion of the previous section allows us to shed some new light on the issue
of whether a debt default becomes more likely in EMU, so that the risk of having
to organize a costly bailout also increases.

From our previous discussion one might conclude that since the member states of
the EMU will not behave in a less disciplined way than they did before joining EMU,
the risk of default should not increase in EMU.

There are other considerations, however, that one should add here to arrive at a
correct appreciation of the risk of default in EMU. One has been stressed by McKinnon
(1996), the other by Eichengreen and von Hagen (1995).

Sovereign nations can default on their debt in two ways. One is an outright default
(e.g. stopping payment of interest on the outstanding debt). The other is an implicit
default by creating surprise inflation and devaluation, which reduces the real value of
the debt. Sovereign nations who control their own national banks can always resort
to surprise inflation and devaluation to reduce the burden of their debt. They often do
this to avoid outright default.

As soon as a country joins a monetary union it loses control over the central bank,
and therefore cannot create surprise inflation to reduce the burden of its debt any
more. As a result, pressure on the government to organize an outright default may
actually increase in a monetary union. McKinnon (1996) argued that this would happen in EMU. The level of the debt of certain EU-countries is so high that in the absence
of implicit defaults by inflation and devaluation, the probability that outright default
will occur increases.

Differences in interest rates allow us to obtain an idea about the nature of the risks
involved. In Table 9.2 we present interest spreads for long-term bonds between a
number of EU-countries and Germany both before and after the start of EMU. The first
column presents the total spread in 1996. For example, the spread between a ten-year
lira bond issued by the Italian government and a ten-year DM bond issued by the
German government amounted to 444 basis points (4.44%) in March 1996. This differential can be interpreted as a premium the Italian government had to pay for the risk
that the lira may be devalued (implicit default) plus the risk of an outright default (the
credit risk). One can disentangle this risk premium as follows. We compute the interest differential on ten-year bonds issued by the Italian and German governments *in the*

---

[10] Roubini and Sachs (1989) have identified other institutional features that have led to different trends in
budget deficits, i.e. the degree of political cohesion of the governments in power.

Table 9.2 Interest differentials with Germany (ten-year bonds), in basis points (March 1996 and August 1999)

	March 1996		August 1999
	in national currencies	in common currency (DM)	in euros
Guilder	4	5	15
French franc	37	21	11
Belgian franc	50	27	30
Peseta	347	30	26
Lira	444	81	29

Source: J. P. Morgan, Mar. 1996 and *Handelsblatt*, Aug. 1999.

same currency (the DM). This is given in the second column. This differential can be interpreted as the premium for the risk of outright default (credit risk). The difference between the first two columns expresses the devaluation risk (risk of implicit default). The third column shows the spread after the start of EMU. There is no devaluation risk involved after that date since the bonds are expressed in the same currency, the euro. We have a pure estimate of the risk of default (the credit risk).

We observe the following interesting phenomena. The premia for the risk of outright default was small prior to the start of EMU. It remained small afterwards for the EMU-member. In the case of Italy it declined significantly after the start of EMU. Up to now there is no evidence of an increase in the risk of outright default. This can be seen from the fact that the post-EMU differentials have not increased significantly in relation to the pre-EMU differentials (column 2).

Another interesting phenomenon is the fact that the post-EMU interest differentials are low compared to the differentials observed between the bonds issued (in the same currency, the dollar) by American states. This suggests that the default risk of American state bonds is significantly higher than the default risk on bonds issued by EMU-member states. An explanation for this difference has been proposed by Eichengreen and von Hagen (1995). These authors argue, and provide evidence, that member countries of a monetary union who maintain control over a large domestic tax base face a low default risk compared to members of a monetary union with few fiscal responsibilities. Since the European Monetary Union consists of countries maintaining large domestic taxing powers, the risk of default is likely to be small, compared to the risk faced by, say, the American states or the Canadian provinces which, compared to the EU-countries, have limited taxing powers. Eichengreen and von Hagen conclude from this analysis that the need to impose tight rules on the government budgets of member countries in the EMU has been overemphasized.

Default risks will never be zero, however, so that the risk of having to organize a costly bailout will also never be zero. The question then is whether the risk of bailouts is larger when countries are in the EMU than when they stay outside. Let us suppose that Italy defaults on its debt. Is this more likely to lead to a bailout operation if Italy is in the EMU than if it had been left outside the EMU?

The standard argument for an affirmative answer runs as follows. In a monetary union, financial integration increases. As a result, bonds issued by the different national authorities will be more widely distributed across different member countries. Therefore, when one government defaults on its debt this will affect more individuals and financial institutions outside the defaulting country than if the country had not been in the union. The result is that pressure exerted on the other governments to bail out the defaulting government will be stronger when that government is in the union than when it stays outside.

Although it cannot be denied that the strong financial integration of a monetary union provides the potential for a lot of pressure to bail out defaulting governments, this is not the only relevant consideration. There is also the exchange rate issue. When a country, say Italy, is not allowed in the union one can expect that a default will also put a lot of pressure on the other EU-members to bail out the Italian government. This pressure comes from the fact that if Italy is outside the monetary union when it defaults, the lira is likely to collapse in the foreign exchange market, causing industrialists in the rest of the EU to put a lot of pressure on their governments to support the lira. This exchange rate effect is absent if Italy defaults when it is a member of the monetary union. We conclude that if Italy had been kept outside the union this would not necessarily have reduced the risk of a future bailout by EMU-countries. The two effects, the financial integration effect and the exchange rate effect, operate in opposite directions. We simply do not know a priori whether in a monetary union the pressure to bail out a defaulting EU-country will be stronger than when this same EU-country is left outside the EMU.

6 The Stability Pact: an evaluation

NATIONAL fiscal policies in the future EMU must find a balance between two conflicting concerns. The first one has to do with flexibility and is stressed in the theory of optimum currency areas: in the absence of the exchange rate instrument and a centralized European budget, national government budgets are the only available instruments for nation-states to confront asymmetric shocks. Thus, in the future EMU national budgets must continue to play some role of automatic stabilizers when the country is hit by a recession.

A second concern relates to the spillover effects of unsustainable national debts and deficits, which were described in the previous sections. Unsustainable debts and deficits in particular countries may harm other member countries and may exert undue pressure on the ECB.

How does the Stability Pact strike a balance between these two concerns? It is clear that the Stability Pact has been guided more by the fear of unsustainable debts and

Figure 9.5 Increase in budget deficits during 1991–1993

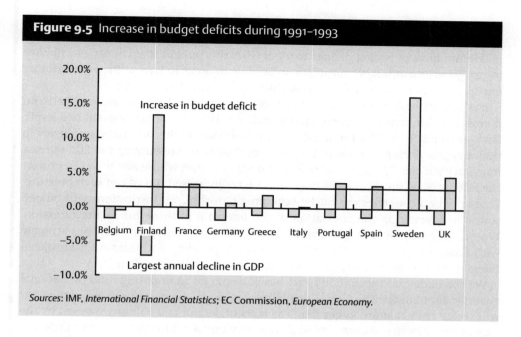

Sources: IMF, *International Financial Statistics*; EC Commission, *European Economy*.

deficits than by the need for flexibility. As a result, it is fair to say that the Stability Pact is quite unbalanced in stressing the need for strict rules at the expense of flexibility. This creates a risk that the capacity of national budgets to function as automatic stabilizers during recessions will be hampered, thereby intensifying recessions. We illustrate the nature of this risk by analysing what happened during the recession of the early 1990s in the EU-countries (see Fig. 9.5). We show the increase of budget deficits in the EU-countries during the recession of the early 1990s.[11] At the same time Fig. 9.5 presents the largest yearly decline in GDP reached during that recession. We observe that six countries (Finland, France, Sweden, Spain, Portugal, and the UK) saw their budget deficit increase by more than 3% during the recession. Some of them (Finland, Sweden, and the UK) would have been able to invoke exceptional circumstances (a decline of GDP by more than 2% for a year) and would have been spared a penalty. The other three countries (France, Portugal, and Spain) would not have been able to invoke these exceptional circumstances, because GDP decline never exceeded 2% a year. These countries therefore would have faced the possibility of being subjected to fines. This could have influenced their behaviour and led them to apply more restrictive fiscal policies during the recession.[12]

From the evidence of Fig. 9.5 it follows that increases in the budget deficit of more than 3% of GDP are not uncommon during recessions. This also happens in countries

---

[11] Note that the timing of the recession is not the same in all countries. In the UK the steepest decline in GDP occurred in 1990, in Sweden and Finland in 1991, and in the other EU-countries in 1993.

[12] Buti and Sapir (1999) come to a different conclusion. They find that the automatic stabilizers in the budgets (the cyclical component in the government budget) are typically smaller than 3% of GDP. According to Buti and Sapir, the Stability Pact allows for enough flexibility in the budgets, provided countries achieve a balanced budget.

that experience recessions involving a decline in their GDP of less than 2% (the benchmark for avoiding fines in the Stability Pact). Since the stability pact sets the maximum limit of budget deficits to 3% of GDP, this implies that countries will have to run government budget surpluses on average in order to have sufficient flexibility during recessions, i.e. in order to avoid hitting the ceiling of 3% of GDP.

The lack of budgetary flexibility to face recessions will create tensions between national governments and European institutions. This tension will exist at two levels. First, as countries will be hindered in their desire to use the automatic stabilizers in their budgets during recessions, they will increase their pressure on the ECB to relax monetary policies. Thus, paradoxically, the Stability Pact whose aim it was to protect the ECB from political pressure may in fact have increased the risk of such pressure. Second, when countries are hit by economic hardship, EU institutions will be perceived as preventing the alleviation of the hardship of those hit by the recession. Worse, they will be seen handing out fines and penalties when countries struggle with economic problems. This will certainly not promote enthusiasm for European integration. On the contrary, it is likely to intensify Euro-scepticism.

We conclude that the Stability Pact has gone too far in imposing rules on national government budgets. The lack of flexibility of national budgetary policies in the EMU will create risks that are larger than the risks of default and bailouts stressed by the proponents of rules. As we argued in the previous sections, there is very little evidence that a monetary union increases fiscal indiscipline and the risks of default and bailouts compared to a situation without a monetary union.

One can of course argue that the Stability Pact will not function, and therefore should not worry us unduly. There is indeed a serious possibility that the implementation of the Stability Pact will be very difficult. We mentioned earlier that in countries where rules on budgetary policies are imposed, all kinds of creative accounting emerge. In addition, any imposition of fines will have to be decided by a majority of two-thirds in the Council (Maastricht Treaty art. 104c–13). Since most recessions are correlated across countries, it is very unlikely that the majority required to impose fines will easily be found. If this is true, the Stability Pact may well become a dead letter.

Our criticism of the Stability Pact should not be misinterpreted. We criticize it because we believe that centrally imposed sanctions and rigid rules are not a good idea. The underlying objective of the Stability Pact, however, is a good one. This is that budget deficits and debt levels should be reduced in many countries. In addition, and quite paradoxically, the reduction of debts and deficits will increase the flexibility and the automatic stabilizing properties of national budgets. When countries like Belgium and Italy have reduced their debts, and when their budgets are in equilibrium on average, an increase in the deficit due to a recession will not easily lead to an unsustainable explosion of government debt. As we have seen, debt explosion has limited the capacity of these nations to use automatic stabilizers during the recent recessions. Thus, restoring fiscal rectitude creates the conditions for using the budget as a tool for absorbing asymmetric shocks and for stabilizing the economy. In that sense fiscal orthodoxy is badly needed to increase the flexibility of a monetary union.

Box 15 How much centralization of government budgets in a monetary union?

The theory of optimum currency areas stresses the desirability of a significant centralization of the national budgets to accommodate for asymmetric shocks in the different regions (countries). What is the limit to such centralization? In order to answer this question it is important to realize that budgetary transfers should be used to cope only with *temporary* shocks, or, when shocks are permanent, these transfers should be used only temporarily. A country or a region that faces a permanent shock (e.g. a permanent decline in the demand for its output) should adjust by wage and price changes or by moving factors of production. The budgetary transfers can be used only temporarily to alleviate these adjustment problems.

The experience with regional budgetary transfers within nations (Italy and Belgium, for example), however, is that it is very difficult to use these transfers in a temporary way. Quite often, when a region experiences a negative shock (the Mezzogiorno in Italy, Wallonia in Belgium), the transfers through the centralized social security system tend to acquire a permanent character. The reason is that these social security transfers reduce the need to adjust. They tend to keep real wages in the depressed regions too high and they reduce the incentive of the population of the region to move out to more prosperous regions. As a result, these transfers tend to become self-perpetuating. This is illustrated by the fact that the Mezzogiorno has been a recipient of transfers (from the rest of Italy) representing 20–30% of the Mezzogiorno's regional output during most of the last twenty-five years.[13] Although less important in size, similar regional transfers exist in other countries (e.g. Belgium).

These large and permanent regional transfers then create new political problems, when the inhabitants of the prosperous regions increasingly oppose paying for them. In some countries these political problems can even lead to calling into question the unity of the nation. When the sense of national identity is weak, this can effectively lead to a break-up of the country.

The experience with regional transfers within European nations is important to bear in mind when considering the limits that should be imposed on the centralization of national budgets (including social security) in Europe. Surely, a centralization of the social security system at the European level would almost certainly create Mezzogiorno problems involving whole countries. This would lead to quasi-permanent transfers from one group of countries to another. The sense of national identification being much less developed at the European level than at the country level, this would certainly lead to great political problems. These would in turn endanger the unity of the European Union. Thus, although Europe needs some further centralization of the national budgets (including the social security systems) to have a workable monetary union, the degree of centralization should stop far short from the level achieved within the present-day European nations. Some schemes of limited centralization of the social security systems (in particular, the unemployment benefit systems) have been proposed and worked out by a number of economists (see Italianer and Vanheukelen (1992), EC Commission (1993), Hammond and von Hagen (1993), and Mélitz and Vori (1993)). These proposals suggest that a limited centralization can be quite effective in taking care of (temporary) asymmetric shocks.

[13] See Micossi and Tullio (1991).

7 Conclusion

According to the theory of optimum currency areas, a monetary union in Europe should go together with some centralization of the national budgets. Such a centralization of the budgetary process allows for *automatic* transfers to regions and countries hit by negative shocks.

Monetary unification in Europe has been realized, despite the fact that no significant central European budget exists. This poses the question of how national fiscal policies should be conducted in a monetary union.

In this chapter we discussed two views about this problem. The first one is based on the theory of optimum currency areas and suggests that national fiscal authorities should maintain a sufficient amount of flexibility and autonomy. The second found its reflection in the Maastricht Treaty and the Stability Pact. According to this view, the conduct of fiscal policies in the monetary union has to be disciplined by explicit rules on the size of the national budget deficits.

We have evaluated these two views. The optimum currency area view is probably overly optimistic about the possibility of national budgetary authorities using budget deficits as instruments to absorb negative shocks. Although there are situations in which countries will need the freedom to allow the budget to accommodate for these negative shocks, the sustainability of these policies limits their effectiveness.

We also argued, however, that the case for strict rules on the size of national government budget deficits is weak. There is little evidence that these rules are enforceable. In addition, the fact that national governments in a future monetary union will not have the same access to monetary financing as most of them have today 'hardens' the budget constraint and reduces the incentives to run large budget deficits. The fear that national authorities will be less disciplined in a monetary union than in other monetary regimes does not seem to be well founded.

From the discussion of this chapter it will be clear that there are many unresolved issues concerning the design and the use of fiscal policies in a monetary union. There are two issues worth mentioning here. First, the EMU will most likely have to operate without a centralized European budget of a significant size. As a result, there will be no automatic mechanism redistributing income between the regions. Assuming that labour mobility between countries will remain small, the adjustment mechanism needed to deal with asymmetric shocks will take the form of relative price changes. It is unclear today whether this mechanism will be flexible enough to deal with such disturbances. We cannot exclude the possibility that some countries will find it difficult to adjust.

Secondly, many issues concerning the interaction between the European central bank and the national fiscal authorities will have to be resolved. It is one thing to legislate that the national authorities will have no access to monetary financing. It is quite another to enforce such a rule. When large countries are affected by negative disturbances, the authorities of these countries are likely to pressure the European central bank to follow accommodative policies. Thus, the absence of a reliable mechanism able to deal with asymmetric shocks is likely to put pressure on the European monetary authorities.

The decision to go ahead with monetary union has clearly been inspired by the political objective of European unification. In this drive towards political union, the economic arguments both in favour of and against monetary union have often played a secondary role. They are important, however, because a failure to take them into account may lead to disillusion and political tensions. Only the future will tell for sure whether the decision to form a monetary union in Europe will be beneficial for all countries concerned.

Chapter 10
The Euro and Financial Markets

The start of EMU will have important implications for financial markets in Europe and for the international monetary relations in the world. In this chapter we analyse some of these issues.

1 EMU and financial market integration in Europe

In principle, the introduction of the euro should speed up financial market integration in Europe. The main reason is that the elimination of the exchange risk also eliminates an obstacle to the free flow of financial assets and services. As long as national moneys existed there was an exchange risk preventing a full integration of financial markets. To give an example, consider the corporate bond market. Before the start of EMU there were (small) corporate bond markets in France and Germany. A FF bond issued by Peugeot and a DM bond issued by Volkswagen were very different assets with different risks, not so much because the two companies were following different strategies, but mainly because of macroeconomic reasons: the FF/DM rate could always be changed in the future. As a result the differences in the risk-return composition of these two bonds were dominated by the risk of future exchange rate changes, upon which these two companies had no influence. In Euroland this should change. When Peugeot and Volkswagen issue bonds in the same currency, the market will be able to price the inherent risks of these two bonds based on the pure corporate risk. When pricing the risk of these two bonds the market will not have to take into account the risk of a change in the exchange rate between two national currencies. This should facilitate the movement towards one unified bond market in Euroland.

The same can be said about the equity markets, the government bond market, the insurance markets, and other financial markets. The elimination of the national currencies has eliminated an important obstacle for the complete integration of these financial markets.

Not all obstacles, however, have been eliminated at the start of EMU. There remain important differences in legal systems that create obstacles for the full integration of financial markets in Euroland. We will discuss the bond market, the equity market and the banking sector consecutively.

1.1 The integration of the bond and equity markets

The government bond markets will be the easiest to integrate into one. After all the bonds issued by the French and German governments will be very close substitutes, since the risk of these two bonds will be almost indistinguishable.

Things are not as simple in other segments of the bond market. The corporate bond market will face the problem that national legal systems differ. Accounting rules, corporate taxation, shareholders' rights, and laws governing take-overs continue to be very different across countries in Euroland. As a result, it will continue to be true that a euro-bond issued by Peugeot and one by Volkswagen will be somewhat different products. This could lead to divergent movements in the price of these bonds not because of exchange risks but because of unforeseen changes in national legislation of corporate taxes or changes in the rules governing take-over bids.

One of the main forces leading to the strong increase in the size of the private bond market is securitization. Increasingly, banks have taken out of their balance sheet loans with the same characteristics (e.g. mortgage loans), repackaged them as bonds, i.e. claims on a fixed stream of future cash flow, and sold them in the market. This securitization has led to a very large market of mortgage-backed bonds in the USA.[1] Should one expect a similar mortgage-backed bond market in Euroland? Again legal obstacles will make such a development in Euroland difficult. The national housing and mortgage markets are governed by very different rules and regulations. (For a description of these differences, see Maclennan, Muellbauer, and Stephens (1999).) To give just a few examples. In some countries banks require 80% collateral or more (e.g. the UK, Belgium, Ireland), in other countries this is only 40% (Italy). In some countries mortgage rates are required by law to be adjusted to market interest rates. In other countries this is not required so that mortgage rates remain fixed for the whole period of the mortgage contract (e.g. France, Denmark). All this makes it very difficult to pool these mortgages from different countries and to sell them as bonds in one Euro-wide market. As long as these national rules and regulations differ, it is more likely that the mortgage-backed bonds will be traded in relatively segmented national bond markets.

Similar obstacles exist for the full integration of the equity markets in Euroland. These obstacles have also to do with legal and regulatory differences. Large differ-

[1] See Bishop (1999) on this issue.

ences in corporate taxation and tax deductions create difficulties in comparing the value of firms. More importantly, changes in these laws and regulations in one country will affect the value of the firms incorporated in these countries. As a result, there will continue to be a country risk attached to shares, despite the fact that the exchange risk (a typical country risk) has disappeared. The continuing existence of country risks will slow down the full integration of the equity markets in Euroland

1.2 The integration of the banking sectors

Today (in 2000) the banking markets are still pretty much segmented in Euroland. In Chapter 7 we showed the evidence (see Table 7.2). More than 85% of the loans granted by banks in Euroland countries are to domestic residents. There is still very little cross-border activity. This contrasts a great deal with other sectors of the economy. For example, sectors like the chemical, the pharmaceutical, the automobile, the computer, and the software industries have become truly international. The banking industry has remained primarily national. An important reason for this national segmentation undoubtedly was the existence of national currencies, which, as in the case of the bond and equity markets, created an obstacle for the full integration of the national banking markets. The abolition of national currencies should foster integration. However, more will have to be done to achieve a full integration of the banking sector in Euroland. And, as in the case of the bond and equity markets, harmonization of national legislation will be the key.

Some progress has been made on the road to harmonization. In particular, the Second Banking Directive of 1989 boosted the harmonization process. This directive introduced the important principle of mutual recognition. This implies that member states have to recognize any financial institution licensed in another member state.[2] Despite this progress, it must be admitted that substantial impediments continue to exist. Here we concentrate on just one obstacle, i.e. the continuing existence of national regulators of the banking systems. As argued in Chapter 7, the lack of centralization of the regulation and supervision of banks creates a threat to the stability of the banking system. It also slows down the process of cross-border bank mergers in Euroland. The reason is that many national bank regulators, who have to give their agreement for bank mergers, show a (not so surprising) reluctance to allow take-overs of their national bank 'champions' by foreign banks. Recent examples in France and Portugal illustrate this tendency. It is not surprising that this happens: the principle of home country control implies that such take-overs reduce the power of the national regulators. The latter typically will fight to keep their power. Although the European Commission can act as a watchdog to make sure that national regulators do not discriminate, i.e. favour national mergers over cross-border mergers, in practice, the Commission cannot prevent such discrimination easily. As a result, the existence

---

[2] See Danthine *et al.* (1999) for more detail.

of a decentralized national regulatory system will work as an obstacle slowing down the integration of the banking sector in Euroland.

2 Why financial market integration is important in a monetary union

FINANCIAL market integration is of great importance for the smooth functioning of EMU. The main reason is that it can facilitate the adjustment to asymmetric shocks. In order to see this, let us return to the two-country model of the first chapter, which we repeat here (see Fig. 10.1). We assume, as before an asymmetric shock, hitting France negatively and Germany positively. Suppose that the financial markets of France and Germany are completely integrated. Thus, there is one bond market, one equity market, and the banking sector is also completely integrated.

Let us concentrate first on how an integrated bond and equity market facilitates the adjustment. In France, as a result of the negative shock, firms make losses, pushing down the stock prices of French firms. Since the equity market is fully integrated, French stocks are also held by German residents. Thus, the latter pay part of the price of the drop in economic activity in France. Conversely, the boom in Germany raises stock prices of German firms. Since these are also held by French residents, the latter find some compensation for the hard economic times in France. Put differently, an integrated stock market works as an insurance system. The risk of a negative shock in

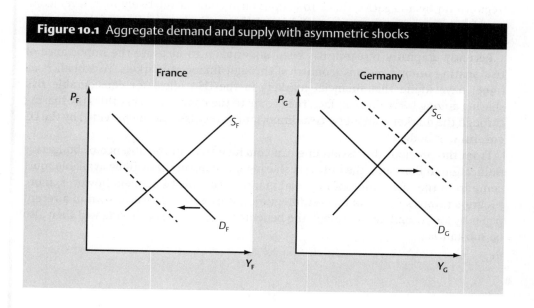

Figure 10.1 Aggregate demand and supply with asymmetric shocks

one country is shared by all countries. As a result, the impact of the negative output shock in one country on the income of the residents of that country is mitigated.

A similar mechanism works through the integrated bond market. Firms in France make losses, some also go bankrupt. This lowers the value of the outstanding French bonds. Part of these French bonds are held by German residents, so that they also pay the price of the economic duress in France.

An integrated mortgage market has similar effects on the degree of risk sharing. When as a result of the negative shock in France, French real estate prices drop this negatively affects the value of outstanding mortgage-backed bonds. The opposite occurs in Germany. The positive shock there is likely to lead to a housing boom, increasing the value of German mortgage-backed bonds. Again, this will allow for risk sharing between France and Germany. The economically unfortunate French are compensated by the fact that they hold part of the German mortgage-backed bonds, while the economically fortunate Germans share in the French economic mis-fortunes by holding French mortgage-backed bonds.

Finally, the integration of the banking sectors also facilitates risk sharing. Suppose the banking sector is fully integrated. This means that the banks operating in France and Germany are the same. Thus, Deutsche Bank has a large portfolio of French loans (to French firms, consumers, home-owners), and so does Credit Lyonnais in Germany. The negative shock in France has the effect of making a part of the French loans 'non-performing', i.e. some French firms and consumers fail to service their debt. As a result, Deutsche Bank loses revenue. It will be able to compensate for this by better revenues in Germany, where the boom boosts the value of the outstanding loans. Similarly, Credit Lyonnais will be able to compensate for its losses on its French loans by higher profits from its German activities.

We conclude that in a monetary union, financial market integration provides different channels of risk sharing. These make it possible for the residents of countries (regions) hit by a negative shock to keep their income at relatively high level (compared to output). The counterpart of this risk sharing is that residents of the booming country see their income increase at a lower rate than their output.

Recently empirical research has been undertaken to measure the importance of risk sharing among regions (countries) through financial markets. Asdrubali *et al.* (1996) have found that financial markets in the USA allow for considerable risk sharing among US regions. In fact, they come to the conclusion that this risk sharing through the market is about twice as important as the risk sharing provided by the US government budget.

From the previous discussion one can conclude that, in the absence of budgetary unification in Euroland, the only risk sharing mechanism that will be available must come from the integration of financial markets. For this to happen, however, more progress towards financial market integration is essential. As was shown in a recent paper by Mélitz and Zumer (1999), the benefits in terms of risk sharing will then also be substantial.

3 Conditions for the euro to become an international currency

THERE is no doubt that the euro can become a major currency challenging the dollar and that the euro financial markets have the potential of becoming a pole of attraction for investors and borrowers very much like the US financial markets are today. How this will happen and at what speed remains very much uncertain, however.

In order to analyse these questions it is important to study the factors that lead to emergence of an international currency. We will distinguish between structural factors that define the necessary conditions, and policy factors without which a currency cannot graduate to an international status even if the structural factors are met.

3.1 Structural factors[3]

Size matters as a condition for a currency to graduate to international status. Surely, Euroland is big. In terms of output and trade (see Fig. 10.2) it surpasses the USA (at least if the UK joins EMU; if not, the USA and Euroland are of approximately equal size). In terms of the size of financial markets Euroland has some way to go (see Fig. 10.3). We observe that the US equity and bond markets as a whole have about twice the size of the equity and bond markets of the EU. Thus, although the 'real' economy of Euroland is as big as the US real economy, the same cannot be said about the financial economy. The US financial size is about twice Euroland's financial dimension.

Financial size influences the liquidity of financial assets, and therefore the ease with which large investors can adjust their portfolios. In addition, size increases the diversity and the choice of investment opportunities. Thus, the fact that the US financial markets are about twice as large as the unified euro financial markets implies that the USA enjoys a strong competitive advantage at the start of EMU.

Economies are dynamic, however, and one should expect that the monetary integration in Europe will accelerate the growth of debt and equity markets in Euroland, so that the financial size of Euroland will come closer to its 'real' size. This process, however, will take time. In addition, as we argued in the previous sections, many legal and regulatory obstacles will have to be removed to make a full integration of the euro financial markets a reality. This full integration is a *conditio sine qua non* for the Euroland to develop financial markets equal in size to the US financial markets. Since this will also take time one should not expect that the euro will displace the dollar in the near future.

Not only size matters for the growth potential of an international currency. The

---

[3] For a path-breaking analysis, see Portes and Rey (1998).

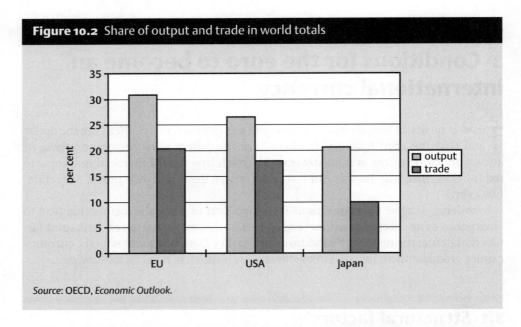

Figure 10.2 Share of output and trade in world totals

Source: OECD, *Economic Outlook*.

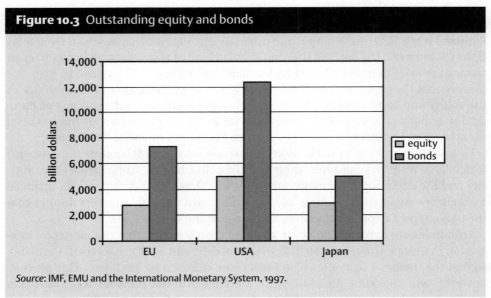

Figure 10.3 Outstanding equity and bonds

Source: IMF, EMU and the International Monetary System, 1997.

degree of *financial liberalization* is equally important. Derivative markets, for example, can only thrive in competitive and free financial markets. Overregulated financial markets do not provide the breeding ground for financial innovations and the development of new financial products and markets. There is no doubt that the USA has a head start in this area. The move to liberalize financial markets has been initiated in the USA at least ten years before the EU (with the possible exception of the UK). As a result, the US financial markets present not only more depth and liquidity but also a wider spectrum of sophisticated financial instruments. The difference between the USA and Europe is well illustrated by the securitization ratio, which is the ratio of outstanding debt and equity over GDP. We can see from Fig. 10.4 that the US securitization ratio is more than twice the size of the EU securitization ratio.

Again one should expect that monetary integration will intensify competition and the liberalization dynamics in Europe. In particular, it is quite likely that it will lead to a shift away from bank financing towards the use of capital markets. It will take time, however, for the European securitization ratios to match the American one. As a result, the conclusion here also should be that the dollar is likely to keep its privileged position in the world for a while.

3.2 The policy environment

A currency can only graduate to an international role if there exists monetary and financial stability at home. This stability in turn depends on monetary and financial policies pursued at home. Where does Euroland stand here, as compared to the USA?

We look at some recent macroeconomic developments in both the EU and in the USA. The foremost indicator of *monetary stability* is the rate of inflation (which measures the stability of the purchasing power of money). As far as inflation is concerned (see Fig. 10.5) we observe a process of strong disinflation in both Europe and the USA during the 1990s. As a result, both countries have entered the twenty-first century with low inflation. This development is to a large extent due to a significant change in the policy preferences of monetary authorities. In both Europe and the USA, price stability has become the major objective of policy-making. This is not likely to change

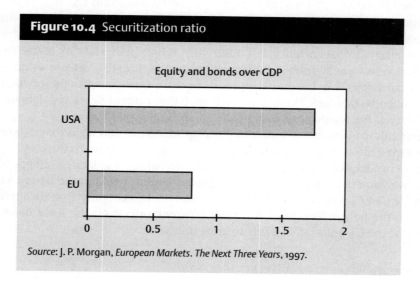

Figure 10.4 Securitization ratio

Equity and bonds over GDP

USA

EU

0   0.5   1   1.5   2

Source: J. P. Morgan, *European Markets. The Next Three Years*, 1997.

Figure 10.5 Inflation in the EU, USA, and Japan

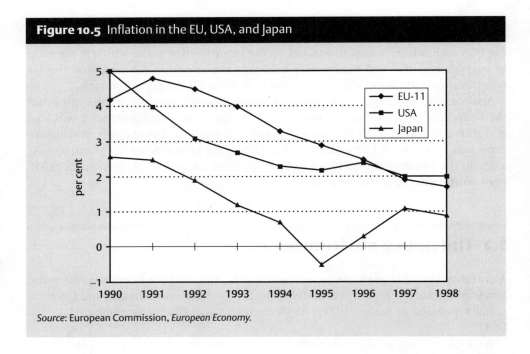

Source: European Commission, *European Economy*.

much in the future, so that one can expect considerable price stability in the future. This conclusion is reinforced in the case of Europe by the institutional design of the ECB. The latter has a mandate for price stability, and has been made politically independent. This will boost the prospect for the euro to become a strong international currency.

Although necessary, price stability alone does not guarantee *financial stability*. This is very well illustrated by the case of Japan. As can be seen from Fig. 10.5, Japan was even more successful in maintaining price stability than Europe and the USA during the 1990s, and yet a financial crisis erupted that has led to a serious setback for the yen as an international currency. Put differently, if only price stability mattered, the yen would now benefit from a large stability bonus, boosting its use as an international currency. This has not happened, because other conditions for financial stability must be satisfied. These have to do with government debts and deficits, and the stability of the financial system.

It is difficult to evaluate the future in this respect. All one can say is that in terms of government debts and deficits, Euroland faces a handicap relative to the USA (see our discussion in Chapter 6). In addition, as we argued earlier, the lack of integration of bank supervision in Euroland may lead to greater bank fragility in the latter country than in the USA.[4] There are, however, also risks in the US economy. One such risk has to do with the bubble-like development of US stock prices. A significant downturn may expose the US financial markets to great upheaval.

---

[4] See Lannoo and Gros (1998), and Wihlborg (1999) on this issue.

Box 16 Will the euro be a strong currency?

In the previous sections we analysed the conditions under which the euro may become an international currency like the dollar. Another widely discussed question is whether the euro will be a strong currency in the future, i.e. whether it will have a tendency to appreciate vis-à-vis other major currencies, like the dollar.

It is important to realize that this second issue is very different from the first one. The factors that determine whether a currency will be used internationally both by investors and by issuers of debt and equity have very little to do with the factors that determine whether a currency will appreciate or depreciate. During the post-war period the dollar developed as the major international currency providing ample opportunities to investors in the world to buy dollar-denominated assets and to foreign firms and institutions to issue bonds and stocks. This happened while the dollar was sometimes appreciating and sometimes depreciating against other major currencies.

We have identified the factors that determine whether a currency will become an international currency in the previous sections. These factors are economic size and the size of financial markets; freedom to buy and to sell assets; a financial environment free of stifling regulations; and reasonable financial and monetary stability.

Except for the last one, these factors are unrelated to those that affect the strength of a currency. Take, for example, the size of countries (economic and financial). This has nothing to do with strength (or weakness) of a currency. Large and small countries can have strong or weak currencies. This point has often been misunderstood during discussions prior to the start of EMU. Up to 1999 many observers believed that the euro would become a strong currency. This belief was based on a fallacious size argument. It went like this: Euroland would suddenly become a new and large economic and financial entity with its own currency. International investors would be very attracted by the new opportunities of a large bond and equity market in euros. As a result, investors from all over the world (both private and official) would start investing in euro assets. In order to do so they would have to sell dollars, yen, and other currencies in the foreign exchange market to buy euros. This would then inevitably increase the price of the euro. The euro was condemned to become a strong currency.

The argument is fallacious because it is only half of the story. With the start of Euroland, euro-bonds and euro-equity became attractive both for international investors wishing to hold more euro-assets in their portfolios *and* for foreign institutions (firms, official institutions) wishing to issue bonds and stocks. While the investors buy euros, the issuers of bonds and equities sell euros. An example will make the latter clear. Suppose a Brazilian company issues a bond denominated in euros. It will then use the proceeds of this euro-bond issue for its investments in Brazil, or possibly elsewhere. Thus, this company will sell the euros obtained by the bond issue to acquire the local currency, or possibly other currencies. This will put downward pressure on the euro.

The upshot of this is that when the foreigners are attracted to use euro-assets either as investors or as issuers of debt, the effect on the value of the euro in terms of, say, the dollar cannot be determined a priori. It can go both ways. In fact, during the first six months of 1999 (when everybody expected a strong euro) the debt issue effect dominated the portfolio effect. More foreigners issued euro-bonds than other foreigners were willing to acquire euro-bonds. The euro went down in the foreign exchange markets.

The price of a currency is determined by the present and expected values of fundamental variables, like interest rates, inflation rates, economic activity, the current account, etc. Thus the euro may appreciate or depreciate in the future depending on how these variables will evolve relative to how the same variables that affect the dollar will evolve. It is generally very difficult to predict this. Therefore, it is very difficult to predict whether the euro will appreciate or depreciate relative to the dollar. All this will not prevent the euro from becoming a major international currency, provided the conditions that we identified in the previous section are satisfied.

One can conclude that the handicaps the euro faces relative to the dollar are structural in nature. In order for the euro financial markets to reach the size (and thus the attraction) of the US financial markets, more will have to be done to integrate fully Euroland's financial markets. In the end this is likely to happen, but it will take time.

References

Aizenman, J., and Frenkel, J. (1985) 'Optimal Wage Indexation, Foreign Exchange Intervention, and Monetary Policy', *American Economic Review*, 75: 402–23.

Akerlof, G., Dickens, W., and Perry, G. (1996) 'The Macroeconomics of Low Inflation', *Brookings Papers on Economic Activity*, no. 1, 1–76.

Alesina, A. (1989) 'Politics and Business Cycles in Industrial Democracies', *Economic Policy*, 8: 55–98.

—— and Grilli, V. (1993) 'On the Feasibility of a One- or Multi-Speed European Monetary Union', NBER Working Paper, no. 4350.

—— and Summers, L. (1993) 'Central Bank Independence and Macroeconomic Performance: Some Comparative Evidence', *Journal of Money, Credit and Banking*, 25.

—— and Tabellini, G. (1987) 'A Positive Theory of Fiscal Deficits and Government Debt in a Democracy', NBER Working Paper, no. 2308.

'All Saints' Day Manifesto', *The Economist*, 1 Nov. 1975.

Arnold, I., and de Vries, C. (1997) 'The Euro, Prudent Coherence', draft, Erasmus University and Tinbergen Institute, Rotterdam.

—— —— (1998) 'Endogenous Financial Structure and the Transmission of the ECB Policy', paper presented at the conference 'Common Money, Uncommon Regions', organized by the ZEI, Bonn, 24–5 July.

—— —— (1999). Endogenous Financial Structure and the Transmission of ECB Policy, (unpublished manuscript), Tinbergen Institute, Erasmus University Rotterdam, March 1999.

Artis, M. J., and Taylor, M. P. (1988) 'Exchange Rates, Interest Rates, Capital Controls and the European Monetary System: Assessing the Track Record', in F. Giavazzi *et al.* (1988).

—— and Zhang, W. (1995) 'International Business Cycles and the ERM: Is There a European Business Cycle?' CEPR Discussion Paper, no. 1191.

Asdrubali, P., Sørensen, B., and Yosha, O. (1996) 'Channels of Interstate Risk-sharing: United States 1963–1990', *Quarterly Journal of Economics*, iii: 1081–110.

Backus, D., and Driffill, J. (1985) 'Inflation and Reputation', *American Economic Review*, 75: 530–8.

Bade, R., and Parkin, M. (1978) 'Central Bank Laws and Monetary Policies. A Preliminary Investigation: The Australian Monetary System in the 1970s', Clayton: Monash University.

Balassa, B. (1961) *The Theory of Economic Integration*, London: Allen & Unwin.

—— (1964) 'The Purchasing Power Parity Doctrine: A Reappraisal', *Journal of Political Economy*, 72: 584–96.

Baldwin, R. (1989) 'On the Growth Effects of 1992', *Economic Policy*, 11.

Barro, R. (1972) 'Inflationary Finance and the Welfare Cost of Inflation', *Journal of Political Economy*, 80: 978–1001.

—— and Gordon, D. (1983) 'Rules, Discretion and Reputation in a Model of Monetary Policy', *Journal of Monetary Economics*, 12: 101–21.

Bayoumi, T., and Eichengreen, B. (1993) 'Shocking Aspects of European Monetary Integration', in F. Torres and F. Giavazzi (eds.), *Adjustment and Growth in the European Monetary Union*, London: CEPR, and Cambridge: CUP.

—— —— (1996) 'Operationalizing the Theory of Optimum Currency Areas', CEPR Discussion Paper, no. 1484.

—— —— (1997) 'Ever Close to Heaven. An Optimum Currency Area Index for

European Countries', *European Economic Review*, 41(3–5): 761–70.

Bayoumi, T., and Masson, P. (1994) 'Fiscal Flows in the United States and Canada: Lessons for Monetary Union in Europe', CEPR Discussion Paper, no. 1057.

—— and Prassad, E. (1995) 'Currency Unions, Economic Fluctuations and Adjustment: Some Empirical Evidence', CEPR Discussion Paper, no. 1172.

Begg, D., and Wyplosz, C. (1987) 'Why the EMS? Dynamic Games and the Equilibrium Policy Regime', in R. Bryant and R. Portes (eds.), *Global Macroeconomics: Policy Conflict and Cooperation*, New York: St Martin's Press.

—— Chappori, P., Giavazzi, F., Mayer, C., Neven, D., Spaventa, L., *et al.* (1991) *Monitoring European Integration: The Making of the Monetary Union*, London: CEPR.

—— De Grauwe, P., Giavazzi, F., Uhlig, H., and Wyplosz, C. (1998) 'The ECB: Safe at Any Speed', *Monitoring the European Central Bank 1*, London: CEPR.

—— Giavazzi, F., von Hagen, J., and Wyplosz, C. (1997) *EMU. Getting the End-game Right*, London: CEPR.

Bernanke, B., and Mihov, I. (1997) 'What does the Bundesbank Target?', *European Economic Review*, 41: 1025–52.

—— Laubach, T., Mishkin, F., and Posen, A. (1999) *Inflation Targeting. Lessons from the International Experience*, Princeton University Press.

Bertola, C., and Svensson, L. (1993) 'Stochastic Devaluation Risk and the Empirical Fit of Target-Zone Models', *Review of Economic Studies*, 60: 689–712.

Bini-Smaghi, L., and Gros, D. (1999) 'Open Issues in European Central Banking', unpublished MS.

—— and Vori, S. (1993) 'Rating the EC as an Optimal Currency Area: Is it Worse than the US?', Banca d'Italia Discussion Paper, no. 187.

—— Padoa-Schioppa, T., and Papadia, F. (1993) 'The Policy History of the Maastricht Treaty: The Transition to the Final Stage of EMU', Banca d'Italia.

Bishop, G. (1999) 'New Capital Market Opportunities in Euroland', *European Investment Bank Papers*, 4 (1).

Blanchard, O., and Muet, P.-A. (1993) 'Competitiveness through Disinflation: An Assessment of the French Macroeconomic Strategy', *Economic Policy*, 16: 11–56.

Bofinger, P. (1999) 'The Conduct of Monetary Policy by the European Central Bank', Briefing paper for the Monetary Subcommittee of the European Parliament, Brussels.

Boyd, C., Gielens, C., and Gros, D. (1990) 'Bid-Ask Spreads in the Foreign Exchange Markets', mimeo, Brussels.

Bruno, M., and Sachs, J. (1985) *Economics of Worldwide Stagflation*, Oxford: Basil Blackwell.

Buchanan, J., and Tullock, T. (1962) *The Calculus of Consent*, Ann Arbor: University of Michigan Press.

Buiter, W. (1999) 'Alice in Euroland', *CEPR Policy Paper*, 1, London: CEPR.

—— and Kletzer, K. (1990) 'Reflections on the Fiscal Implications of a Common Currency', CEPR Discussion Paper, no. 418.

—— —— (1991) 'Reflections on the Fiscal Implications of a Common Currency', in A. Giovannini and C. Mayer (eds.), *European Financial Integration*, Cambridge: CUP.

—— Corsetti, G., and Roubini, N. (1993) 'Sense and Nonsense in the Treaty of Maastricht', *Economic Policy*, 16.

Bundesministerium der Finanzen (1996) *Finanzbericht 1997*, Bonn.

Buti, M., and Sapir, A. (eds.)(1998) *Economic Policy in EMU*, Oxford: Clarendon Press.

Cagan, P. (1956) 'The Monetary Dynamics of Hyperinflation', in M. Friedman (ed.), *Studies in Quantity Theory of Money*, Chicago: Chicago University Press.

Calmfors, L., and Driffill, J. (1988) 'Bargaining Structure, Corporatism and Macroeconomic Performance', *Economic Policy*, 6: 13–61.

Canzoneri, M., Cumby, R., and Diba, B. (1996) 'Relative Labor Productivity and the Real Exchange Rate in the Long Run: Evidence for a Panel of OECD Countries', Discussion Paper, Dept. of Economics, Georgetown University.

Canzoneri, M., Valles, J., and Vinals, J. (1996) 'Do Exchange Rates Have to Address International Macroeconomic Imbalances?', CEPR Discussion Paper, no. 1498.

Carlin, W., and Soskice, D. (1990) *Macroeconomics and the Wage Bargain*, Oxford: OUP.

Cecchetti, S. G. (1999) 'Legal Structure, Financial Structure and Monetary Policy Transmission Mechanism', mimeo, Federal Reserve Bank of New York.

Clarida, R., and Gertler, M. (1996) 'How Does the Bundesbank Conduct Monetary Policy?', NBER Working Paper, no. 5581.

—— Gali, J., and Gertler, M. (1999) 'The Science of Monetary Policy: A New Keynesian Perspective', CEPR Dicussion Paper, no. 2139, May.

Cohen, D. (1983) 'La Coopération monétaire européenne: du SME á l'Union monétaire', *Revue d'économie financière*, 8/9.

—— and Wyplosz, C. (1989) 'The European Monetary Union: An Agnostic Evaluation', unpub. typescript.

Collins, S. (1988) 'Inflation and the European Monetary System', in Giavazzi *et al.* (1988) *The European Monetary System*, Cambridge: CUP.

Committee on the Study of Economic and Monetary Union (the Delors Committee) (1989) *Report on Economic and Monetary Union in the European Community (Delors Report)* (with Collection of Papers), Luxemburg: Office for Official Publications of the European Communities.

Connolly, B. (1995) *The Rotten Heart of Europe: The Dirty War for Europe's Money*, London: Faber & Faber.

Corden, M. (1972) 'Monetary Integration', *Essays in International Finance*, no. 93, Princeton.

Costa, C. (1996) 'Exchange Rate Pass-Through: The Case of Portuguese Imports and Exports', unpub. typescript, University of Leuven.

Cukierman, A. (1992) *Central Bank Strategy, Credibility and Independence, Theory and Evidence*, Cambridge, Mass.: MIT Press.

Danthine, J. P., Giavazzi, F., Vives, X., and von Thadden, E. (1999) 'The Future of European Banking', *Monitoring European Integration*, 9, London: CEPR.

David, R (1985) 'CLIO and the Economics of QWERTY', *American Economic Review*, 75: 332–7.

Davis, S., Haltiwanger, J., and Schuh, S. (1996) *Job Creation and Destruction*, Cambridge, Mass.: MIT Press.

De Cecco, M., and Giovannini, A. (eds.) (1989) *A European Central Bank? Perspectives on Monetary Unification after Ten Years of the EMS*, Cambridge: CUP.

De Grauwe, P. (1975) 'Conditions for Monetary Integration: A Geometric Interpretation', *Weltwirtschaftliches Archiv*, 111: 634–46.

—— (1983) *Macroeconomic Theory for the Open Economy*, Aldershot: Gower.

—— (1987) 'International Trade and Economic Growth in the EMS', *European Economic Review*, 31: 389–98.

—— (1990) 'The Cost of Disinflation and the European Monetary System', *Open Economies Review*, 1: 147–73.

—— (1991) 'Is the EMS a DM-Zone?', in A. Steinherr and D. Weiserbs (eds.), *Evolution of the International and Regional Monetary Systems*, London: Macmillan.

—— Dewachter, H., and Aksoy, Y. (1999) 'The European Central Bank: Decisions, Rules and Macroeconomic Performance', CEPR Discussion Paper, no. 2067.

—— —— and Veestraeten, D. (1999) 'Explaining Recent Exchange Rate Stability', *International Finance*, 2(1).

—— and Heens, H. (1993) 'Real Exchange Rate Variability in Monetary Unions', *Recherches Économiques de Louvain*, 59/1–2.

—— and Peeters, T. (eds.) (1989) *The ECU and European Monetary Integration*, London: Macmillan.

De Grauwe, P., and Spaventa, L. (1997) 'Setting Conversion Rates for the Third Stage of EMU', CEPR Discussion Paper, no. 1638.

—— and Vanhaverbeke, W. (1990) 'Exchange Rate Experiences of Small EMS Countries. The Cases of Belgium, Denmark and the Netherlands', in V. Argy and P. De Grauwe (eds.), *Choosing an Exchange Rate Regime*, Washington, DC: International Monetary Fund.

—— —— (1993) 'Is Europe an Optimum Currency Area?: Evidence from Regional Data', in P. R. Masson and M. P. Taylor (eds.), *Policy Issues in the Operation of Currency Unions*, Cambridge: CUP.

de Haan, J., and Eijffinger, S. (1994) 'De Politieke Economie van Centrale Bank Onafhankelijkheid', *Rotterdamse Monetaire Studies*, no.2.

Demopoulos, C., Katsimbris, G., and Miller, S. (1987) 'Monetary Policy and Central Bank Financing of Government Budget Deficits: A Cross-Country Comparison', *European Economic Review*, 31: 1023–50.

Dominguez, K., and Frankel, J. (1993) *Does Foreign Exchange Intervention Work?*, Washington, DC: Institute for International Economics.

Dornbusch, R. (1976;) 'Money and Finance in European Integration', mimeo, Cambridge, Mass.: MIT.

—— (1988), 'The European Monetary System, the Dollar and the Yen', in Giavazzi *et al.* (1988), *The European Monetary System*, Cambridge: CUP.

—— Favero, C., and Giavazzi, F. (1998) 'Immediate Challenges for the European Central Bank', *Economic Policy*, 26 (Apr.).

—— and Fischer, S. (1978) *Macroeconomics*, New York: McGraw-Hill.

Driffill, J. (1988) 'The Stability and Sustainability of the European Monetary System with Perfect Capital Markets', in Giavazzi *et al.* (1988) *The European Monetary System*, Cambridge: CUP.

EC Commission (1977) Report of the Study Group on the Role of Public Finance in European Integration (MacDougall Report), Brussels.

—— (1988) 'The Economics of 1992', *European Economy*, 35.

—— (1990) 'One Market, One Money', *European Economy*, 44.

—— (1993) 'Stable Money—Sound Finances, Community Public Finance in the Perspective of EMU', *European Economy*, 53.

Eichengreen, B. (1990) 'Is Europe an Optimum Currency Area?', CEPR Discussion Paper, no. 478.

—— (1992) 'Designing a Central Bank for Europe: A Cautionary Tale from the Early Years of the Federal Reserve System', in M. Canzoneri, V. Grilli, and P. Masson (eds.), *Establishing a Central Bank: Issues in Europe and Lessons from the US*, Cambridge: Cambridge University Press.

—— and von Hagen, J. (1995) 'Fiscal Policy and Monetary Union: Federalism, Fiscal Restrictions and the No-Bailout Rule', CEPR Discussion Paper, no. 1247.

—— and Wyplosz, C. (1993) 'The Unstable EMS', CEPR Discussion Paper, no. 817.

Eijffinger, S., and de Haan, J. (1999) 'European Money and Fiscal Policy', mimeo, forthcoming Oxford University Press.

—— and Schaling, E. (1995) 'The Ultimate Determinants of Central Bank Independence', in S. Eijffinger and H. Huizinga (eds.), *Positive Political Economy: Theory and Evidence*, New York: Wiley & Sons.

Engel, C., and Rogers, J. (1995) 'How Wide is the Border?', International Finance Discussion Paper, no. 498, Washington, DC: Board of Governors of the Federal Reserve System.

Erkel-Rousse, H., and Mélitz, J. (1995) 'New Empirical Evidence on the Costs of Monetary Union', CEPR Discussion Paper, no. 1169.

European Central Bank (1999) *Monthly Report*, Frankfurt, January.

European Commission (various years) *Car Prices within the European Union*, Brussels.

European Monetary Institute (1997) 'The Single Monetary Policy in Stage Three', Frankfurt, September.

Fischer, S. (1982) 'Seigniorage and the Case for a National Money', *Journal of Political Economy*, 90: 295–307.

Frankel, J., and Rose, A. (1996) 'The Endogeneity of the Optimum Currency Area Criteria', NBER Discussion Paper, no. 5700.

Fratianni, M. (1988) 'The European Monetary System: How Well has it Worked? Return to an Adjustable-Peg Arrangement', *Cato Journal*, 8: 477–501.

—— and Peeters, T. (eds.) (1978) *One Money for Europe*, London: Macmillan.

—— and von Hagen, J. (1990) 'German Dominance in the EMS: The Empirical Evidence', *Open Economies Review*, 1: 86–7.

—— —— (1992) *The European Monetary System and European Monetary Union*, Boulder, Colo.: Westview Press.

—— —— and Waller, C. (1992) 'The Maastricht Way to EMU', *Essays in International Finance*, no. 187, Princeton.

Friedman, M. (1967) 'The Role of Monetary Policy', *American Economic Review* 58: 1–17.

—— (1969 edn.) 'The Optimum Quantity of Money', in M. Friedman (ed.), *The Optimum Quantity of Money and Other Essays*, Chicago: Aldine.

—— and Schwartz, A. (1963) *A Monetary History of the United States, 1867–1960*, Princeton: Princeton University Press.

Froot, R., and Obstfeld, M. (1989) 'Exchange Rate Dynamics under Stochastic Regime Shifts', NBER Working Paper, no. 2835.

Giavazzi, F., and Giovannini, A. (1989) *Limiting Exchange Rate Flexibility: The European Monetary System*, Cambridge, Mass.: MIT Press.

—— and Pagano, M. (1985) 'Capital Controls and the European Monetary System', in *Capital Controls and Foreign Exchange Legislation*, Euromobiliare, Occasional Paper 1.

—— —— (1988) 'The Advantage of Tying One's Hands: EMS Discipline and Central Bank Credibility', *European Economic Review*, 32: 1055–82.

—— —— (1990) 'Can Severe Fiscal Contractions be Expansionary? Tales of Two Small European Countries', *NBER Macroeconomic Annual*: 75–111.

—— and Spaventa, L. (1990) 'The "New" EMS', in P. De Grauwe and L. Papademos (eds.), *The European Monetary System in the 1990s*, London: Longman.

—— Micossi, S., and Miller, M. (eds.) (1988) *The European Monetary System*, Cambridge: CUP.

Giersch, H. (1973) 'On the Desirable Degree of Flexibility of Exchange Rates', *Weltwirtschaftliches Archiv*, 109: 191–213.

Giovannini, A., and Spaventa, L. (1991) 'Fiscal Rules in the European Monetary Union: A No-Entry Clause', CEPR Discussion Paper, no. 516.

Goodhart, C. (1989) '*The Delors Report*: Was Lawson's Reaction Justifiable?', London: Financial Markets Group, London School of Economics (unpub.).

Gordon, R. (1996) 'Problems in the Measurement and Performance of Service-Sector Productivity in the US', NBER Working Paper, no. 5519.

Grilli, V. (1989) 'Seigniorage in Europe', in De Cecco and Giovannini (1989).

—— Masciandro, D., and Tabellini, C. (1991) 'Political and Monetary Institutions and Public Financial Policies in the Industrial Countries', *Economic Policy*, 13: 341–92.

Gros, D. (1990) 'Seigniorage and EMS Discipline', in P. De Grauwe and L. Papademos (eds.), *The European Monetary System in the 1990s*, London: Longman.

—— (1995) 'Towards a Credible Excessive Deficits Procedure', Brussels: Centre for European Policy Studies.

—— (1996) 'A Reconsideration of the Optimum Currency Approach: The Role of External Shocks and Labour Mobility', Brussels: Centre for European Policy Studies.

—— and Lannoo, K. (1996) *The Passage to the Euro*, CEPS Working Party Report, no. 16.

Gros, D., and Tabellini, G. (1998) 'The Institutional Framework for Monetary Policy', CEPS Working Document, no. 126, Brussels.

—— and Thygesen, N. (1988) 'The EMS: Achievements, Current Issues and Directions for the Future', CEPS Paper, no. 35, Brussels: Centre for European Policy Studies.

—— —— (1992) *European Monetary Integration: From the European Monetary System towards Monetary Union*, London: Longman.

Grubb, D., Jackman, R., and Layard, R. (1983) 'Wage Rigidity and Unemployment in OECD Countries', *European Economic Review*.

Hammond, G., and von Hagen, J. (1993) 'Regional Insurance against Asymmetric Shocks: An Empirical Study for the European Community', University of Mannheim, typescript.

Hayek, F. (1978) *Denationalization of Money*, London: Institute of Economic Affairs.

Hayo, Bernd (1998) 'Inflation Culture, Central Bank Independence and Price Stability', *European Journal of Political Economy*, 14: 241–63.

HM Treasury (1989) *An Evolutionary Approach to Economic and Monetary Union*, London: HMSO.

—— (1990) 'The Hard ECU Proposal', mimeo.

Holtfrerich, C.-L. (1989) 'The Monetary Unification Process in Nineteenth-Century Germany: Relevance and Lessons for Europe Today', in De Cecco and Giovannini (1989).

Ingram, J. (1959) 'State and Regional Payments Mechanisms', *Quarterly Journal of Economics*, 73: 619–32.

International Monetary Fund (1984) 'Exchange Rate Volatility and World Trade: A Study by the Research Department of the International Monetary Fund', *Occasional Papers*, no. 28.

—— (1998), *International Capital Markets*, Wahington, DC.

Ishiyama, Y., The theory of optimum currency areas: A survey, IMF Staff Papers, 22, pp. 344–83, 1975.

Issing, O. (1999) 'The Eurosystem: Transparent and Accountable or "Willem in Euroland" ', *CEPR Policy Paper*, no. 2, London: CEPR.

Italianer, A., and Vanheukelen, M. (1992) 'Proposals for Community Stabilization Mechanisms', in 'The Economics of Community Public Finances', *European Economy*, Special Issue.

Jozzo, A. (1989) 'The Use of the ECU as an Invoicing Currency', in P. De Grauwe and T. Peeters (eds.), *The ECU and European Monetary Integration*, London: Macmillan.

Kaldor, N. (1966) *The Causes of the Slow Growth of the United Kingdom*, Cambridge: CUP.

Kenen, R (1969) 'The Theory of Optimum Currency Areas: An Eclectic View', in R. Mundell and A. Swobodaa (eds.), *Monetary Problems of the International Economy*, Chicago,: University of Chicago Press.

Klein, B. (1978) 'Competing Monies, European Monetary Union and the Dollar', in Fratianni and Peeters (1978).

Krugman, P. (1987) 'Trigger Strategies and Price Dynamics in Equity and Foreign Exchange Markets', NBER Working Paper, no. 2459.

—— (1989) 'Differences in Income Elasticities and Trends in Real Exchange Rates', *European Economic Review*, 33: 1031–47.

—— (1990) 'Policy Problems of a Monetary Union', in P. De Grauwe and L. Papademos (eds.), *The European Monetary System in the 1990s*, London: Longman.

—— (1991) *Geography and Trade*, Cambridge, Mass.: MIT Press.

—— (1993) 'Lessons of Massachusetts for EMU', in F. Torres and F. Giavazzi (eds.), *Adjustment and Growth in the European Monetary Union*, London: CEPR, and Cambridge: CUP.

Kydland, E., and Prescott, E. (1977) 'Rules Rather than Discretion: The Inconsistency of Optimal Plans', *Journal of Political Economy*, 85.

Lamfalussy, A. (1989) 'Macro-coordination of Fiscal Policies in an Economic and Monetary Union', in Committee on the Study of Economic and Monetary Union (1989).

Lannoo, K. (1998) 'From 1992 to EMU, The Implications for Prudential Supervision', Centre for European Studies, Research Report, no. 23, May.

—— and Gros, D. (1998) *Capital Market, and EMU*, Report of a CEPS Working Party, Brussels: Centre for European Policy Studies.

Leiderman, L., and Svensson, L. (eds.) (1995) *Inflation Targets*, London: CEPR.

Lippi, F. (1999) 'Revisiting the Case for a Populist Banker: the Real Effects of Nominal Wage Bargaining', mimeo, Bank of Italy

Lomax, D. (1989) 'The ECU as an Investment Currency,' in P. De Grauwe and T. Peeters (eds.), *The ECU and European Monetary Integration*, London: Macmillan.

Ludlow, R (1982) *The Making of the European Monetary System*, London: Butterworths.

Maastricht Treaty (Treaty on European Union) (1992) CONF-UP-UEM 2002/92, Brussels, 1 Feb.

McDonald, I., and Solow, R. (1981) 'Wage Bargaining and Employment', *American Economic Review*, 71: 896–908.

McKinnon, R. (1963) 'Optimum Currency Areas', *American Economic Review*, 53: 717–25.

—— (1996) *Default Risk in Monetary Unions*, background report for the Swedish Government Commission on EMU, Stockholm.

Maclennan, D., Muellbauer, J., and Stephens, M. (1999) 'Assymetries in Housing and Financial Market Institutions and EMU', CEPR Discussion Paper, no. 2062.

Mastropasqua, C., Micossi, S., and Rinalid, R. (1988) 'Interventions, Sterilization and Monetary Policy in the EMS Countries (1979–1987)', in Giavazzi *et al.* (1988).

Mélitz, J. (1985) 'The Welfare Cost of the European Monetary System', *Journal of International Money and Finance*, 4: 485–506.

—— (1988) 'Monetary Discipline, Germany and the European Monetary System: A Synthesis', in Giavazzi *et al.* (1988).

—— and Vori, S. (1993) 'National Insurance against Unevenly Distributed Shocks in a European Monetary Union', *Recherches Économiques de Louvain*, 59: 1–2.

—— and Zumer, F. (1999) 'Interregional and International Risk Sharing and Lessons for EMU', CEPR Discussion Paper, no. 2154.

Micossi, S., and Tullio, G. (1991) 'Fiscal Imbalances, Economic Distortions, and the Long Run Performance of the Italian Economy', OCSM Working Paper, no. 9, LUISS.

Moesen, W., and Van Rompuy, P. (1990) 'The Growth of Government Size and Fiscal Decentralization', paper prepared for the IIPF Congress, Brussels.

Monticelli, C., and Papi, U. (1996) *European Integration, Monetary Co-ordination, and the Demand for Money*, Oxford: Oxford University Press.

Morales, A., and Padilla, A. J. (1994) 'Designing Institutions for International Monetary Co-operation', unpub., Madrid: CEMFI.

Morgan J. P., *European Markets. The Next Three Years*, London: 1997.

Mundell, R. (1961) 'A Theory of Optimal Currency Areas', *American Economic Review*, 51.

Mussa, M. (1979) 'Empirical Regularities in the Behaviour of Exchange Rates and Theories of the Foreign Exchange Markets', in Carnegie Rochester Conference Series on Public Policy, *Journal of Monetary Economics*.

Myrdal, G. (1957) *Economic Theory and Underdeveloped Regions*, New York: Duckworth.

Neumann, M. (1990) 'Central Bank Independence as a Prerequisite of Price Stability', mimeo, University of Bonn.

—— and von Hagen, J. (1991) 'Real Exchange Rates within and between Currency Areas: How far away is EMU?', Discussion Paper, Indiana University.

Obstfeld, M. (1986) 'Rational and Self-Fulfilling Balance of Payments Crises', *American Economic Review*, 76: 72–81.

OECD (1990) *Economic Outlook*, Paris.

—— (1999) *EMU: Facts, Challenges and Policies*, Paris.

Padoa-Schioppa, T. (1988) 'The European Monetary System: A Long-Term View', in Giavazzi *et al.* (1988).

—— (1999) 'EMU and Banking Supervision', lecture at the London School of Economics, 24 February.

Parkin, M., and Bade, R. (1988) *Modern Macroeconomics*, 2nd edn., Oxford: Philip Allan.

Persson, T., and Svensson, L. (1989) 'Why a Stubborn Conservative would Run a Deficit: Policy with Time Inconsistent Preferences', *Quarterly Journal of Economics*, 104.

—— and Tabellini, G. (1996) 'Monetary Cohabitation in Europe', NBER Working Paper, no. 5532.

Phelps, E. (1968) 'Money-Wage Dynamics and Labour Market Equilibrium', *Journal of Political Economy*, 76: 678–711.

Poole, W. (1970) 'Optimal Choice of Monetary Policy Instruments in a Simple Stochastic Macro Model', *Quarterly Journal of Economics*, 85.

Portes, R. (1989) 'Macroeconomic Policy Coordination and the European Monetary System', CEPR Discussion Paper, no. 342.

—— (1993) 'EMS and EMU After the Fall', *World Economy*, 16: 1–16.

—— and Rey, H. (1998) 'The Emergence of the Euro as an International Currency', *Economic Policy*, Cambridge, Mass.: MIT Press.

Posen, A. (1994) 'Is Central Bank Independence the Result of Effective Opposition to Inflation? Evidence of Endogenous Monetary Policy Institutions', mimeo, Harvard University.

Prati, A., and Schinasi, G. (1998) 'The ECB and the Stability of the Financial System', IMF Working Paper, Washington, DC.

Rogoff, K. (1985a) 'Can Exchange Rate Predictability be Achieved without Monetary Convergence? Evidence from the EMS', *European Economic Review*, 28: 93–115.

—— (1985b) 'The Optimal Degree of Commitment to an Intermediate Monetary Target', *Quarterly Journal of Economics*, 100: 1169–90.

Roll, E. (1993) 'Independent and Accountable: A New Mandate for the Bank of England', Report of an Independent Panel chaired by Eric Roll, London: CEPR.

Romer, P. (1986) 'Increasing Returns and Long-Term Growth', *Journal of Political Economy*.

Rose, A., and Svensson, L. (1993) 'European Exchange Rate Credibility Before the Fall', NBER Working Paper, no. 4495.

Roubini, N., and Sachs, J. (1989) 'Government Spending and Budget Deficits in the Industrial Countries', *Economic Policy*, 11: 100–32.

Russo, M., and Tullio, G. (1988) 'Monetary Policy Coordination within the European Monetary System: Is there a Rule?' in Giavazzi *et al.* (1988).

Sachs, J., and Sala-i-Martin, X. (1989) 'Federal Fiscal Policy and Optimum Currency Areas', Harvard University Working Paper, Cambridge, Mass.

—— and Wyplosz, C. (1986) 'The Economic Consequences of President Mitterand', *Economic Policy*, 2.

Sachverständigenrat zur Begutachtung der Gesamtwirtschaftlichen Entwicklung, 'Sondergutachten', 20 Jan. 1990.

Salin, P. (ed.) (1984) *Currency Competition and Monetary Union*, The Hague: Martinus Nijhoff.

Sannucci, V. (1989) 'The Establishment of a Central Bank: Italy in the Nineteenth Century', in De Cecco and Giovannini (1989).

Sargent, T., and Wallace, N. (1981) 'Some Unpleasant Monetarist Arithmetic', *Federal Reserve Bank of Minneapolis Quarterly Review*, 5: 1–17.

Shapiro, M., and Wilcox, D. (1996) 'Mismeasurement in the Consumer Price

Index: An Evaluation', NBER Working Paper, no. 5590.

Steinherr, A. (1989) *Concrete Steps for Developing the ECU*, Report prepared by the ECU Banking Association Macrofinancial Study Group, Brussels.

Stiglitz, J., and Weiss, A. (1981) 'Credit Rationing in Markets with Imperfect Information', *American Economic Review*, 71: 393–410.

Straubhaar, T. (1988) 'International Labour Migration within a Common Market: Some Aspects of the EC Experience', *Journal of Common Market Studies*, 27.

Svensson, L. (1992) 'The Foreign Exchange Risk Premium in a Target Zone with a Devaluation Risk', *Journal of International Economics*, 33: 21–40.

—— (1995) 'Optimal Inflation Targets, Conservative Central Banks, and Linear Inflation Contracts', CEPR Discussion Paper, no. 1249.

—— (1997) 'Inflation Forecast Targeting: Implementing and Monitoring Inflation Targets', *European Economic Review*, 41: 111–46.

—— (1998) 'Inflation Targeting as a Monetary Policy Rule', CEPR Discussion Paper, no. 1998.

Tavlas, C. (1993) 'The "New" Theory of Optimum Currency Areas', *World Economy*, 33: 663–82.

Thygesen, N. (1988) 'Decentralization and Accountability within the Central Bank: Any Lessons from the US Experience for the Potential Organization of a European Central Banking Institution?' (with comment by Jean-Jacques Rey), in P. De Grauwe and T. Peeters (eds.), *The ECU and European Monetary Integration*, Basingstoke: Macmillan.

—— (1989) 'A European Central Banking System: Some Analytical and Operational Considerations', in Collection of Papers of Delors Report, 157–75.

Tower, E., and Willett, T. (1976) 'The Theory of Optimum Currency Areas and Exchange Rate Flexibility', *Special Papers in International Finance*, no. 11, Princeton, NJ: Princeton University.

Turnovsky, S. (1984) 'Exchange Market Intervention under Alternative Forms of Exogenous Disturbances', *Journal of International Economics*, 17: 279–97.

Ungerer, H., Evans, O., and Byberg, P. (1986) 'The European Monetary System: Recent Developments', International Monetary Fund Occasional Paper, no. 48.

van der Ploeg, F. (1991) 'Macroeconomic Policy Coordination during the Various Phases of Economic and Monetary Integration in Europe', in EC Commission, *European Economy*, Special edn., 1.

Van Neder, N., and Vanhaverbeke, W. (1990) 'The Causes of Price Differences in the European Car Markets', International Economics Discussion Paper, University of Leuven.

Van Rompuy, P., Abraham, F., and Heremans, D. (1991) 'Economic Federalism and the EMU', in EC Commission, *European Economy*, Special edn., 1.

van Ypersele, J. (1985) *The European Monetary System*, Cambridge: Woodhead.

Vaubel, R. (1978) *Strategies for Currency Unification*, Kieler Studien, no. 156, Tübingen: Mohr & Siebeck.

—— (1989) 'Uberholte Glaubenssätze', *Wirtschaftsdienst*, 69: 276–9.

—— (1990) 'Currency Competition and European Monetary Integration', *Economic Journal*, 100: 936–46.

von Hagen, J. (1991) 'A Note on the Empirical Effectiveness of Formal Fiscal Restraints', *Journal of Public Economics*, 44: 199–210.

—— (1991) 'Fiscal Arrangements in a Monetary Union. Evidence from the US', Working Paper, Indiana University.

—— and Fratianni, M. (1990) 'Asymmetries and Realignments in the EMS', in P. De Grauwe and L. Papademos (eds.), *The European Monetary System in the 1990s*, London: Longman.

—— and Hammond, G. (1995) 'Regional Insurance against Asymmetric Shocks: An

Empirical Study for the European Community', CEPR Discussion Paper, no. 1170.

—— and Lutz, S. (1996) 'Fiscal and Monetary Policy on the Way to EMU', *Open Economies Review*, 7: 299–325.

Walsh, C. (1995) 'Optimal Contracts for Independent Central Banks', *American Economic Review*, 85: 150–67.

—— (1998) *Monetary Theory and Policy*, Cambridge, Mass.: MIT Press.

Walters, A. (1986) *Britain's Economic Renaissance*, Oxford: OUP.

Weber, A. (1990) 'European Economic and Monetary Union and Asymmetric and Adjustment Problems in the European Monetary System: Some Empirical Evidence', University of Siegen Discussion Paper, no. 9–90.

Wickens, M. (1993) 'The Sustainability of Fiscal Policy and the Maastricht Conditions', London Business School Discussion Paper, no. 10–93.

Wihlborg, C. (1999) 'Supervision of Banks after EMU', *European Investment Bank Papers*, 4(1).

Williamson, J. (1983) *The Exchange Rate System*, Washington, DC: Institute of International Economics.

Winkler, B. (1994) 'Reputation for EMU: An Economic Defence of the Maastricht Criteria', unpub MS, European University Institute.

Wyplosz, C. (1989) 'Asymmetry in the EMS: Intentional or Systemic?', *European Economic Review*, 33: 310–20.

—— (1991) 'Monetary Union and Fiscal Policy Discipline', in EC Commission, *European Economy*, Special edn., 1.

Zimmerman, H. (1989) 'Fiscal Equalization between States in West Germany', *Government and Policy*, 7: 385–93.

Index